Mother Goose,
Mother Jones,
Mommie Dearest

Society of Biblical Literature

Semeia Studies

Number 61

MOTHER GOOSE,
MOTHER JONES,
MOMMIE DEAREST
Biblical Mothers and Their Children

edited by
Cheryl A. Kirk-Duggan and Tina Pippin

Mother Goose, Mother Jones, Mommie Dearest

Biblical Mothers and Their Children

edited by
Cheryl A. Kirk-Duggan
Tina Pippin

Society of Biblical Literature
Atlanta

MOTHER GOOSE,
MOTHER JONES,
MOMMIE DEAREST
Biblical Mothers and Their Children

Copyright © 2009 by the Society of Biblical Literature

Library of Congress Cataloging-in-Publication Data

Mother Goose, Mother Jones, Mommie Dearest : biblical mothers and their children / edited by Cheryl A. Kirk-Duggan and Tina Pippin.
    p.   cm. — (Society of Biblical Literature Semeia studies ; no. 61)
Includes bibliographical references and indexes.
ISBN 978-1-58983-441-5 (pbk. : alk. paper)
    1. Mothers in the Bible. 2. Motherhood in popular culture. I. Kirk-Duggan, Cheryl A. II. Pippin, Tina, 1956–
BS579.M65M68 2009b
220.8'3068743—dc22   2009035122

16 15 14 13 12 11 10 09   5 4 3 2 1

Printed in the United States of America on acid-free, recycled paper conforming to ANSI/NISO Z39.48-1992 (R1997) and ISO 9706:1994 standards for paper permanence.

Contents

Responses

Acknowledgements

We offer our deepest thanks to the named and unnamed women, mothers and daughters, whose stories appear in ancient, biblical texts.

We hold much gratitude for the legacy of the *Women's Bible*, feminist, womanist global scholarship, and for all scholars with courage to name the tensions and injustices in the text, and for those who champion a hermeneutics of transformation.

To Gale Yee, we give thanks for staying the course with us, for shepherding the editorial process, and for her wise, discerning hermeneutical eye.

We thank the authors in this volume for stepping up to the challenge of deciphering mother-daughter and mother-son relationships that are often overlooked and hidden from view in majority biblical resources, lectionaries, and commentaries.

We are so grateful to all students, particularly those students in our biblical studies courses at Shaw University Divinity School and Agnes Scott College, who as teacher-learners press us to examine these texts in new ways.

And we offer our profound thanks to our families for celebrating our creativity and for understanding the times when we needed to be enmeshed in this work.

Abbreviations

AB	Anchor Bible
ABD	*Anchor Bible Dictionary*. Edited by David Noel Freedman. 6 vols. New York: Doubleday, 1992.
ABRL	Anchor Bible Reference Library
AThR	*Anglican Theological Review*
BRev	*Bible Review*
BZAW	Beiheft zur Zeitschrift für die alttestamentliche Wissenschaft
CBQ	*Catholic Biblical Quarterly*
CC	Continental Commentary
CSHJ	Chicago Studies in the History of Judaism
ETR	*Etudes théologiques et religieuses*
FCB	Feminist Companion to the Bible
JFSR	*Journal of Feminist Studies in Religion*
FOTL	Forms of the Old Testament Literature
GBS	Guides to Biblical Scholarship
HBC	*Harper's Bible Commentary*
HBD	*Harper's Bible Dictionary*
HSM	Harvard Semitic Monograph
ICC	International Critical Commentary
IBC	Interpretation: A Bible Commentary for Teaching and Preaching
Int	*Interpretation*
JBL	*Journal of Biblical Literature*
JIT	*Journal of Inculturation Theology*
JSNT	*Journal for the Study of the New Testament*
JSOT	*Journal for the Study of the Old Testament*
JSOTSup	Journal for the Study of the Old Testament Supplement Series
LHB/OTS	Library of Hebrew Bible/Old Testament Studies
NAC	The New American Commentary
NIB	*New Interpreter's Bible*. 13 vols. Nashville: Abingdon, 1994–2004.
NIBC	New International Biblical Commentary
OBT	Overtures to Biblical Theology
OTL	Old Testament Library

SBEJL	Society of Biblical Literature Early Judaism and Its Literature
SBLMS	Society of Biblical Literature Monograph Series
SBT	Studies in Biblical Theology
SemeiaSt	Semeia Studies
SP	Sacra Pagina
ThTo	*Theology Today*
ThViat	*Theologia Viatorum*
TOTC	Tyndale Old Testament Commentaries
TSAJ	Texte und Studien zum antiken Judentum
USQR	*Union Seminary Quarterly Review*
VT	*Vetus Testamentum*
WBC	Word Biblical Commentary
ZAW	Zeitschrift für die alttestamentliche Wissenschaft

Introduction

MOTHER GOOSE, MOTHER JONES, MOMMIE DEAREST:
BIBLICAL MOTHERS AND THEIR CHILDREN

Cheryl A. Kirk-Duggan
Tina Pippin

Mothers are loved and despised, glorified and caricatured, idolized and scandalized in life and literature. Many children do not know or grow up with their fathers but have strong images or experiences of mother, whether she is alive or dead. Recalling mother stories brings up a range of emotions: from nostalgia, gentleness, and affection to horror and mistrust. Some view the role of mother as an asexual institution, a devoted being who must sacrifice everything for husband/partner and children. Many tend to forget that mother is female, was once a little girl, and is a sexual being, with needs and wants. Within the historical, literary, artistic, psychological, and sociological landscape of the United States, our American civil religious dogmas rank Mom's apple pie, and thus mothers, along with flag and country. Mothers hold such a place of honor and adoration throughout history to the present day that many governments globally have set aside a day to honor them.

Do mothers hold such a place of honor in the book that consistently outsells all other books worldwide? Are mothers that important in the Bible? Why has a conversation that engages a comparative analysis between mothers, their sons and daughters in the Bible, and other mother-children relationships not emerged in the twenty-first century? Christianity as a global religion takes seriously the biblical text in matters of faith and life. In the United States, where most of the authors of this volume live, mothers are a part of civil religious praxis and are important, of course, to the well-being of families. Not only are there many kinds of paradigms of families; there are more single-parent and extended families headed by women, by mothers. Mothers have a tremendous impact on the rearing of children, and many who are Christian and Jewish live their lives according to so-called biblical principles. The former head of state, President George W. Bush, pressed his agenda of compassionate conservatism, adapting biblical language to his political platform. To begin to understand some of the complexities facing contemporary mothers and their families, it can be eye-opening to reflect, critique, and analyze the actual roles, actions, and experiences of biblical mothers and how they related to their children. Such an analysis is particularly vital, since in the patriarchal ancient Near East, a woman only had value when she married the right man and became a mother. Her value was also linked to her birthing the right son who would inherit the land, following the covenantal promise of Gen 12:1–3. Women and girls were property of their husbands and fathers. Thus, a rape or assault against a woman was not a personal crime against her; it was a crime against the property of her father or spouse. Though they had no rights, mothers were still vital in helping to create and sustain the family. Though there was little celebration of her, this reality did change during the Greco-Roman era.

There are conflicting opinions, but most agree that the earliest Mother's Day celebratory tributes occurred in ancient Greece to honor Rhea, the mother of many ancient Greek gods, and to the offerings ancient Romans made to their Great Mother of Gods, Cybele. During the seventeenth century, England began to celebrate "Mothering Sunday," and today it is celebrated on the fourth Sunday of Lent (the forty-day period leading up to Easter). In the United States, Mother's Day holiday is celebrated on the second Sunday in May; children honor their mothers with cards, gifts, and flowers. The first observance occurred in Philadelphia in 1907, based on suggestions by Julia Ward Howe in 1872, and it was dedicated to peace. Today peace groups such as Women's Action for New Directions link their fundraisers to Mother's Day. Most credit Anna Jarvis of Philadelphia with bringing about the official observance of Mother's Day. Her campaign to establish such a holiday began as a remembrance of her mother, who died in 1905 and who had, in the late nineteenth century, tried to establish "Mother's Friendship Days" as a way to heal the scars of the Civil War. Anna Jarvis began her campaign in 1907, and the national observance dates from 1914, when President Woodrow Wilson officially proclaimed Mother's Day as a national holiday to be held on the second Sunday of May. But Jarvis's accomplishment soon turned bitter for her. Enraged by the commercialization of the holiday, she filed a lawsuit to stop a 1923 Mother's Day festival and was even arrested for disturbing the peace at a war mothers' convention where women sold white carnations—Jarvis's symbol for mothers—to raise money. Shortly before her death, Jarvis told a reporter that she was sorry she had ever started Mother's Day. While some countries adapted the same date as the United States, others established their days in conjunction with celebrations already existing honoring motherhood. Some countries celebrate International Women's Day, rather than Mother's Day; others celebrate both. Even celebrations of mothers have a checkered history. Similarly, representations of mothers are mixed: some are jaded; others are repulsive.

The media, for example, has portrayed mothers in simplistic and complex ways. The 1950s and 1960s version of mother resided in the likes of June Cleaver, Lucy Ricardo, and later Julia, the first single TV mother who worked outside of the home. Many of these mothers had a fairytale-like sensibility, not unlike Mother Goose. Mother Goose is a mythological mother whose name is synonymous with collections of folk stories read to children. The mother who comes closest to being a real-life Mother Goose would have probably been an eighth-century noblewoman named Bertrada II of Laon, who married Pepin the Short, king of the Franks, in 740; in 742 she bore his son Charles, celebrated as Charlemagne, the de facto founder of the Holy Roman Empire. Bertrada, a patroness of children, who was her son's only teacher, was known as *Berte aux grand pied*, or Bertha Greatfoot, or Queen Goosefoot. By the mid-seventeenth century a mythical Mother Goose—*mère l'oye*—was widely acknowledged by French citizens as a fairy bird mother who told charming tales to children. Charles Perrault produced the first collection of stories to bear the name "Mother Goose" in 1697.

Born almost fifty years after the American Revolution ended, and dead on the eve of the New Deal, Mary Harris "Mother" Jones was a self-avowed "hell raiser." Known in the U.S. Senate as the grandmother of all agitators, she was a great storyteller and could invoke a wide range of emotions. Born in Ireland, she grew up in Toronto after her parents were forced to flee. After losing her husband, a staunch union member, and four children to a yellow fever epidemic in 1867 and losing everything, she owned in the great Chicago fire of 1871, Jones, a seamstress, got involved in the labor movement. Wherever there were labor troubles, there was Mother Jones—the "Miners' Angel." Jones made Chicago her base as she traveled back and forth across the country, doing union organizing, from industrial area to industrial area. She adopted U.S. laborers, and they called her "Mother." For over fifty years, she helped to stoke class conflict. At ninety-three years of age, she worked among coal miners in West Virginia. She came to national attention in 1912–13, because of the publicity resulting from frequent violence, and she was known for attracting government attention for the cause of workers. She led a march of miners' wives and the children's crusade to make the case for abolishing child labor.

Film star Joan Crawford joins the ranks of Augustine's mother Monica and Alexandria, Czarina at the time of the Russian Revolution, in their embodiment of "Mommie Dearest": abusive, self-centered, manipulative mothers. *Mommie Dearest* is a biographical account of Crawford, a great Hollywood actress, written by her adopted daughter. The actress decides to adopt children to fill a void in her life. Yet her problems with alcohol, men, and the pressures of show business disrupt her personal life, turning her into a mentally abusive wreck. Other biological, adoptive, or symbolic mothers have brought much love, care, and action for social justice in the lives of Saint Katherine Drexel, Dorothy Day, Mother Hale, Sojourner Truth, Hillary Clinton, Marian Wright Edelman, Amy Tan, the Mothers of the farm workers movement, and the Mothers of the Disappeared in Latin America. Hundreds of fiction and nonfiction books and articles have been written about mothers.

In those works and in the biblical text, one begins to see the complexities of the personas and roles of mothers. Many are not idyllic; some come from privilege, the others are poor. The relationships with mothers and their children vary. Some mothers are controlling, manipulative, brutal, conniving, violent, and abusive. Other mothers are gentle, supportive, loving, kind, and generous. Some mothers have had horrific lives and thus pass this type of behavior on to their children. Most societies have their image of who they think mothers ought to be— above and beyond that of saint. In some cultures the lives of mothers are made public as a matter of course, particularly when they are the spouses of governmental officials. Some mothers' lives are made public because they committed a crime, committed infanticide by taking the lives of their own children. Some mothers have joined their adult children in sordid lives of crime. Some mothers are the matriarchs of large, extended families. There is no one model of mother. While many in society assume that one such paradigm exists, a most engaging analysis can ensue when comparing biblical mothers, who cover a spectrum, with the more recent tapestry of fiction and nonfiction mothers.

The role of mother, then, is a literary, political, theological, ethical, biological, psychological, philosophical, economic construct. When the rhetoric of family values based on alleged biblical norms blared across the television during the 1996 presidential elections in the United States, families and paradigms for mothers surfaced yet again. But who are the mothers in the biblical text? What do they do? What kinds of power do they have? Liz Curtis Higgs and Barbara Essex have both authored books entitled *Bad Girls of the Bible*; Higgs's most recent text in that genre is entitled *Really Bad Girls of the Bible: More Lessons from Less-Than-Perfect Women.* Are these Bad Girls Bad Mothers? Is Badness here part signification and part reality? That is, are the girls so bad because they are really outstandingly good, or are they bad because they do evil things? Are the mothers in the Bible the same ones we meet in the lists cited above? How many mothers are there among the unnamed women in the Bible? Who gets to be a mother in the Bible? Given the press for political correctness, inclusiveness, and the overwhelming numbers of women and girls in faith communities, those enrolled in seminaries, and those who are taking leadership roles in the world, it presses us to wrestle with the ideology around mothers and mothering, particularly concerning biblical mothers.

This volume of Semeia Studies explores the role, place, and politics of identity of biblical mothers and their relationships with their daughters and their sons. The authors in this volume participate in a comparative analysis between biblical mothers and mothers in popular media, history, literature, the arts; they employ interdisciplinary analysis and engage their exegetical issues in conversation with critical theory, the dynamics of representation, and arguments that ponder matters of sociology, anthropology, class, race, gender, biology, economics, and the law. Method varies based upon author interest, texts engaged, and the types of tools the author deems necessary to engage a creative, comprehensive critique. In other words, a diversity of methods offers a rich discussion on what can be a sensitive matter: the deconstruction of motherhood.

The essays in this volume reflect a variety of ways of re-membering motherhood in the Bible. Themes shared by our authors include mythology, violence, race, sexuality, identity, authority, and power around the popular icons of Mother Goose, Mother Jones, and Mommie Dearest. Several authors utilize womanist hermeneutics to explore biblical motherhood. Madeline McClenney-Sadler discusses violence in her rereading of the legal tradition against incest in her article, "For God's Sake, Mommie, Help! The Mother-Daughter Dyad in Leviticus 18 and the Biblical Directive for Equity in the Family." McClenney-Sadler makes connections to the contemporary context of women and girls and how to continue the conversation with the biblical texts.

Wil Gafney considers the intricacies of motherhood in Ruth in "Mother Knows Best: Messianic Surrogacy and Sexploitation in Ruth." Gafney shows how motherhood is not so straightforward; women are forced into maternal roles, and one, Naomi, becomes a "messianic maternal surrogate." Gafney further compares Ruth, who is used to give a male child to the landowner-relative, to the slave women of the African diaspora to show how the sexual exploitation of women and girls continues to be a real danger.

Taking a different gaze, Brian Britt also reflects on Ruth in his essay, "Sacrifice and the Displacement of Mothers in Ruth and Coetzee's *Disgrace*," as he examines sacrificial and displaced mothers. By reading the biblical Ruth and South African novelist Coetzee together, Britt shows the further possibilities of comparative literature in exploring biblical motherhood and the mother-daughter bond. Britt relates, "Is it necessary for sacrifice to occur without the mother, even at the expense of the mother?"

Frank M. Yamada ventures into popular cultural representations of the biblical mother in "Of Virtue and of Eating Shorts: Breaking Down the Configuration of Faithful Mother and Wayward Son in Judges 13 and *The Simpsons*." Yamada reads the story of Sampson and his mother in Judg 13 against the relationship of Marge and Bart in *The Simpsons* and finds both to be examples of stories of the faithful mother and wayward son. When the relationship breaks down, chaos ensues.

Mothers also assume leadership roles in the biblical narrative. Mignon R. Jacobs explores this leadership identity in "Mothering a Leader: 1 Kings 1–2's Portrayal of Bathsheba as Model of Relational and Functional Identities." She examines mothers whose sons are rulers—Maacah (1 Kgs 15:1–15) and Athaliah (2 Kgs 11)—and the various roles and identities these mothers exemplify.

In "Parturition (Childbirth), Pain, and Piety: Physicians and Gen 3:16a," Linda Schearing examines childbirth and perspectives on pain during the process from an Anglo-American exegetical reading of obstetrical technology in the last two centuries. Schearing'focuses on the development of anesthesia, and the so-called curse factor around childbirth of Genesis 3.

Cheryl A. Kirk-Duggan explores the famous superwoman of Prov 31 in "Rethinking the 'Virtuous' Woman (Proverbs 31): A Mother in Need of Holiday." Kirk-Duggan asks, Is the wife/mother reflected in Prov 31 an admirable and persuasive role model? Or is she abusive to self and her children, a combination of a Mother Goose, Mother Jones, and Mommie Dearest? In her essay Kirk-Duggan questions this picture of the ideal woman while offering liberating, and less violent, alternatives to motherhood.

Mark Roncace and Deborah Whitehead bridge the Testaments in their exploration of sexuality and motherhood in contemporary Christian culture in their study, "Reading the Religious Romance: Sexuality, Spirituality, and Motherhood in the Bible and Today." They scrutinize evangelical Christian devotional literature that highlights women's sexuality (especially in relation to Jesus) and analyze the constructions of motherhood.

The relationship of Jesus and his mother Mary, as widow, is the center of Andrew Mbuvi's study in "Jesus and His Mother: An Analysis of Their Public Relationship as a Paradigm for African Women (Widows) Who Must Circumvent Traditional Authority in Order to Thrive in Society." The presence of Mary, absence of Joseph, and family dynamics in the Gospel accounts of Jesus are the focus of Mbuvi, who wants to know, "Is Mary exercising a cultural mandate to be the overseer of the family following the demise of her husband, therefore assuming the role of the *paterfamilias*, as widow?" Tina Pippin also explores motherhood images in the Jesus narrative in examining the role of "Jesus as Fantasy Mother." Utilizing fantasy criticism she questions the image of Jesus as mother hen in Matt 23:37–39 as a positive, maternal image.

In, "BMW: Biblical Mother Working/Wrecking, Black Mother Working/Wrecking," Stephanie Buckhanon Crowder continues to expand a womanist hermeneutic. She examines the way the Canaanite woman is portrayed (Matt 15:21–28 // Mark 7:24–30). She parallels this biblical treatment of the Canaanite woman to modern stereotypes of African American women. Buckhanon Crowder uses a womanist maternal theological framework to reveal the racial, ethnic, and gendered nature of the work of black mothers and the role of Jesus on these boundaries. She asks, "In other words, does a biblical mother working or a black mother working, in effect, become a biblical mother wrecking/black mother wrecking, one who wrecks or dismantles mother-to-child bonds and relationships in the name of work?"

Brenda Wallace engages a comparative analysis between a textual woman of justice, the widow in Luke 18 and a contemporary woman of justice, Mother Mary Harris Jones. She explores the widow in Luke 18 from feminine instinctual qualities that form the basis for archetypal mothers of justice movements.

Lastly, Paul gets a word in on motherhood in Margaret Aymer's "'Mother Knows Best': The Story of Mother Paul Revisited." Aymer rereads the Pauline language of motherhood in 1 Cor 3:1–2; 1 Thess 2:7b; and Gal 4:19 with a womanist lens, offering a critique of previous scholarship in this area with a refocus on race, gender, and sexuality. Is Paul "an accommodationist, bicultural mother teaching survival or a colonized mother teaching assimilation?" Does the motherhood language and image Paul uses for himself show "the identity and presence or absence of Paul's 'baby-daddy' in light of his trans-gendered rhetorical identity as mother?"

Respondents Allison Jasper and Tat-siong Benny Liew engage the various essays with helpful insight and learned critique at the close of the volume.

Issues of identity, authority, violence (self and external and eschatological), gender, sexuality, race, ethnicity, mother-bond(age), sexual exploitation and rape-marriage, murder, and role and relation to God have haunted the characters and characterization of motherhood from Eve to Mary and beyond. These images speak potent messages to contemporary women, and we intend this volume to be part of a conversation that examines and disrupts the violence and turns toward new ways of envisioning biblical (and beyond) motherhood—always with the biblical mothers alongside.

1

For God's Sake, Mommie, Help!

The Mother-Daughter Dyad in Leviticus 18
and the Biblical Directive for Equity in the Family

Madeline McClenney-Sadler

For centuries, biblical scholars have questioned the presence or absence of an explicit father-daughter incest prohibition in the biblical text. In light of research that I present in *Recovering the Daughter's Nakedness* (McClennny-Sadler 2007), our main question can be put to rest. There is an explicit father-daughter prohibition in Lev 18. An unexpected outcome of my research is evidence that mothers in the Iron Age household were the legal heads of the family. When studied through an anthropological lens, it becomes clear that the internal logic of Lev 18 provides theological and social equity for women in the family. Yet, as long as current popular thinking and biblical scholarship continue to perpetuate the Aristotelian hierarchy of male over female, men and women will continue to operate with the presumption of a theological disparity in their standing with each other and reinforce those disparities in their relationships. In households where incestuous assaults occur, daughters pay a heavy price for a mother who adopts the socially constructed role of second-class citizen. As we explore the mother-daughter dyad in Lev 18, I use the case below to illustrate the need to update our understanding of the biblical directive for theological and social equity in the family.

"I wish you were my mother." "What?" I said. "I wish you were my mother!" "Thank you, Linda. I would be very proud to have you as a daughter. [long pause, speaking almost in a whisper] Linda, your mother doesn't understand, that's why she doesn't listen to you, but one day she will. I know it's hard on you. Don't forget you have a lot of other grownups who are here to help."

By the time I met Linda, I had been doing research on the topic of incest since seminary, a total of four years. All of my doctoral papers addressed some aspect of incest in the biblical text. This topic was not chosen by choice but by Heaven's leading. As I was about to graduate from seminary, the horror of incest and the number of women who came to me disclosing stories of family rapes made it clear to me that I was unprepared for sanctuaries holding survivors of rape. I had an independent study elective to fill. Here was my opportunity to be better prepared to serve the body of Christ. I chose to work one-on-one with our human development specialist, who had a thriving family therapy practice. Our course title was "Counseling Survivors of Rape." My professor made it clear to me that what we were doing was only preparing me for brief crisis counseling. Among all forms of rape, I knew the least about the after-effects of incest in general, and father-daughter incest in particular. My father is the epitome of what every father should be; thus, father-daughter incest was almost unfathomable to me. Sadly, with such high defenses, I knew I would be of no ecclesiastical use. If I did not completely disabuse myself of the psychological safety and security from incest that was familiar to me, like so many people in the church, I would likely want to explain away the horror of incest if it were ever brought to my attention in a living example. Consequently, we made counseling survivors of incest our primary focus. For an entire summer, we studied incest and the impact of incest on survivors and how to support survivors in the immediate aftermath of disclosure. Years later, it came as somewhat of a surprise that in the middle of my research on the doctoral level, I was involved in the life of a family under siege by social services. A father had been accused of raping his eleven-year-old daughter. This was not just any father who did not know right from wrong, but a father who was supposed to know better—a father who was also an ordained minister.

The following discussion is part autobiography, part exegesis, part exhortation. Identification markers, like names, have been concealed to protect the innocent and the guilty in the encounter I present. The unfolding and substance of this case is based on my notes and personal memory. We are also examining the most important chapter in the Bible for mothers who love their daughters, Lev 18:6–18, commonly known as the incest prohibitions.

The number of boys being sexually abused by their mothers and fathers is as alarming as the statistics related to girls. I recognize that the particularities of their sufferings as males are finally coming to the light of day in the helping services and in the public domain. We must continue to create avenues for boys and adult males who have survived sexual abuse to disclose their stories without any fear of emasculation. Notwithstanding the focus of this volume of Semeia Studies on mothers and daughters and mothers and sons, the horror of incest and its detrimental impact is certainly not limited to females.

This is a tribute to the Divine Mystery that calls all mothers to stand at attention when their children are hurting and that calls all fathers to keep their sexual dysfunctions away from their daughters or face execution (Lev 20:14). In contradistinction to other avenues for scholarly reflection, this volume of Semeia Studies provides an opportunity for me to enlarge the range of intellectual expression to include reports of encounters with the Holy Other that have import for biblical interpretation. I have lost patience with an academy that views rationality and spirituality as mutually exclusive, as if encountering the voice of God in sacred space negates the operation of human reason. We may focus on one or the other, but the practice of making rationality and spirituality antithetical to each other in the academy is outdated. We acknowledge secretly, over coffee at SBL meetings, that *maybe* God still speaks to us. Yet, the secrecy itself allows biblical scholars to continue to treat Heaven's communications, as depicted in the biblical text, as *primarily* fairytale, myth, and allegory (Gen 6:13–17; Isa 1:1; Luke 1:26–28). Should we continue in this way, liberal scholarship, with all of its gifts to conservative scholarship, will become irrelevant to modern practitioners who regularly experience annunciations, still small voices, and theophanic encounters.

In addition to proposing new readings of the biblical text for the academy, seminarians, and pastors, the objective here is to embolden Christian mothers to defend Christian daughters raped by Christian fathers. Over twelve years later, I am honoring the pain and courage of a little girl emotionally abandoned by her mother who felt so disowned that she wished that I, one of her advocates, were her birth mother. I remember the hatred of her mother carried in that speculation of me as mother. I remember the seriousness of her brow as we ate in a Mexican restaurant, finishing our dinner on one of our weekly check-in meetings approved by social services. What she did not have the courage to say to her mother, at least not in my presence, was simply this, "For God's sake, Mommie, help! Your husband, my father, is raping me!" As long as mothers view fathers as the heads of the household, the malignancy of nonintervention will continue.

I concur with the prevailing view among psychologists that mothers who do not recognize the abuse and mothers to whom abuse is not disclosed are not to blame. I concur that patriarchal family structures make incest and other abuse possible. As an eyewitness to the practice of maternal alienation, I can also confirm that it is indeed true that offenders do all in their power to create mistrust between mother and daughter. Psychologist Anne Morris notes:

> There is a growing body of evidence that describes the tactics used by offenders to constantly and actively shape the realities, beliefs and relationships of his victim and those people surrounding the child. . . . The offender sets up a web-like structure of traps, lies and distortions to isolate the victim and to re-create the child as problematic in the eyes of siblings, the mother, friends, family and neighbors. In particular, the offenders

admit that their prime target is to destroy the child's relationship of trust
with the mother. (Morris 2003)

Nonetheless, I tell this story from what I perceive to be the viewpoint of
the one assaulted. To the one who has not reached adulthood and college-
level reading, highly reasoned intellectual discourse sounds like little more
than an excuse. This account is told through eyes that have not been exposed to postmodern psychology or twentieth-century feminism. I relate
this account from the perspective of one empathetic to the perspective of
the daughter who has disclosed abuse but whose mother does not believe
her. As we shall see, biblical law puts mothers in charge, and it is time for
mothers to reclaim their equity within the abusive and ungodly patriarchal structures that render them silent. In the film *Woman Thou Art Loosed*,
Bishop T. D. Jakes has produced a story that aptly depicts the anguish that
embodies a daughter's soul when mommie does not believe and protect.
The torment caused by a mother's disbelief is to a daughter a spiritual
assault. From the daughter's perspective, the weapon is a lack of love in
favor of self- or family-preservation. To the daughter, the lack of love is a
form of hate. Yet, the family has long since been destroyed by the rape;
there is nothing to preserve but Mommie Dearest's fiction. To whom it applies, even though you are not the mother of that child that you suspect
is being molested, your common kinship in the household of faith makes
every younger girl your daughter. The finger in this article that points
to Mommie Dearest charging her to consider, take action, and speak out
points to us all (Judg 19:30).

We begin with the phenomenological background to this story, a risky
endeavor in itself. As previously noted, I will not treat phenomenological
experiences[1] as off-limits to intellectual discourse. I choose to acknowledge the omnipresence of God's Spirit and the regularity with which She
speaks to us, if we believe She speaks, if we slow down and listen, and if
we surrender to her will and way. After providing the phenomenological backdrop to this story, we move to a summary of the historical-critical
research that I present in *Recovering the Daughter's Nakedness: A Formal
Analysis of Israelite Kinship Terminology and the Internal Logic of Leviticus 18*
(McClenney-Sadler 2007). We close with the implications for mothers and
daughters today and recommendations for seminary professors, pastors,
social workers, and people of faith who interpret the biblical text and encounter incest in the life of the church and beyond.

After moving to a new city, there we sat in the pews of the church that
Heaven had finally given us the green light to join. We only knew the pastor and a few other members. It was a sunny spring Sunday. We entered
and sat on the left side of our new home church—a small family church. It

---

1. Also known as miracles, signs, and wonders.

must have once been a rural church. By this time, it was experiencing the encroachment of new development. Church members were so welcoming and the pastor was so gifted a preacher and servant of the Lord that chairs had to be placed in both aisles to accommodate more worshipers. It was easy to see this sacred space would have to be enlarged.

At 10:50 a.m., the pulpit was empty. Behind the pulpit, the choir began to take its place. A man followed by a teenage girl entered the pulpit. As they came into my direct line of view, time stopped. I do not mean that metaphorically. For me, someone hit the pause button on time and space. Everything froze. My husband and everything to my left formed a vertical wall of particulate gray like a channel that has gone off the air on an old television screen. Simultaneously, the same thing happened to my immediate right. I saw rows of people sitting in pews waiting for the service to begin, and then suddenly, everything to my right turned into a wall of fuzzy gray particles. I could see no one. I could hear nothing. All sound had ceased its travel. The atoms of all earthly matter—solids, liquids, and gases—ceased their normal rate of vibration and stood at attention. What remained was a telescopic view connecting me to this unfamiliar man and the teenage girl who followed him. Their movement was suspended in time as well. From the pulpit to my being, complete Evil disrobed before me. It felt impenetrable and thick enough to cut. This was the most uncomfortable encounter with a diabolical presence I had ever experienced. There are no English words that can relate the magnitude of this evil. C. S. Lewis speaks of Satan's lieutenants in the *Screwtape Letters*. This was no emissary. It seemed to be the General himself. Evil entered the sanctuary, and I felt the young girl's sensations replace my own. I was feeling both a demonic presence in the midst of this encounter and the shame of incest all at once. The man walking in front of me had touched me inappropriately; he betrayed my trust, he violently assaulted me, and I was in deep pain, without identity, without agency, completely lost.

This was not spiritual warfare; there was no need to rebuke the devil. This was Heaven drawing the curtain on evil. The air was so thick with disembodied Evil that I wanted to stop this extremely painful transmission, but I had erred in the past by stopping such a transmission—withdrawing my soul from it. I said, "Okay, Lord, I will receive what you are showing me." I relaxed and allowed Heaven to complete its presentation (Gen 6:11–22; Exod 11; 1 Sam 3:1–18; Luke 2: 9–14). As suddenly as it began, it ended, and the man and the teenager found their seats and sat down in the pulpit. I could see my husband and everything to my left and right again. The clock continued its drone. The sounds of whispers and laughter pervaded the sanctuary; the hum of electricity continued its song. Particles of matter yet to be named by science resumed their movement. I had one question of God: "What do you want me to do?" The Holy Spirit said simply "support her." I said "okay" and forgot about it for a few months.

Several months later, I was at the church late one evening; I ran into another female minister on staff. "Did you hear what happened?" "No," I said. "It was all over the news," she said, "But we are keeping it quiet. You didn't hear?" "No, what happened? "They arrested him." "They arrested who?" "They arrested Rev. Jake." "You know, the man from Vermont with two girls." I did not know he had *two* girls. "Yeah, they say he touched them. You know that older one was enjoying it. She's fifteen and all hot in the pants. The younger one doesn't even know what she is talking about; she's four yearsold." I was as shocked by this female minister's perspective as I was by the news that there was another daughter. She continued, "The church is going to help the father get a lawyer. You know how those white people at Social Services are. They don't care if they destroy our families." Immediately, I remembered the unveiling of this situation that happened several months prior, but the key relationship of support that actually formed was with the younger daughter, not the soul I saw in the pulpit that day. The months rolled by, and the juvenile court prosecutor went about establishing her case. Eventually, Rev. Jake was removed from the home. I met with the mother to tell her that I believed her daughter and to encourage her to accept Linda's disclosure. She responded with incredulity, saying that her daughter had an active imagination and that she "makes up things." The mother's angst and inability to digest all that was happening was clear.

One Saturday afternoon, as Linda and I played in the park, I made a terrible mistake and teased her about the way she threw the frisbee far away from where I was standing. In utter frustration, she quit playing. "I can't do anything right!" I apologized and asked her repeatedly what was wrong. She said "Nothing." We sat on our blanket. She looked directly at me and asked, "Why can't God stop evil?" "What do you mean, Linda?" "Evil can't be stopped, right?" "No, Linda, God can stop evil." I learned later that against the court's instructions that no one talk to the children about the matter, a member of the church, also an assistant to the public defender, along with other members, visited Linda that morning and she recanted. It was recorded on tape. I was concerned that, in a matter of weeks, the father could be back in bed with his daughters. I was given permission to continue ministering to the children when they were placed in foster care. The whole situation had become a hornet's nest. I would have no peace until I asked Linda why she recanted. One of our regular visits would give me the opportunity, and the Highest Court of All gave me permission to disregard the juvenile court's gag order as well.

I asked the question. Linda responded, "My mother said it would make things better." I asked her to affirm to me that her original account of abuse was true. She gave several nonverbal "yeses," motioning with her head up and down as she yawned. Finally, I asked her to be very clear. She finally whispered, "Yes. I told you already." I asked her what she wanted of me; she said, "Talk to my father." I told her directly for the first time that I believed her, that God hated what had happened, and that the Bible prohibited it (Lev 18:17). I told her that God wept when she wept and that she would grow into a strong young woman. Since she had been coerced to change her story, I asked her what she wanted me to say if I were questioned by authorities. She was worried that if I disclosed our conversation, "people will get mad at you." I told her I did not care. I only wanted to respect her wishes. More than anything else, many children who have had their wills and bodies transgressed need at least one adult to affirm that their yes means yes and that their no means no. It is an important gift to their recovery in adulthood as they reflect back and learn to trust again. She responded as any conscientious, straight-A eleven-year-old might respond, "Well, you can't lie." Somehow she understood that her recantation was coerced and whatever I said was not. I took her father to lunch and told him that she wanted him to stop abusing her. I did what the daughter told me to do. When I was subpoenaed, under oath, I did what the daughter told me to do—tell the truth. For that crisis, I saw myself as the priest of Linda and her siblings only. The judge stated that even if all the other witnesses' testimonies were impeachable, he could make a ruling based solely on my testimony. It seemed to me that Heaven was the real testifier—I, its pawn. With the recantation, Evil tried to close the curtain again, but God was in control of the stage. None can close a curtain that God wants open. After I testified, court was adjourned. I went to the back of the courtroom where we—church members—gathered. Husband and wife stood together. The wife was both stoic and gentle. She cowered when Rev. Jake, her husband, approached, and she straightened up when he moved away. Her husband played the part of an innocent man caught in a mess. He was kind to me. During the two years of this ordeal, wherever I saw him, I always greeted him; he always greeted me. The theatrical nature of this couple's relationship brought me to silent tears at the back of the courtroom. Linda's mother stood in front of me smiling. "Why are you crying? You did what you had to do." I just shrugged my shoulders. Gently, like a mother consoling her daughter, she wiped the tears from my cheeks with her bare hands, wiping one side first, and then the other. I welcomed her kind and genuine care but wept for her nonetheless. Her children were safe in foster care. She was going home with the monster.

One Friday

Long before the juvenile court closed its case, our small family church had outgrown itself. We were in a new sanctuary, and I had a new passion, informed by my walk with Linda. I had to get to the heart of centuries-old questions about the incest prohibitions of Lev 18. Why were certain relatives explicitly listed, but an explicit father-daughter prohibition appeared to be absent? The curtain was about to open here as well. My research demonstrates that the father-daughter prohibition was concealed because the Holiness Code transmitter knew something that we had not considered. The incest prohibitions protect relationships between two people who have a special claim to mutual love, protection, and affection with one another. The relationship between two close family members is protected whether their relationship is sexual or not. The violation of a daughter is a violation of a *mother's right* to unhindered affection and love with her daughter, that is, without sexual exploitation and competition for the father, his favor, or resources. Verse 6 of Lev 18 clarifies that both consensual and nonconsensual sex with a biological family member is an abomination. A father-daughter prohibition is implicit here. Given that other relatives are explicitly listed, that has not been enough for scholars throughout the ages.

In *Recovering the Daughter's Nakedness* (McClenney-Sadler 2007), I demonstrate that verse 17 provides an explicit father-daughter prohibition because it protects a wife's right to peace, tranquility, and unhindered affection to people with whom she is closely related: "You shall not uncover the nakedness of a wife and her daughter, you shall not take her son's daughter or her daughter's daughter to uncover her nakedness; they are her flesh (17); it is depravity." Each of the incest prohibitions is written according to whose rights are being protected. The catalogue begins with the rights of Yahweh to the nuclear family (v. 6) followed by the mother's rights (7a), and ending with the wife's rights (17, 18). The first is last and the last is first. This merism informs us that in the ancient Israelite family the mother's rights are second only to those of Yahweh.

It was through an interdisciplinary evaluation of the prohibitions of Lev 18 that the results summarized here came to the fore. Specifically, my research necessitated a six-pronged analysis of over three thousand Hebrew kinship terms, a formal analysis as invented by comparative ethnographers who study incest cross-culturally, and a structural examination of descent, marriage rules, and postmarital residence in the biblical text. The bulk of my research culminated with much prayer on a Friday afternoon when the internal logic of Lev 18 became transparent with three short assertions from Heaven. According to the incest prohibitions of Leviticus, incest is prohibited between: (1) Ego and Ego's close kin (vv. 6–11); (2) Ego and Ego's close kin's kin (vv. 12–16); and (3) Ego and two people who are close kin to each other (vv. 17–18). Not only is there an explicit daughter prohibition; there is also an explicit full-sister prohibition in verse 9. Furthermore, the kinship system of ancient Israel was not Eskimo; it was normal Hawaiian, which means descent was not determined patrilineally. In ancient Israel it was determined bilaterally, that is, through males and females (McClenney-Sadler 2007, 72). Cross-culturally, throughout the world, wherever descent is determined bilaterally, through both parents, the status of women is higher or nearly equal to that of men. Bilateral descent is reflected in the bilateral extension of the incest taboos and also in the descent markers of the Pentateuch.[2] Our assessments of "patriarchal" behavior in the biblical text, derived from a patrilineal descent rule, are incorrect. Critical texts need to be reanalyzed in light of the ethnographic evidence that in normal Hawaiian kinship systems women are treated as equals in the family. As reflected in biblical accounts of male ancestors, the efforts of the Leviticus Holiness Code transmitters to attenuate the brute force of unholy male domination in ancient Israelite families was not always successful. However, there is growing evidence that the "exceptional" women with power in the Hebrew Bible were not so exceptional. With rights second only to Yahweh, Lev 18 gave women jural and cultic authority to fight and subvert male domination if it appeared, and it conditioned males to share authority within the operative Hawaiian kinship system. It should be no surprise that the Lord says to Abraham, "Do whatever Sarah says" (Gen 21:12), or that King Josiah is instructed to take the rediscovered law to the prophetess Huldah for authentification (2 Kgs 22:13, 14). Like incest, male domination is an abomination.

The same rights that Lev 18 protected for ancient Israelite women accrue to the women, mothers, and wives who find sacral authority in the Hebrew Bible today. You may articulate this right to protect yourself, your daughter(s), and other female relatives. Men may articulate the rights of women as advocates of their female kin and advocates of egalitarian familial relationships. When revisited, we find that even troubling passages that address the consequences of rape echo this fundamental truth: the God of the Hebrew Bible values women's rights. The Torah militates against the manipulation of brute force. Where the rights of women are respected, incest and other forms of abuse cannot survive. The case of the concubine's Levite in Judg 19 illustrates the cognitive dissonance created by the biblical retelling of stories of rape and abuse and the assumptions that underlie the retelling. The retelling itself has theological and revelatory purpose. Judges 19:1–30 is not concerned about inhospitality toward men, as some have argued (Trible 1984; Fewell 1992). The only person actually denied hospitality is the concubine. This pericope is about inhospitality toward women in general and daughters in particular. We have taken such offense at the barbaric domination and rape explicit in this story that we have missed the antithetical parallelism that sets up its instructive agenda to warn males not to behave this way. Two fathers are juxtaposed to each other: a "good" father (Judg 1:1–15) who tries to protect his daughter's

---

2. This can only be understood in light of the seven marriage forms attested in the Genesis–Exodus narratives: Milcah-Nahor (Gen 11:29); Sarah-Abraham (Gen 12:13); Rebekah-Isaac (Gen 24:4); Mahalath-Esau (Gen 28:9); Leah-Jacob-Rachel (Gen 29:30); Aaron-Elisheba (Exod 6:23); and Amram-Jochebed (Exod 6:20).

safety and beckons her stay in her mother's household, and a "bad" father who offers his daughter and the concubine to a rapacious crowd (Judg 19:22–26).

The repetition of kinship terms in the first ten verses provides clues to the reader that this story is about family ties. The instructive nature of this narrative is that the consequence of inhospitality toward daughters is the total annihilation of the offending clan (Judg 20:8–48). Inhospitality toward daughters will not be tolerated. Offended families are licensed to kill. The redactor's hand aptly clarifies that there was "no king in Israel." Atrocities like these occur because men rule and Yahweh does not. The commonly held view that women are represented as the property of men in the biblical text does not take into account how social systems operate in prestate societies. Until a social system grows beyond kin ties and develops its own police force that takes over the role of protector, defender, and enforcer, brothers and fathers must police the tribal networks. Sometimes they do this well, sometimes horribly. When a band of raiding males arrives to take water, women, and food, the simple biological fact of greater physical strength places males in the line of fire. It is far too simplistic to describe women as the property of men, especially in societies where the kinship system grants women rights equal to that of men, but there is no separate police system to enforce it. The case of slavery in ancient Israel is a separate matter. It is not clear that either men or women have full command of their bodies. We cannot address slavery here.[3] In this analysis, we are addressing the rights of family members. In Judg 19, males who fail to respect women are executed, and no recipient of this tradition can miss that the "bad" father neglected his responsibility by offering his daughter and the concubine. We must keep in mind that, in a Hawaiian kinship system, one who is a "father" has certain expected duties to care for one who is a "daughter" while under his roof. Whether the relationship is a blood-tie or not is immaterial. The "bad" father failed in every respect.

Housed under the roof of the "bad" father, the silence and absence of the mother figure magnifies the concubine's betrayal. Where was the mother of the household? Why did she not object? What an interesting coincidence that in the few biblical accounts where fathers behave badly toward daughters, mothers are noticeably silent (Gen 19; Judg 11; 2 Sam 13). This may very well be the structural representation of a truth in human conditioning that cannot be delimited by historical period, culture, or geographical location: oppression silences resistance. From daughter's perspective, Mommie's silence wins her the appellation of Mommie Dear-

---

3. It is noteworthy, however, that Lev 19:20 suggests that laying carnally with a slave woman was frowned upon. The slavewoman is protected from execution because it is understood that she would feel unable to assert a right of refusal even if she were betrothed to another.

est. Because she is silent, we cannot comment on Mommie Dearest in the biblical text without an analysis comparative to the continuing silence of mothers facing father-daughter incest today. In the biblical text, there are indeed representations of maternal instincts gone awry, but these are women who have embraced their God-given status. They become Mommie Dearest by seeking to use their equal status coercively; such is the case in Sarah's treatment of Ishmael and his mother Hagar and Rebecca's treatment of Esau. Yet, these are not mother-daughter dyads. The mother-daughter dyad that is protected by Lev 18 prevents the silencing of mothers. According to psychologist Patricia Bell, modern-day mothers who accept the social construction of motherhood "impose upon themselves unrealistic standards of ideal motherhood" (Bell 2003, 135). The only power they have within the family is attached to mothering; however, they must yield to abusive patriarchal structures and the dominance of the father in the home. This ensures their silence in the face of evidence or suspected evidence of sexual abuse. To rebut the father is to rebut the authority of God who put the father in charge. God-fearing women obey God, even at the expense of their children. Mothers like Linda's mother enter into marriage already silenced by the implicit rules of the marriage contract: preserve the fiction of superior mothering that would never miss abuse and do so while preserving the fiction that God says that the father must rule. Mothers who have been trained in this way never have an opportunity to be Mother Joneses to their children because the average marriage contract and its traditional vows place no emphasis on the mutuality of loving and parenting expected in the biblical canon (Gen 2:24; Song of Songs).

By virtue of the jural-legal authority given to women in Lev 18 by the prophet Moses, according to tradition, on behalf of the deity, according to the text, neither Iron Age mothers nor twenty-first-century mothers who accept its constitutional value in faith have biblical permission to remain silent in the face of a father who thinks his rule is supreme. Mothers of incest victims must reclaim the Levitical authority given to them to consider it, take counsel, and speak out (Judg 19:30; Lev 18) when their rights and the rights of their daughters are violated. Their efforts must be supported and not subverted by those who seek to maintain the father's right to be the king of his castle, even if he behaves like a barbarian.

One Day Soon

Remaining Mommie Dearest to a young girl is to let the curtain remain closed at all costs and to align oneself with the ill father whose sexual domination in the family is often encouraged by demonic disembodied entities. His demons tell the mother that she could be wrong and that she will look foolish if she confronts him, her ruler. The man who thinks he rules has already put in place specious web-like mental whispers about how silly and confused children can be. What can be done? At this point, I wish to directly address the Mommie Dearest who seeks to become Mother Jones, and I wish to directly address those who must now act as Mother Jones, if Mommie Dearest is unable to summon her voice and authority. If Heaven has led you to this article, it is probably time to act.

If more confirmation is needed from Heaven, ask for more confirmation. Consider taking action as if the abuse were actually happening in front of you. In my context, the denial was so complete and the religious support was thrown so clearly around the Reverend father that I needed to be shown what was happening in advance to trust the actions that I was being led to take. One of the reasons I was sent to the church described above was so that this article could appear now to you, in support of you as mother or surrogate mother, and in support of what you have been contemplating. Let the Divine Mystery guide you, but be certain, once evil has been unveiled to us by Heaven, to do nothing is to incur guilt as if we had actually committed the abomination ourselves (Lev 19:18). There are a multitude of networks and resources to guide you.[4]

What is at stake? A woman's entire life and mental health is at stake. The enduring consequences of father-daughter rape includes a startling and horrifying range of effects the severity of which is determined by the age of the overcomer or survivor at the time of the abuse and the duration and extent of the abuse. According to Cole, the effect of incest on self and social functioning include: difficulty setting boundaries; self-mutilation; borderline personality disorder; multiple personality disorder; substance abuse; disruption in self-development; deviations in the ability to experience a sense of trust and confidence in relationships; identity confusion; poorly modulated affect and impulse control; insecurity in relationships, particularly distrust, suspiciousness, lack of intimacy, and isolation; low self-esteem; anxiety disorders; depression; suicide; and many developmental problems that may plague a survivor for years (Cole and Putnam 1992, 174–84).

My interlocutor's proposition that the older daughter somehow "enjoyed" the abuse revealed her own dysfunction while aptly capturing a lurking thought in the minds of people who are not dysfunctional at all: Suppose the sex is consensual? Psychologist Sue Blume said it best in *Secret Survivors*: "if her 'no' has no power, her 'yes' has no meaning" (1991, 23). Children do what they are told. True consent cannot be given because children know that refusal is not allowed.

The biblical directive of Lev 18 is for families to protect the rights of girls and women in the household. The nonoffending parent must be supported as disclosures are made. The seriousness of a failure to protect

---

4. See Help for Recovery website: http://www.way2hope.org/incest_survivors _help.htm; and Fortune 1983. FaithTrust Institute does workshops and trainings related to identifying and addressing sexual and domestic violence, including when clergy are perpetrators. See also Cooper-White 1995.

women in the family is exemplified in Judg 19 and again in King David's mishandling of the rape of his daughter Tamar by her brother Amnon. David is censured in the biblical text (2 Sam 14). David is portrayed as a horribly neglectful father. He is implicated in the rape of his own daughter because he fails to avenge according to biblical law. The incest laws punish consensual half-sibling sex with communal alienation (Lev 20:17). The Deuteronomic influence in this account demonstrates that Absalom behaved in a priestly fashion, ensuring that the execution of his brother was carried out as required by the rape laws (Deut 22:25).

Without communal support for maternal authority in the family, as bestowed by the sacred texts, mothers will continue to cower before fathers who believe they rule. Mothers and daughters will continue to be alienated from each other, and girls like Linda will continue to view their mothers as Mommie Dearest. According to a reliable anonymous source from the court, Linda's own Mommie Dearest admitted knowing what was happening between her husband, Rev. Jake, and his daughters. All the while, she stood by him and lied for him before an entire congregation. To Linda, her own mother was also the perpetrator. Pastors and practitioners must begin to face the unthinkable incest taboo with the courage and the determination to learn and understand an experience that impacts 30–50 percent of all women and 20–40 percent of boys. We must unravel erroneous assumptions about the acceptability of incest in biblical narratives and law. Mommie Dearest must be empowered to become Mother Jones through prophetic preaching that identifies her authority in the household as second only to that of Yahweh. Believers, social workers, and practitioners who read the Hebrew Scriptures must inform Mommie Dearest of her biblically authorized joint headship, if not sole headship, in the household. When the entire community refuses to let evil close the curtain on itself and provides support to Mommie Dearest against her own domination by the offender, she is more likely to develop the courage to transform into Mother Jones. She will begin to see what has been disclosed with new eyes. The offending father can be held responsible for all the guilt he bears, and she will bear guilt no more. At that time, the tears that Mother Jones wipes away will be those of her own daughter after she herself has testified that she believes her daughter and that she has indeed come to help.

Works Cited

Alaggia, Ramona. 2002. Balancing Acts: Reconceptualizing Support in Maternal Response to Intra-Familial Child Sexual Abuse. *Clinical Social Work Journal* 30.1:41–56.

Bell, Patricia. 2002. Factors Contributing to a Mother's Ability to Recognize Incestuous Abuse of Her Child. *Women's Studies International Forum* 25.3:347–57.

———. 2003. "I'm a Good Mother Really!" Gendered Parenting Roles and Responses to the Disclosure of Incest. *Children and Society* 17:126–36.

Blume, Sue. 1991. *Secret Survivors: Uncovering Incest and Its Aftereffects in Women.* New York: Ballantine Books.

Bolen, Rebecca M., and J. Leah Lamb. 2004. Ambivalence of Nonoffending Guardians after Child Sexual Abuse Disclosure. *Journal of Interpersonal Violence* 19:185–211.

Candib, Lucy M. 1999. Incest and Other Harms to Daughters across Cultures: Maternal Complicity and Patriarchal Power. *Women's Studies International Forum* 22.2:185–201.

Cole, Pamela M., and Frank W. Putnam. 1992. Effect of Incest on Self and Social Functioning: A Developmental Psychopathology Perspective. *Journal of Consulting and Clinical Psychology* 60.2:174–84.

Cooper-White, Pamela. 1995. *The Cry of Tamar: Violence against Women and the Church's Response.* Minneapolis: Fortress, 1995.

Fewell, Danna Nolan. 1992. Judges. Pages 67–77 in *The Women's Bible Commentary.* Edited by Carol Newsom and Sharon Ringe. Louisville: Westminster John Knox.

Fortune, Marie. 1983. *Sexual Violence: The Unmentionable Sin.* Cleveland: Pilgrim.

Grand, Sue, and Judith Alpert. 1993. The Core Trauma of Incest. An Object Relations View. *Professional Psychology: Research and Practice* 24.3:330–34.

Howard, Carol A. 1993. Factors Influencing a Mother's Response to Her Child's Disclosure of Incest. *Professional Psychology: Research and Practice* 24.2:176–81.

Koralewski, Mary A. 1993. Review of Janis Tyler Johnson, *Mothers of Incest Survivors: Another Side of the Story. Journal of Sex Research* 30.3:283–85

McClenney-Sadler, Madeline. 2007. *Recovering the Daughter's Nakedness: A Formal Analysis of Israelite Kinship Terminology and the Internal Logic of Leviticus 18.* Library of Hebrew Bible/Old Testament Studies 476. New York: T&T Clark.

Morris, Anne. 2003. The Mother of the Victim as Potential Supporter and Protector: Considerations and Challenges. Paper presented at the Child Sexual Abuse: Justice Response or Alternative Resolution Conference convened by the Australian Institute of Criminology.

Poling, James Newton. 1991. *The Abuse of Power: A Theological Problem.* Nashville: Abingdon.

Rice, Marnie E., and Grant T. Harris. 2002. Men Who Molest Their Sexually Immature Daughters: Is a Special Explanation Required? *Journal of Abnormal Psychology* 111.2:329–39.

Trible, Phyllis. 1984. *Texts of Terror: Literary Feminist Readings of Biblical Narratives.* Philadelphia: Fortress.

Turell, Susan C. 2000. Differentiating Incest Survivors Who Self-Mutilate. *Child Abuse & Neglect* 24.2:237–49.

2

Mother Knows Best

MESSIANIC SURROGACY AND SEXPLOITATION IN RUTH

Wil Gafney

The Bible remains a paradigmatic text in the West for exploration and analysis of human and divine relationships. In some contexts, the authority imputed to the Bible makes it normative and definitive (within specific communal interpretive frameworks). In other contexts, the biblical text represents normalization of hierarchy and androcentrism. The impact of biblical narratives and their underlying tropes on religious discourse in the West cannot be overstated, particularly in the characterizations and expectations of women, of mothers.

In human experience, motherhood remains ubiquitous and paradoxical. Not all are or will become mothers, but all have had mothers. Yet, motherhood is regularly obscured in the genealogies that describe the emergence of key characters in the Jewish and Christian Scriptures. Patrilineality is the dominant (but not the only)[1] form of relational identity in those two canons. Their genealogies regularly detail fathers (or significant male ancestors) without naming or mentioning the women who give birth

---

Portions of this paper were initially presented at the Annual Meeting of the Society of Biblical Literature (Gafney 2005b) and at the Midwestern Regional Conference of the Society of Biblical Literature (Gafney 2006).

1. Rebekah's father is identified by a matronymic in Gen 24:15, 24; he is Bethuel the son of Milcah. Milcah is his mother. Rebekah's household is also matrilineal; it is identified as her mother's household in verse 28. (Other matrilineal households in the scriptures include the families of origin of Ruth and Orpah in Ruth 1:8 and the bride in Song 3:4 and 8:2.) Other persons in the scriptures identified by their mother's names include Jacob, who identifies himself as the son of Rebekah (*ben Rivkah*) but does not mention Isaac or even Abraham in Gen 29:12, and David's chief warriors—and nephews—Joab, Abner, and Abishai, the sons of Zeruiah, their mother, in 1 and 2 Samuel (Gafney 2005b).

to the children-cum-ancestors in those lists.[2] The naming of Ruth as an ancestor of David in Jewish Scripture (Ruth 4:13–17) and of David and of Jesus in Christian Scripture (Matt 1:5–15) is significant in both corpora.

This essay explores one biblical configuration of motherhood through the notion of maternal nurture, which I find to be inverted and subverted in Naomi's relationship with Ruth. I examine Naomi's motivations in furthering Ruth's relationship with Boaz, asking the questions: Is Naomi seeing Ruth's well-being or her own? And, if Naomi is motivated by self-preservation, does that make her a type of "Mommie Dearest"? This hermeneutic explores the characters, relationships, and motherhood in Ruth from the underside. I examine the marriages of Ruth and Orpah as paradigms of rape-marriage characterized by the use of the verb נשא, *ns'*. This essay examines the seizure and sexual exploitation of women for the purposes of providing Israelite progeny, the legitimization of maternity by force, in the broader literary context of the Hebrew Scriptures. Under consideration are the literary transformations of Ruth from race-traitor to warrior-(heart)- woman (*eshet chayil*, אשת חיל), Orpah from cultural exemplar to extraneous outsider, and Naomi from purveyor of Ruth's body to messianic maternal surrogate. This essay explores Ruth's covenant with Naomi from the perspective of a non-Israelite cultural outsider. I analyze Ruth's abandonment of her family, land, ancestors, and gods through the lens of the abducted, enslaved, and sexually exploited and Orpah's return to her family, land, ancestors, and gods through the lens of the abducted, enslaved, and sexually exploited and through the perspective of those who escaped a similar fate. Then I consider Naomi's conduct in securing a kinsman to provide for her material needs at the cost of Ruth's and (initially) Orpah's bodies, from Naomi's textual silence at the abduction of Orpah and Ruth to her exploitation of Boaz's ego and desire, and Ruth's sexuality.

Finally, a contemporary hermeneutic applied to the book of Ruth compares the characters in Ruth and women in the African diaspora (African slaves in the Americas, contemporary Tutsi and Darfurian women) who have been abducted and sexually assaulted to provide progeny for an alien culture. This essay also considers the conduct and motives of women who facilitate the sexual exploitation of other women and rejects the sacralization of the practices of rape-marriage, forced impregnation, and sexual exploitation, particularly for material gain, because they pose a continuing danger to women and girls. And, I revaluate and rearticulate Ruth's maternal relationship to messianic figures in Judaism and Christianity.

Ruth as Messianic Mother

Ruth 4:13. So Boaz took Ruth, and she became his woman. When he went to her, Yhwh gave her conception, and she gave birth to a son. 14. Then the

---

2. A notable exception is the extended genealogy in 1 Chr 1–9.

women[3] said to Naomi, "Blessed be YHWH, who has not left you woman, without redeeming kin this day; and may that[4] name be proclaimed in Israel! 15. That one shall be to you woman, a restorer of life and a provider when your hair grays woman; for your daughter-in-law, she who loves you woman, she has given birth—she who is more to you woman, than seven sons." 16. Then Naomi took the child and laid him in her bosom, and became his nurturer. 17. The women of the neighborhood gave him a name, saying, "A son has been born to Naomi." The women named him Oved;[5] he became the father of Yishai, the father of David.[6]

Matthew 1:1. This is the genealogy of Yeshua the Messiah, son of David, son of Avraham:

2. Avraham was the father of Yitzchak;
Yitzchak was the father of Yaakov;
Yaakov was the father of Yehudah, his brothers and sisters;
3. Yehudah was the father of Peretz and Zerach; their mother was
Tamar;
Peretz was the father of Hetzron;
Hetzron was the father of Ram;
4. Ram was the father of Amminadav;
Amminadav was the father of Nachshon;
Nachshon was the father of Salmon;
5. Salmon was the father of Boaz; his mother was Rachav;
Boaz was the father of Oved; his mother was Ruth;
Oved was the father of Yishai;
6. Yishai was the father of David the king . . .;
16 Yaakov was the father of Yosef, the husband of Miryam,
from whom was born Yeshua, the One who is called "Messiah."

Ruth is configured as the (fore)mother of the Messiah in both Jewish and Christian Scriptures and traditions. Both David and Jesus are identified as "Messiah" in the Scriptures.[7] (Saul is the original biblical messiah, but YHWH revokes his messianic status.[8] This may be somewhat difficult

---

3. Because the scriptures are androcentric, it is important to identify each female person and her agency when the text does so. Therefore, I make patent each grammatical feminine construct pertaining to women.

4. Literally, "his name"; ironically, it is not clear whether the Divine Name or Yishai's name is meant here.

5. I use the names by which biblical characters were known in their own time and space, given by their parents, in their language, and not those imposed upon them by later European scholarship. (Remembering that there is no "J" in Hebrew, Greek or even Latin, the names "Jesse" and "Jesus" are more German than Hebrew.)

6. Unless otherwise noted, all translations are mine.

7. For larger discussions of David's complicated identity, see Halpern, 2001; Lenowitz 1998; Werblowsky 1992.

8. In 1 Sam 24:7 LXX, David refuses to assassinate Saul, whom he recognized as God's messiah. God will have to remove Saul, Godself: "David said to his men,

to track in English, since both JPS and NRSV use "anointed" to translate משיח, *meshiach*, rather than "messiah.") The Greek Septuagint uses *christos* (χριστός, Christ, anointed) for David, just as the Greek New Testament does for Jesus.[9] Consider the following texts where the respective messiahs are identified as the "Christ":

> 2 Sam 23:1 LXX These are the last words of David: Faithful is David, the son of Yishai, and faithful is the man whom the Lord raised up as messiah of the God [*christon theou*, χριστὸν Θεοῦ] of Yaakov, and beautiful are the psalms of Israel.

> Mark 8:29 Yeshua asked them, "But who do you say that I am?" Kefa (Peter) answered him, "You are the Messiah [*ho christos*, ὁ χριστός]."

In the Matthean Christic genealogy, Yeshua is identified as Christ (1:1, 16), son of David (1:1), and the offspring of Ruth (1:6). The other women in his genealogy, Tamar (1:3), Rahab (1:5), and Miryam ("Mary" of Nazareth, 1:16) will not be addressed in the present work. (It should be noted that Ruth is blessed in the name of Tamar in Ruth 4:12.)

Rape-Marriage in the Scriptures of Israel

Ruth's entry into the messianic family tree is more brutal than traditional translators have been comfortable relaying: "They abducted Moabite women; the name of the first woman was Orpah, and the name of the second woman was Ruth" (Ruth 1:4). Ruth's and Orpah's marriages were rape-marriages. Ruth's abductors are not identifiable. The masculine (and common) plural in biblical Hebrew regularly masks the presence of women. For example, in most instances בני ישראל, *beney yisrael*, means "Israelites," that is, all of the Israelites, female and male (Gafney 2008). Yet the gendered grammar of biblical Hebrew in which ninety-nine women with one male in their midst must be designated by the masculine plural may obscure the presence of an untold number of women in groups that were previously understood to be all male. The masculine plural here, "they abducted," likely refers to Machlon and Kilyon, the sons of Naomi and Elimelek. There is no reason to presume that Naomi was not involved. In fact, given the level and nature of Naomi's recorded activities, particularly her focus on obtaining a grandson, there is every reason to believe that she was involved. The abduction of Orpah and Naomi occurred on Naomi's watch as the surviving parent. What is clear is that Scripture does not record any protest from Naomi against the abduction of Ruth and Orpah.

The Lord forbid it me, that I should do this thing to my lord (Saul) the anointed of the Lord [*to christo kuriou*, τῷ χριστῷ κυρίου], to lift my hand against him; for he is the anointed of the Lord [*christos kuriou*, χριστὸς κυρίου]." The MT uses *meshiach*, משיח.

9. I am identifying the LXX as Jewish scripture in that it was produced by Jews for Jews.

For the course of this work, I am defining rape-marriage as forcible conjugal cohabitation. In the Israelite context, it is typified by the seizing of sexually immature and inexperienced girls as conjugal partners, particularly, although not exclusively, in the course of armed conflict as "the spoils of war" (השלל, *hashalal*), "booty" (המלקח, *hamalqoach*), or "plunder" (הבז, *habaz*). The concept has passed almost unnoticed into the lexicon of American English and African American cultural rhetoric, where "booty" has been reduced from a whole person to a person's anal and genital orifices, usually accessed from the back, along with the most recent expansion of the lexicon to include "bootylicious."[10]

I am describing these unions as marriages because they are legitimate conjugal unions in the text that produce children who are recognized as legitimate members of the Israelite community. There even developed statutes regulating the practice that offered some limited protections to the abducted women and their children. And I am describing these unions as rape-marriages because, not only is there no consent to these unions and concomitant sexual intercourse in the contemporary sense, but more important, there is no consent to these unions in these narratives. The normative practices associated with conjugal unions in the Hebrew Scriptures—negotiations between families, consent of the parents or the woman herself—are not present in these narratives.

Beginning in the Torah (Num 31), in spite of his own marriage to a Midianite woman, and in spite of his relationship with his father-in-law by any name—Yitro/Reuel/Hobab—which leads to the establishment of the judicial system in the wilderness, Moshe calls for the virtual annihilation of the Midianite people. To be fair, it is YHWH who calls for the vengeance (נקמת, *niqmath*) for an unspecified offense.[11] The text presents the notion of these rape-marriages as Moshe's own notion, apart from the divine in-

---

10. Given the ongoing colonization and exploitation of African American sexuality, particularly female sexuality, I find the veneration of young women who proclaim the deliciousness of their own "booty" fascinating. I am referring to the song "Bootylicious" by Destiny's Child, from the album *Survivor* (2001). The term is now defined in the Webster and Oxford English Dictionary as "sexually attractive, especially in the buttocks."

11. Num 31:9: "The Israelites took the women of Midian and their little ones captive; they plundered their flocks and all their wealth [or their whole army]. . . . 15. Moshe said to them, 'Have you allowed all the women to live? 16. These women here, on Balaam's advice, made the Israelites act treacherously against YHWH in the affair of Peor, so that the plague came among the congregation of YHWH. 17. Now then, kill every male among the little ones, and kill every woman who has known a man by sleeping with him. 18. But all the young girls who have not known a man by sleeping with him, keep alive for yourselves. . . .' 32. The booty remaining from the plunder that the troops had taken totaled 675,000 sheep, 33. 72,000 oxen, 34. 61,000 donkeys, 35. and 32,000 human souls in all, from women who had not known a man by sleeping with him."

struction. All of the Midianite men and boys with the exception of the infants and toddlers had already been killed. Moshe instructs the Israelites to execute all males among those too young to walk, and they slaughtered all of the male infants. According to the text, the Israelites captured 32,000 sexually uninitiated young girls. In Deuteronomy, the practice becomes standardized.[12]

The key differences between the Deuteronomy texts, particularly chapter 21, and the Numbers text are: (1) the women of any group designated as "the enemy" are now available for forced conjugal cohabitation; (2) the Israelite men may choose women for conjugal relations based on their appearance; (3) abducted women are no longer required to be sexually uninitiated; and (4) the Israelites have developed a protocol for breaking in their new women. The humiliation-based breaking-in process consists of shaving the woman's head, cutting her nails (this may also be a practical, protective step on the part of the rapist-husband), and stripping her (the use of the *hiphil* makes the act extraordinarily forceful); no mention is made of clothing her. Finally, she is to be given a month to mourn her mother and father and to accept her new situation. Then, whether she is ready or not, the male Israelite who chose her because he desired her is given divine/Mosaic authority—the two voices are presented as one—to penetrate her, literally to "come over her," presumably holding her down if necessary.

In Judg 20 the Benjaminites refuse to hand over the men of Gibeah who raped and murdered the Levite's *pilegish*-wife, or wife of secondary status.[13] Israel goes to war against Benjamin, killing 25,000 male warriors.

---

12. Deut 20:1 "When you go out to war against your enemies . . . 14. You may plunder for yourselves the women, the children, livestock, and everything else in the town, all its spoil. You may enjoy the spoil of your enemies, which YHWH your God has given you. . . . 21:10. When you go out to war against your enemies and YHWH your God hands them over to you and you take them captive, 11. suppose you see among the captives a woman beautiful in form whom you desire and want to take as your woman/wife, 12. and you bring her home to your house: she shall shave her head, pare her nails, 13. strip the garments of her captivity from her, and shall remain in your house a full month, mourning for her father and mother; after that you may penetrate her and marry/rule over her, and she shall be your woman/wife. 14. But if you take no delight in her, you shall release her person, and under no circumstances shall you sell her for money. You must not shackle her, since you have violated her."

13. In the polygynous (multiple wives, versus polyandrous, multiple husbands) polygamy of ancient Israel, there were two types of wives, primary and secondary. A primary wife (אשה, *isshah*, the same word as woman) had full societal recognition, legal status, and her children had full inheritance rights. A secondary wife (פילגש, *pilegesh*) also had full societal recognition and legal status, but her children had limited or no inheritance rights. Some translators have called secondary wives "concubines." This is incorrect because these women were also wives. The

The remaining Israelite tribes swear not to give their daughters in marriage to the six hundred survivors of Benjamin. Since the Gadite warriors of Yavesh-gil'ad did not join in the battle, it was decided to annihilate their warriors, men and boys, and sexually active women.[14]

Since the four hundred sexually uninitiated girls were insufficient for the Benjaminite survivors, the decision was made to abduct the innocent daughters of faithful Israelites from the house of God. Young women performing a religious service at the Shiloh shrine, in this case, liturgical dance, would be abducted for the Benjaminites.[15]

The verbs נשא, ns', and חטף, chtph, are used to describe the abduction and rape of the Shilonite women; נשא, ns', means "to lift" or pick up anything, including a person; חטף, chtph, which is used only in Ps 10:9 and the Judges passage, means "to capture." The abduction of Ruth and Orpah is described with the verb נשא, ns' in Ruth 1:4.[16]

Before I return to Ruth's messianic motherhood, I would like to make a final observation about the language of rape-marriage in the Hebrew Scriptures. In the case of each text discussed above, the scholarly convention in translation has been to describe the victims of rapine as "women"

---

type of marriage agreement, not the order of the marriages, determined the status of the wife. Judg 19:1, 2 Sam 15:16, and 2 Sam 20:3 all use both terms together, with *pilegesh* as secondary in rank to modify wife, *isshah*, making the relationship clear. Some translators fail to translate *isshah*, woman/wife, when it is combined with *pilegesh*, secondary. However, Judg 19:1 reads "A certain Levite . . . took a wife (אשה, *isshah*) for himself of secondary status (פילגש, *pilegesh*)" (Gafney 2005b).

14. Judg 21:10. "The congregation sent twelve thousand soldiers there and commanded them, 'Go, put the inhabitants of Yavesh-gil'ad to the sword, including the women and the little ones. 11. This is what you shall do; every male and every woman that has lain with a male you shall devote to destruction.' 12 And they found among the inhabitants of Yavesh-gil'ad four hundred innocent girls who had never slept with a man and brought them to the camp at Shiloh, which is in the land of Canaan. 13 Then the whole congregation sent word to the Benjaminites who were at the rock of Rimmon and proclaimed peace to them. 14 Benjamin returned at that time, and they gave them the women whom they had saved alive of the women of Yavesh-gil'ad, but they did not suffice for them."

15. Judg 21:20. "And they instructed the Benjaminites, saying, 'Go and lie in wait in the vineyards, 21. and watch; when the daughters of Shiloh come out to dance in the dances, then come out of the vineyards, and each of you seize a woman for himself from the daughters of Shiloh, and go to the land of Benjamin. 22. Then if their fathers or their brothers come to complain to us, we will say to them, "Be generous and allow us to have them, because we did not capture in battle a woman for each man. But neither did you incur guilt by giving your daughters to them."' 23. The Benjaminites did so; they carried away women for each of them from the dancers whom they stole."

16. The usage of נשא, ns', in the Writings may indicate that abduction was primarily carried out against foreign women: the Moabite Ruth and Orpah; foreign women in Ezra 10:44.

and not girls, even when the text is careful to stipulate that the persons in question are pubescent and prepubescent; one reason is that the text uses הנשים, *hanashim* (women), to describe these persons; Judg 21 uses both הנשים and נערות בתולות, *na'aroth betuloth* (virgin girls). Whether these young people were considered adult women before their abduction and forced marriages is uncertain; what is clear is that their initiation into womanhood was brutal.

Naomi's Sexploitation of Ruth

According to the text of Ruth, it was in the context of a famine and widowhood that Naomi began to use Ruth's youth and potential fertility to her own advantage. With the death of her husband Elimelek, Naomi was bereft of her provider. She needed to provide for her own material needs by any means necessary. She did not insist that Machlon and Kilyon return to the land of her (or Elimelek's) ancestors for a suitable bride. As argued earlier, the masculine plural construction of the abductors does not eliminate Naomi as a perpetrator. What is clear is that she never said a mumbling word. Given her loquaciousness and audaciousness in the rest of the saga, my reading is that she authorized and orchestrated the abduction of the women. When Machlon and Kilyon follow their father in death, Naomi has no more use for two foreign women who have not even provided her with grandchildren.

Naomi's urging that Orpah and Ruth return to their mothers' households and be blessed by YHWH and find security in the households of their husbands is provocative. Were Orpah and Ruth from a matrilineal family? Were their fathers killed in battle? Were they abducted in a battle? Did their fathers lose their lives trying to save their daughters? Were Ruth and Orpah sexually naïve when they were abducted, or were they simply desirable? Are there husbands for them to return to? Will they be accepted as potential conjugal partners as former abductees? How will they provide for themselves? Where will they live? Do they both initially cling to Naomi out of what we now call Stockholm syndrome? Why does Orpah leave? Why does Ruth stay?

Perhaps Ruth stays because she knows she will be shunned when she returns to her people. She is a childless widow and, as such, a less-than-desirable bride. She may be presumed to be infertile. And if she were to marry and give birth soon after, the paternity of her child would always be suspect. Ruth stays. After Ruth commits herself to Naomi with vows that are regularly taken out of their woman-to-woman context and changed to fit a heterosexual context in many communions that would not consider adapting a heterosexual text to a homosexual context, Orpah leaves and Ruth stays with Naomi. How telling that Naomi cannot think of any reason for them to stay, apart from the foolish hope of her bearing sons to be their husbands. The plot of this story turns on the axes of progeny and provision. When Ruth becomes the ancestral mother of the messiah, it will be as Naomi's surrogate.

Naomi's self-concern and willingness to use Ruth's body to meet her own material needs are demonstrated at several points in their saga. In chapter 3 Naomi masks her concern for her own material provision by cloaking her instructions to Ruth in concern for Ruth's well-being (3:1): "My daughter, am I not seeking a resting-place for you, that it may be well with you?" My response to Naomi's rhetorical question on Ruth's behalf is "No, you are using my body for your own purposes, again, and now, Boaz's, too." Naomi's instructions are for Ruth to wash and anoint herself; more than hygiene is at stake here: Naomi wants Ruth to be fragrant and inviting. She also tells her to dress herself and go to the threshing floor where Boaz and his workers are celebrating the end of the barley harvest, but not to reveal herself. Naomi tells Ruth to wait until Boaz is satiated and inebriated before approaching him, and still not to reveal herself to him. In 3:4, Naomi instructs Ruth in the fine art of stalking: "When he lies down, memorize the place where he lies; then go and uncover his thighs and lie down; and he will tell you what to do." I am translating מרגלתיו, *margelotayv*, as "his thighs," because רגלים, *raglayim* (feet), includes everything from navel to toenails.[17] Naomi's final counsel to Ruth is that he will tell her what to do.

Naomi is not just exploiting Ruth, her body, her commitment to her; she is also exploiting Boaz's drunken, human sexuality. When he discovers her, Boaz signals his intent to become her husband under the redemption practices of his people. But that does not conclude their business. He tells her to resume her position. And she lay, with her face at the juncture of his thighs until the morning. The text does not tell us his next set of instructions to her, but his inebriation is wearing off, and they have all night for Ruth to do whatever Boaz tells her to do.

Naomi's motives in using Ruth, Orpah, and Boaz are revealed in the speech and songs of the women of Bethlehem:

> 4:14. "Blessed be YHWH, who has not left you woman, without redeeming kin this day; and may that name be proclaimed in Israel! 15. That one shall be to you woman, a restorer of life and a provider when your hair grays woman; for your daughter-in-law, she who loves you woman, she has given birth—she who is more to you woman, than seven sons." 16. Then Naomi took the child and laid him in her bosom and became his nurturer. 17. The women of the neighborhood gave him a name, saying, "A son has been born to Naomi."

Naomi has received her social security; she has become the surrogate mother of the messiah. Ruth is a non-Israelite cultural outsider who aban-

---

17. Susan Niditch presents a very fine collection of translations of the account of Sisera's death between the thighs of Yael (1999, 308).

dons her family, land, ancestors, and gods, siding with her abductors and those who exploited her. For her troubles, she is not permitted to name her own child, as was the custom among Israelite women, nor is she named in the first genealogy of her most famous descendant in 4:17: "The women of the neighborhood gave him a name, saying, 'A son has been born to Naomi.' They named him Oved; he became the father of Yishai, the father of David." She will always be remembered as an outsider. After she has pledged herself to Naomi, after Boaz has pledged himself to her, they still call her "Ruth, the Moabite woman." She will never be one of them, no matter what she does; whether she is remembered as the grandmother of David, Israel's messiah-king, or the ancestress of Yeshua, the Christian Messiah, Ruth is remembered as a non-Israelite.

Because her body is used to provide progeny for a people who are not her people and to worship a god she never knew, she is also remembered as a woman with a warrior's noble heart (*eshet chayil*, אשת חיל). There is great irony in this. One of the chief Israelite virtues is fidelity, fidelity to god, ancestors, and land. Ruth becomes a woman of virtue by abandoning her gods, ancestors, and land. When Boaz signals—by spreading his garment over her—that he will become Ruth's (and Naomi's) provider, he commends Ruth with the affirmation in 3:12: "all the assembly of my people know that you are a warrior-woman." And when Boaz completes the ritual and legal transaction that will make him become Ruth's and Naomi's provider, all of the people including the elders of Bethlehem bless Boaz in his access to Ruth's body in 4:11–12: "May Yhwh make the woman who is coming into your house like Rachel and Leah, who together built up the house of Israel. May you produce children in Ephrathah and bestow a name in Bethlehem; and, through the children that Yhwh will give you by this young woman, may your house be like the house of Perez, whom Tamar bore to Judah." Alternatively, "Blessed are you to have the body and procreative power of this woman who was abducted from her family, land, and gods and has chosen not to return to them but to bind herself to your people, land and god."

Orpah the True-Hearted Woman

Orpah is perhaps the most overlooked character in this narrative. She returns to her family, land, ancestors, and gods; she chooses liberation and rematriation. She is an exemplar of the kind of covenant fidelity that is most valued by Israel and its ancestral familial god.[18] At one time the Torah-framers recognized that there were other gods who had every right to expect their worshipers to be as loyal them as Israel was (or was supposed to have been) to Yhwh. Of course, in the Scriptures of Israel it is

---

18. Laura Donaldson (1999) also reads Orpah positively, from an indigenous perspective, resisting "imperial exegesis."

clear that YHWH is sovereign of those gods but still lets them have their servants, including, I would argue, Orpah—Deut 32:8: "When the Most High apportioned the nations, when God divided humankind, God fixed the boundaries of the peoples according to the number of the gods."

By returning to her family, land, ancestors, and gods, Orpah is simply returning to the life the Most High, YHWH, the God of Israel ordained for her. She evinces the kind of covenant fidelity advocated by the framers of Scripture: loyalty to one's god/s; loyalty to one's land; loyalty to one's ancestors. Perhaps she has decided that the uncertainties of home are preferable to the uncertainties of exile. Perhaps she cannot stay another moment among the people who abducted her. Perhaps she hopes that there is still a home for her to return to. Hope is enough.

Orpah is not commended in the biblical text for her virtues. Her unwillingness to allow her body to be colonized to gestate the hopes of patriarchy means that she is simply written out of Israel's history. Their story is not her story.

Contemporary Sex-Crimes

The abduction of women and girls for forced exogamous procreation and unwelcome conjugal unions did not end "in the days when the judges judged," the literary setting of Ruth. Each story cited below illuminates the experiences of contemporary women, experiences that like those contained in the story of Ruth resonate with sexual exploitation, rape, abduction and or forced impregnation.

The following is an analysis of forced procreation between Tutsis and Hutus.

> Although not the norm, conjugal unions between the Tutsis and Hutus were not uncommon in the decades preceding the genocide. Marriages between Tutsi women and Hutu men, however, were much more common than marriages between Tutsi men and Hutu women. Since ethnicity was determined along patrilineal lines, the offspring of Tutsi women and Hutu men were legally Hutu. As such, these marriages "conferred the full benefits of Hutu citizenship to progeny who were perceived by many as racially impure." Tutsi women's ethnicity and gender made them particularly vulnerable to attack. In fact, the campaign against Tutsi women well preceded the actual genocide. In 1990, four years before the start of the genocide, Tutsi women were frequently the centerpiece of propagandist efforts to heighten ethnic tensions and engender hatred.
>
> Forced impregnation has had deep psychological effects on Tutsi women. Suffered exclusively by women, forced pregnancy involves a violation of, among other things, reproductive freedom and sexual autonomy, and has lasting effects given that the women may then have to raise the offspring. Tutsi women who became pregnant have suffered intense shame and ostracization in a society that is particularly unwilling to accept unwed mothers. Moreover, mistreatment by society, including by

their own families, has led many unmarried mothers to resort to abortion or infanticide. The passage of time is unlikely to cure the psychological harm done to the victims of forced impregnation. (Green 2002)

In "Raped Darfur Women Wrestle with Fate of Babies," Nima Elbagir wrote:

KALMA, Sudan—"The rapes never stop, sometimes there are more, sometimes less," she (Hawa) said, accusing militiamen known as Janjaweed of the crime. "Now the Janjaweed babies are being born and the girls are throwing them down latrines," she said. "Better the babies are lost this way than we carry the burden," she said, falling silent as she stared into her coffee cup.. . .

Hawa's friends point out a woman who gave birth to a child conceived by rape. The victim nods as the women explain how the child died of malnutrition because the mother was too distressed to breast-feed.

The Associated Press distributed this story on 21 June 2005:

ADDIS ABABA, Ethiopia (AP)—Police say three lions rescued a 12–year-old girl kidnapped by men who wanted to force her into marriage, chasing off her abductors and guarding her until police and relatives tracked her down in a remote corner of Ethiopia.

The men had held the girl for seven days, repeatedly beating her, before the lions chased them away and guarded her for half a day before her family and police found her, Sgt. Wondimu Wedajo said Tuesday by telephone from the provincial capital of Bita Genet, some 560 kilometers (348 miles) west of the capital, Addis Ababa.. . .

"If the lions had not come to her rescue then it could have been much worse. Often these young girls are raped and severely beaten to force them to accept the marriage," he said. "Everyone thinks this is some kind of miracle, because normally the lions would attack people," Wondimu said. (Mitchell 2005)

The complicity of women in the sexual abuse of other women is illustrated by Danna Harman's article "A Woman on Trial for Rwanda's Massacre":

ARUSHA, Tanzania—. . .Pauline Nyiramasuhuko is the first woman charged with genocide and using rape as a crime against humanity.... Witnesses, one after another, tell harrowing stories of Nyiramasuhuko personally encouraging Hutu gangs known as *Interahamwe* to "select the nicest" women and rape these victims before killing them. (Harman 2003)

Conclusion

Ruth becomes the mother of the messiah in Jewish and Christian traditions as a surrogate for her mother-in-law, Naomi. Naomi uses Ruth's fertility to produce a grandson who will provide for her in her old age. Naomi's intent is not hostile. Naomi is not "Mommie Dearest." Neither is she "Mother Goose." Naomi is something like Mother Jones, in that she organizes Ruth's physical and reproductive labor for the good of Ruth and their shared community. By exposing her motives, I am not passing judgment on her. Her actions are consistent with the cultural values of her time, perhaps even likely, that Naomi wants only good for Ruth, particularly once she comes to know her. And it is not necessarily the case that Ruth was an unwilling surrogate. Yet it is troubling that Naomi procured her own salvation through the sexual and reproductive services of another woman.

Naomi's use of Ruth as a surrogate calls to mind Sarah's use of Hagar. It is striking to note that, while both women are significant ancestresses in the messianic lineage who take reproductive matters into their own hands, the judgments pronounced on them by the text are quite different. The child conceived for Sarah by her surrogate Hagar will not be the child of promise.

The narratives of Ruth and those of the raped and forcibly impregnated women in Rwanda and Darfur remind us that the violence against women that underlies—and overlays—so many biblical texts is not a thing of the past or simply an issue of interpretation. Violence against women predates, perfuses, and postdates the biblical text. Historical and contemporary violence against women affects the experience of mothering, directly or indirectly.

A final thought on messianic surrogacy is in order here. Miryam of Nazareth serves as a divine surrogate for the holy child, Yeshua. Unlike Ruth, she does not need to trade her body for survival. She consents to the divine impregnation. But her consent may not have mattered. The divine messenger did not ask her permission. Gavriel simply told her what would be—and she submitted. What would have happened if Miryam had said no? Of course, these are the questions of a twenty-first-century woman. The question of consent is rarely considered by the Iron Age writers of the Scriptures of Israel.

Works Cited

Donaldson, Laura. 2006. The Sign of Orpah: Reading Ruth through Native Eyes. Pages 159–70 in *The Postcolonial Biblical Reader*. Edited by R. S. Sugirtharajah. Malden, Mass.: Blackwell.

Elbagir, Nima. 2005. Raped Darfur Women Wrestle with Fate of Babies. *Sudan Tribune* 20 February:3. Online: http://www.sudantribune.com/spip.php?article8120.

Gafney, Wilda. 2005a. Commentary on Genesis. Pages 87–177 in vol. 3 of *The Pastor's Bible Study*. Edited by David Albert Farmer. Nashville: Abingdon.

———. 2005b. A Fem/Womanist Hermeneutic Reading Ruth against the Grain: The Valorization of a Race-Traitor and a Pimp. Paper presented in the Feminist Biblical Hermeneutics Section of the Society of Biblical Literature Annual Meeting. Philadelphia.

———. 2006. Rape-Marriage as Biblical Marriage. Paper presented in the Woman and the Bible Section of the Midwestern Regional Conference of the Society of Biblical Literature, Madison, Wisconsin.

———. 2008. *Daughters of Miriam: Women Prophets in Ancient Israel*. Minneapolis: Fortress.

Green, Llezlie L. 2002. Gender Hate Propaganda and Sexual Violence in the Rwandan Genocide: An Argument for Intersectionality in International Law. *Columbia Human Rights Law Review* 33:733–76.

Halpern, Baruch. 2001. *David's Secret Demons: Messiah, Murderer, Traitor, King*. Grand Rapids: Eerdmans.

Harman, Danna. 2003. A Woman on Trial for Rwanda's Massacre. *The Christian Science Monitor* 7 March. Online: http://www.csmonitor.com/2003/0307/p09s01-woaf.html.

Lenowitz, Harris. 1998. *The Jewish Messiahs: From the Galilee to the Crown Heights*. New York: Oxford University Press.

Mitchell, Anthony. 2005. Lions to the Rescue! Big Cats Save Kidnapped Girl. Associated Press 21 June. Online: http://compositivelive.com/animals/050621_ap_lion.html.

Niditch, Susan. 1999. Eroticism and Death in the Tale of Jael. Pages 305–15 in *Women in the Hebrew Bible*. Edited by Alice Bach. New York: Routledge.

Werblowsky, R. J. Zwi. 1992. Jewish Messianism in Comparative Perspective. Pages 1–13 in *Messiah and Christos: Studies in the Jewish Origins of Christianity Presented to Davis Flusser on the Occasion of His Seventy-Fifth Birthday*. Edited by Ithamar Gruenwald et al. Texte und Studien zum antiken Judentum 32. Tübingen: Mohr Siebeck.

3

Sacrifice and the Displacement of Mothers in the Book of Ruth and Coetzee's *Disgrace*

Brian Britt

For the dirty work of culture, particularly violence and sacrifice, mothers must often be displaced.[1] In the Bible, Sarah is displaced in the Akedah, the story of the binding of Isaac (Gen 22), and Jephthah's wife is displaced from the story of her daughter's sacrifice (Judg 11). The absence of mothers in these stories is striking and perhaps crucial to the fathers' plans to kill their children (Exum 1993, 99, Delaney 1998, 17–23, Gunn 2005, 164). Neither Sarah nor Jephthah's wife protests, but Sarah's death in the next chapter of Genesis has been interpreted as a reaction to the Akedah (Levenson 1993, 133). (More dramatically, in the Greek myth of Iphigeneia, Clytemnestra kills Agamemnon in revenge for his sacrifice of their daughter.) Mothers are also often displaced in birth legends of great warriors and patriarchal heroes like Moses, Sargon, and Oedipus. While it may not be surprising that mothers are absent from the patriarchal domains of war and public life, it is important to consider when, how, and to what effect mothers are displaced from the traditional roles of giving birth and providing care and protection for their children. This essay challenges the axiom that mothers do all the dirty work by showing how they are displaced in the book of Ruth and J. M. Coetzee's *Disgrace*. My method here is to apply social-scientific categories of sacrifice, gender, and ethnic and racial rivalry to literary readings of the book of Ruth and Coetzee's novel.

The book of Ruth and J. M. Coetzee's *Disgrace* depict vulnerable young women living in patriarchal societies; their mothers are displaced, and they lack protection from husbands and fathers. The women, Ruth and Lucy,

---

1. I wish to thank Jerome Copulsky, Cheryl Kirk-Duggan, and Tina Pippin for their comments on this essay.

also face grave dangers tied to conflict between rival groups (Israelites and Moabites, white and black South Africans). Both women take shelter under the wings of powerful men and thereby avoid becoming sacrificial victims. Yet in both texts, these daughters challenge their subordination by acting independently and becoming mothers themselves.

In the book of Ruth, a widow from a foreign ethnic group, the Moabites, surprisingly attaches herself to her Israelite mother-in-law (also a widow) after a famine. The book of Ruth ignores prohibitions on marriage to Moabites and diatribes against them elsewhere in the Bible (Ezra 9:12; Neh 13:1; Num 22; 25:1; Deut 23; Gen 19:30–38), leading some biblical scholars to read the text as a challenge to these ethnic proscriptions. Prompted by Naomi, her mother-in-law, Ruth gains the protection of Naomi's wealthy kinsman, Boaz, and he marries her. Later, after Ruth gives birth, the women of the town celebrate by saying "A son is born to Naomi!" (Ruth 4:17). The book of Ruth has raised abundant questions of scholarly interpretation, one of which is the question of whether Ruth can better be seen as a figure of pious obedience or unconventional self-assertion. (Campbell, for example, tends to regard Ruth as dutiful and obedient, while Trible, LaCocque, and Bal stress her unconventional self-assertion.) This essay suggests how ethnic rivalry and danger affirm both images of Ruth.

In *Disgrace*, the 1999 novel by white South African novelist J. M. Coetzee, David Lurie is a white professor of literature whose affair with a white, female student leads to his dismissal and personal downfall. Parallel to his own indiscretions is the sexual assault of his daughter by her black neighbors. Lurie is powerless to help his daughter or to persuade her to leave the rural farm where she lives alone. By the novel's end, his disgrace complete, Lurie begins to live and work at an animal clinic, bagging and incinerating the carcasses of abandoned dogs. Written and set during the post-Apartheid era, *Disgrace* offers disturbing images of race relations, sexuality, and power during the period of the Truth and Reconciliation Commission. The fate of Lurie's daughter Lucy presents him with a cruel sexual irony, but it also confronts the painful realities of coexistence between races and classes after Apartheid. While the novel focuses on Lurie's personal misery, his daughter Lucy, like Ruth, embodies a powerful combination of self-assertion and self-denial.

With *Disgrace* and the book of Ruth (as well as Gen 22), we can ask: Is it necessary for sacrifice to occur in the absence of the mother, even at the expense of the mother (as well as the child)? Like Isaac, Ruth and Lucy become vulnerable to patriarchal projects in their mothers' absence. The Abrahamic covenant is patriarchal merely insofar as it demands the near-killing of the son by the father in the mother's absence. In the book of Ruth, the relation between Moabites and Israelites, specifically whether a Moabite can be a good wife, daughter, and mother in Israel, addresses gender and ethnicity in the context of death and famine (Kirk-Duggan 1999,

192–97, 205). In *Disgrace*, the fate of Lucy opens up a whole set of questions about gender and race in contemporary South Africa.

Such violent stories of mothers and daughters reveal the anxieties of patriarchal cultures. In *Death and Dissymmetry* (1988), Mieke Bal analyzes several stories in which displaced mothers, like Clytemnestra, enact violence in the book of Judges. For Bal, these stories displace concerns of "daily life" onto "national" issues in a way that reveals the "fragile foundation of fatherhood as the cornerstone of the social system" (229). A related account of biblical violence appears in Nancy Jay's *Throughout Your Generations Forever* (1992), which associates sacrifice with the shift from matrilineal to patrilineal systems, another dimension of the story of Ruth. If such sacrifice performs some expiatory or propitiatory function, then is it worth the cost of eliminating motherhood from the picture? In the context of patriarchal and racist traditions, how can we disentangle the use of sacrifice to achieve transcendence from routine male desire and domination? Are Ruth and Lucy trapped in prison-houses of patriarchy, or does the displacement of their mothers still leave them the option of self-determination?

The book of Ruth and *Disgrace* figuratively depict sacrifices performed at the expense of young women and their bonds to their mothers. This comparison seeks to show that the link between sacrifice and motherhood is biblical as well as literary, that the biblical text can be as complex as Coetzee and that Coetzee can be as tradition-bound as the Bible. A central issue for both texts is whether the women act as independent agents or merely as sacrifices to the dynamics of group conflict. While they are clearly victims of circumstance, Lucy and Ruth both emerge as agents who make choices that direct the stories' action.

The Book of Ruth

In the book of Ruth, Naomi's husband and two sons have died in a famine that takes place during the barley harvest. One of Naomi's daughters-in-law, Orpah, returns to her family of origin, while Ruth famously follows Naomi from Moab back to the Judahite town of Bethlehem. Ruth's Moabite identity evokes a biblical history of war and bitter animosity between two peoples. According to André LaCocque, the book of Ruth subverts the prohibition on intermarriage emphasized in Ezra and Nehemiah (LaCocque 1990, 86). Read in this way, the book of Ruth accepts or even embraces marriage with Moabites in spite of such prohibitions. For many interpreters, though, Ruth simply personifies the covenant virtue of lovingkindness (חסד, 3:10). Such readers regard Ruth as the embodiment of obedience and other values of a pious daughter; she is sometimes identified as the "woman of substance" (3:11, אשת חיל) described in the final, acrostic passage of Proverbs (31:10), which immediately precedes the book of Ruth in the Masoretic Text.

While there is no literal sacrifice in the text, the book of Ruth takes place against the background of the barley harvest, associated with the sacrifice festival of firstfruits in ancient Israel (Exod 23:16; Lev 23:9–14). The phrase "barley harvest" (קציר שערים) only appears in one other biblical text: 2 Sam 21, a text in which Israelite men are killed (one could even say sacrificed) in order to lift a bloodguilt curse and famine (Gosse 1996, 431). The deaths of the three men at the beginning of the book of Ruth coincide with a famine. On the basis of this evidence, I believe the book alludes to sacrifice (Britt 2005, 1–5). Set against the background of a sacrifice festival, Ruth herself performs a kind of self-sacrifice, giving up her identity and placing herself at the mercy of Naomi, Boaz, and the God of Israel. Such a reading makes the category of sacrifice available outside texts that have a specific ritual meaning. Like the Akedah of Gen 22 and many other biblical texts dealing with sacrifice, the canonical, literary text of Ruth contains no "real" sacrifice as such.

As a figure of self-sacrifice, is Ruth a docile, vulnerable daughter or a forceful agent of subversive action? Both images of Ruth can be seen in the text. On the one hand, Ruth treats Naomi and Boaz with deference, yet she creates bonds to each of them. If Ruth's mother is displaced, it is Ruth herself who displaces, by unexpectedly clinging (דבק) to her mother-in-law (Ruth 1:14). Naomi urges her daughters-in-law to return to their mothers, first politely (Ruth 1:8–9, a passage that includes the first of three uses of the term חסד, "lovingkindness," in the book of Ruth), and then with sardonic force (Ruth 1:11–13). Orpah leaves, but Ruth stays with her, making extraordinary claims of loyalty and kinship with Naomi's people and God (Ruth 1:16–17; Britt 2003, 301–2). Almost immediately, as if to reject Ruth's claim on her as a "mother," Naomi renames herself "Bitter One" instead of "Pleasant One" (Ruth 1:20). Having both given themselves identity "makeovers," Ruth and Naomi come to Bethlehem as an odd couple of vulnerable widows, eventually regaining full strength with a bold plan to gain the protection of Boaz (whose name means "strength is in him"). In the end, Ruth has subverted Naomi's (and perhaps the reader's) expectations of a Moabite widow.

What does the subversive work of Ruth achieve? Has she interrupted the status quo simply to establish her own exceptional virtue, or has she contributed to a systemic transformation of the status quo? Mieke Bal suggests the latter with a reading of the book influenced by Victor Hugo's poem "Booz endormi," which emphasizes the vigor of Ruth and the weakness of Boaz. In this reading, it is Ruth who is generous to Boaz, against the conventional reading of Boaz as benefactor (Bal 1987, 70–71). As Bal points out, the biblical comparison of Ruth to Rachel and Leah can be read as an endorsement of her subversive work: "Slowly, a conception of 'collective heroism' comes to the fore. A new form of hero, different from both the filial and the paternal hero, emerges here" (Ruth 4:11–12; Bal 1987, 85). The solidarity between Ruth and Naomi, which could also be extended to include the women who comment on the story in the first and last chapters of the text, allows these women to say a son has been born to Naomi (4:17). Where the displacement of Ruth's mother and Ruth's decision to become a mother herself leaves her; in other words, whether Ruth has performed a self-sacrifice or a self-affirmation depends upon the reader's understanding of the book's conclusion, which proclaims her to be better than seven sons and the ancestor of David.

Disgrace

In *Disgrace*, the racial violence of Apartheid and its aftermath forms the historical background for the story of David Lurie's private life. After his private life becomes public and his daughter has been raped, this background becomes foreground. Lurie is a disappointed white scholar of Romantic literature stranded in a Communication Department at a technical university. Living in a world and an identity in which religious tradition and family structure lie in ruins, Lurie believes he and his colleagues are "clerks in a post-religious age" (Coetzee 1999, 4). He describes his students as secular and inhuman: "Post-Christian, posthistorical, postliterate, they might as well have been hatched from eggs yesterday" (32). In the absence of intellectual fulfillment or cultural standards, Lurie immerses himself in a series of illicit love affairs, forcing himself into the lives of others. A destroyer who becomes destroyed, Lurie becomes fascinated with the family of the prostitute Soraya, who is married with children, and he hires a detective to find her at home. Later, after the affair with his student Melanie, he seeks out her father to explain his actions and spend an awkward evening with her family (9, 163–74). When he fails in these efforts, he finds himself alone and incapable of protecting his own daughter.

Mothers and daughters haunt the novel, which begins with Lurie's infatuation with the "exotic" Soraya. When he desperately follows her to her home and family, he becomes even more interested in her, but she warns him to leave her alone. After a one-night stand with a secretary, Lurie seduces Melanie Isaacs, whom he compares to his daughter; this affair leads to her possible suicide attempt and his dismissal (45). As with Soraya, Lurie becomes fascinated with the family of Melanie, and she takes an interest in his: Melanie sees a photograph of David's mother on the coffee table and asks whether it is his wife. He replies, "My mother. Taken when she was young" (15). The preoccupation with mothers extends even to an unlikely attachment with ducks: after Lurie has left Lucy in the country, pregnant and in the care of her black former employee, Petrus, he misses "the duck family, for instance: Mother Duck tacking about on the surface of the dam, her chest puffed out with pride, while Eenie, Meenie, Minie and Mo paddle busily behind, confident that as long as she is there they are safe from all harm" (178).

Lurie has been married twice before, first to Evelina or Evie (the Dutch mother of Lucy), and then to Rosalind, with whom he has become friends and discusses his problems. After the biblically named Evie divorced Lurie and took Lucy back to Holland (the colonial motherland) with her, Lucy chose to return to South Africa, not to be with her father but to live in a "certain surround, a certain horizon" (161). Lucy and her lesbian partner, Helen, move to a farm in the country, but Helen leaves her; later, when Lucy is raped and robbed, she decides not to press charges and, when she discovers she is pregnant, decides to keep the baby.

Lucy's horrific experience is complicated by the fact that she is an affluent white from the city and the perpetrators, like most of her neighbors, are poor and black. Lurie regards the rape as an outrage, but Lucy accepts her situation with surprising equanimity, even when her rapist, a young relative of her employee Petrus, returns. Like Ruth, Lucy is socially vulnerable as an unmarried pregnant woman in rural South Africa, and Petrus, who already has two wives, decides to marry her, much to Lurie's horror. Lucy explains her resolve to her father (whom she addresses by his first name): "'I don't believe you get the point, David. Petrus is not offering me a church wedding followed by a honeymoon on the Wild Coast. He is offering an alliance, a deal. I contribute the land, in return for which I am allowed to creep in under his wing'" (203; the same language appears earlier, when Bev Shaw tells Lurie that "Petrus will take her under his wing," 140).

Whether Lucy's words allude to Ruth 3:9, in which Ruth seeks shelter under the "wings" of Boaz, can be debated, but the parallel to Ruth is nevertheless striking: the vulnerable but assertive widow survives her victimization and chooses to shelter under the protection of a powerful man (Petrus means "rock," and Boaz means "strength is in him"). As a white woman living in a black community after Apartheid, Lucy accepts her status as a member of a weak minority but refuses to be sacrificed on the altar of racial and economic group conflict. She admits this is humiliation and says she is willing to make sacrifice to keep peace; she keeps her baby, her life in the country, her kennels, and her house (204). For Lurie, of course, nothing could be more disgraceful and outrageous—his racism blinds him to the hypocrisy of his position.

The numerous references and allusions to sacrifice in *Disgrace* make Lucy's status and purpose, like Ruth's, a central question. Is Lucy a sacrificial victim in the struggle between white and black South Africans? Lurie raises the issue when, pleading with her to resist her situation, he invokes the image of Passover sacrifice:

> "Do you think what happened here was an exam: if you come through, you get a diploma and safe conduct into the future, or a sign to paint on the door-lintel that will make the plague pass you by? That is not how vengeance works, Lucy. Vengeance is like a fire. The more it devours, the hungrier it gets." (Coetzee 1999, 112)

Lurie argues, in effect, that Lucy's self-sacrifice has no larger purpose: instead of reducing conflict by channeling the violence of all against all into the violence of all against one (the sacrificial victim), the attack on Lucy is just a single episode in a protracted story of the revenge of blacks against whites. (Other allusions to sacrifice include a gift Lurie makes to Soraya for the Muslim Eid and Lurie's thought of castrating himself like the early Christian thinker Origen [9].)

But even before the rape, Lucy defines herself in opposition to her father:

> "You think I ought to involve myself in more important things. . . . You
> don't approve of friends like Bev and Bill Shaw because they are not
> going to lead me to a higher life. . . . They are not going to lead me to a
> higher life, and the reason is, there is no higher life. This is the only life
> there is. Which we share with animals." (Coetzee 1999, 74)

Later, in an argument with her father, Lucy admits, "I am prepared to do anything, make any sacrifice, for the sake of peace" (208). As it turns out, Lucy's perspective on animals will be borne out by Lurie himself, who begins to assist Bev Shaw at the animal clinic. Shaw, with whom Lurie has a brief affair, serves as a kind of surrogate mother for Lucy and Lurie both. As Shaw treats a goat with injured testicles (echoing Lurie's earlier thoughts on self-castration), he muses on the sacrificial tradition of the scapegoat (82, 126). The sacrificial motif extends further when Lurie helps Shaw to euthanize dogs. Wondering why he does this, Lurie muses, "He saves the honour of corpses because there is no one else stupid enough to do it. That is what he is becoming: stupid, daft, wrongheaded" (146).

The deaths of these animals, together with the sheep Petrus slaughters for a party to celebrate the transfer of Lucy's land to himself (and thus the transfer of fatherhood and protection from Lurie to Petrus), raise the question whether animal "sacrifices" substitute for Lucy or Lurie as sacrificial victims or whether they have any value at all (123–24, 142, 162). Readers of Coetzee's *Elizabeth Costello*, which includes the titular character's lectures endorsing animal rights (2003), may see Lurie's compassion toward animals as a way out of patriarchal violence. How one understands the role of animals in the novel may decide whether the reader sees Lucy and Lurie as utterly destroyed or potentially redeemed in the end.

Displacement, Sacrifice, and Social Conflict

This analysis of Ruth and Lucy combines the categories of displacement and sacrifice. Displacement refers not simply to one taking the place of another, as Naomi displaces Ruth's mother, as the women displace Naomi for Ruth as the mother of Obed, or as Petrus and Bev displace Lucy's mother. By displacement I also refer to Sigmund Freud's psychoanalytic notion that such a change accompanies a transfer of affect; Freud gives the example of an unmarried woman who transfers her affection to animals (Freud 1965, 210). The mechanism of displacement is crucial to Freud's idea of self and his ideas of religion and culture. The "mechanism of displacement," says Freud in 1907 (long before *Civilization and Its Discontents*), is at the heart of obsessional neuroses and religion itself: "In view of these similarities and analogies one might venture to regard obsessional neurosis as a pathological counterpart of the formation of a religion, and to describe that neurosis as an individual religiosity and religion as a universal obsessional neurosis" (Freud 1975, 126–27). For present purposes, displacement refers not to religion as neurosis but to transformations that express cultural anxieties in the texts of Ruth and *Disgrace*.

How does the displacement of mothers work in the book of Ruth and *Disgrace*? For Mieke Bal, mothers are typically displaced from violent stories of murdered daughters and avenging women. In Judges, the scene of Jael serving Sisera milk, covering him, and then killing him in a rape-like way takes place in the absence of a mother; Jael subverts the nurturing identity of a mother in violent fashion (Bal 1988, 212–14). For Bal, such a displacement reflects anxiety about the establishment of patriarchal law and homeland: "The political and military conquest of the land and the slow and difficult implementation of monotheism will then be placed next to, and in interconnection with, the slow enforcement of virilocal fatherhood" (Bal 1988, 230). The displacement of mothers in the book of Ruth and *Disgrace* does not lead immediately to violence, but the violence done to Lucy and the danger of violence to Ruth would be impossible without the displacement of mothers. Displacement of mothers, I suggest, enables Ruth and Lucy to figure centrally in conflicts between rival groups, survive danger, and eventually become mothers themselves.

My understanding of sacrifice draws from René Girard's and Nancy Jay's analyses of the social purpose of sacrifice. For Girard, the goal of sacrifice is not just propitiation of a deity, as Henri Hubert and Marcel Mauss might have it, but the avoidance of all-out conflict between groups (Girard 1977, 8–15; Hubert and Mauss 1964, 9–13). While neither the book of Ruth nor *Disgrace* depicts human sacrifice, the daughters in both stories face mortal danger, and death and sacrifice appear against the background of group conflict in both texts. According to Girard, sacrifice serves primarily to control and limit social violence. By channeling violence in this way, sacrifice serves "to restore harmony to the community, to reinforce the social fabric" (Girard 1977, 8). The social notion of sacrifice, from Girard, considers how sacrifice navigates and equilibrates social conflicts.

At the heart of the book of Ruth and *Disgrace* is conflict between two rival groups: Israelites and Moabites in the first, and white and black South Africans in the second. Both rivalries are bitter, and both texts introduce a young, motherless woman to serve as a middle term, negotiating chip, or sacrifice in the pursuit of a balance between the groups. My suggestion is that in these narratives of daughter sacrifice the mother is displaced by the violent struggle between two groups and that in patriarchal systems it is often the daughters (and their mothers) who symbolically become sacrificial victims in the calculated pursuit of balance between groups. No longer simply human beings, these daughters, like the concubine in Judg 19–20, symbolize and embody violence itself, though *Disgrace* and the book of Ruth narrate the transition of these victimized daughters to motherhood.

For the expiatory or mediating activity to work, there must be a cultural mechanism of exchange. Crucial to all of Girard's analysis are the workings of mimesis and symbolism. Common desire for a single object, which he calls mimetic desire, leads to conflict, the danger of violence, and the subsequent need to implement symbolic substitutions and ritual actions to bring violence under control. As Ruth substitutes for the Moabites, Lucy substitutes for whites, though in the end Ruth and Lucy both transcend the status of victimhood. In the case of Ruth, a vision of danger and scarcity is replaced by one of security and plenty; the unexplainable virtue of lovingkindness (חסד) yields what Phyllis Trible calls a "human comedy." In *Disgrace*, Lucy also avoids the status of victimhood, not by creating racial harmony but by asserting herself against her father's sexism, racism, and, perhaps, "species-ism" (the idea of human superiority over other animals).

As I suggested above, the setting of the book of Ruth during the barley harvest (a sacrifice festival), together with the death of Naomi's two sons (Mahlon and Chilion), makes sacrifice part of the story's context. In a figurative sense, Ruth sacrifices herself by renouncing her Moabite identity and placing herself at the mercy of Boaz on the threshing floor. Though the elevation of Ruth to a model of חסד and the ancestor of King David may in fact be a polemical gesture against the xenophobic tendencies of Ezra and Nehemiah, this Ruth is nevertheless a new Ruth, one who has given up her Moabite family, land, and identity. A similar self-sacrifice can be said to apply to Lucy's decisions in *Disgrace*. Lucy chooses to leave her mother in Holland and chooses to live in a majority black farm district far from her white, urban home. She has abandoned the racial, sexual, economic, and even human-centered ideologies of her upbringing.

Girard locates ritual sacrifice—"real" violence—at the core of all religious tradition: "All religious rituals spring from the surrogate victim, and all the great institutions of mankind, both secular and religious, spring from ritual. Such is the case, as we have seen, with political power, legal institutions, medicine, the theater, philosophy and anthropology itself" (Girard 1977, 306). But in a recent elaboration of his position, Girard avers that the Bible (unlike Greek mythology) represents violence in order to criticize it. On this view, vivid depictions of violence in the Bible are designed to confront the reader with the horrors of injustice, thus laying the groundwork for contemporary ethics of nonviolence: "It is for biblical reasons, paradoxically, that we criticize the Bible" (Girard 1999, 392).

My use of Girard's idea of sacrifice gives this idea of religious self-criticism a literary and feminist turn. While Girard consistently observes the importance of sexuality and marriage practices to ritual violence, he does not enlarge upon how these cultural systems relate to the status and well-being of women and men (Girard 1999, 34–36). Of course, neither Lucy nor Ruth is literally sacrificed; both are figures in literary texts structured by patriarchy and cultural conflict. But in terms of these texts, their experiences function like sacrifice, or self-sacrifice, since both exercise surprising self-determination. Without the background of larger social conflict (between Israelites and Moabites, between white and black South Africans), their stories would have a different and more private meaning. Such a reading of Ruth or *Disgrace* would tend to regard the women characters as strong, exceptional woman. Feminist and nonfeminist readings of Ruth as an extraordinary "woman of substance" (Ruth 3:11) typically overlook the cultural world she inhabits.

According to Nancy Jay, blood sacrifice is used to legitimate patriarchy and patrilineal systems of social order. Sacrifice "can be seen as a historically contingent practice for production of a political ideology in which the perspective of male nobles is elaborated as transcendent divine truth, legitimating one particular historical form of male domination by making it appear universal and eternal" (Jay 1992, 146). Jay argues that sacrifice motifs in the marriage stories of Genesis, between Abraham and Sarah, Isaac and Rebekah, and Jacob and Rachel, help stabilize and establish patrilineal marriage.

> Sacrifice can expiate, get rid of, the consequences of having been born of woman (along with countless other dangers) and at the same time integrate the pure and eternal patrilineage. Sacrificially constituted descent, incorporating women's mortal children into an "eternal" (enduring through generations) kin group, in which membership is recognized by participation in sacrificial ritual, not merely by birth, enables a patrilineal group to transcend mortality in the same process in which it transcends birth. In this sense, sacrifice is doubly a remedy for having been born of woman. (Jay 1992, 40)

Jay's cultural analysis carries over even into modern societies in which real blood sacrifice has declined: "But even if sacrifice may not be a major future means of disempowering women, it is still important to understand sacrificially maintained domination" (150). Cultural conflicts and ambiguities surrounding marriage and gender, Jay argues, are perennial concerns of ritual life.

Combining Bal's notion of displaced mothers with Jay's, one can see how Ruth and *Disgrace* dramatically displace motherhood in the context of conflicts over marriage, property, and ethnicity. The main men in the stories, Boaz and Lurie, fall short in their duties as fathers and husbands, leaving Ruth and Lucy alone as members of hated minority groups. Each story thus betokens a kind of sacrifice in a patriarchal struggle between ethnic and racial groups. In *Disgrace*, predatory, violent male behavior becomes a sacrifice in the absence of a mother's intervention or even witness. In Ruth, the death of the two sons, Mahlon and Chilion, sets the stage for Ruth's famous choice to embrace Naomi's people and God. Ruth's Moabite mother is displaced by her Israelite mother-in-law, who in turn is displaced in the role of protector by Boaz (though barely or comically, as Bal shows).

Like their mothers, the ancestral "motherlands" of Lucy and Ruth, Holland and Moab, have been displaced by new fatherlands (South Africa and Israel). *Disgrace* and the book of Ruth narrate sacrifice attempted in the name of these fatherlands: white colonial South Africa and ethnically pure Israel. But through the actions of Naomi, Ruth, Lucy, and Bev, both narratives offer new, sustaining images of mothers and motherlands. And while Coetzee's novel offers very little hope, the quasi-maternal figure of Bev Shaw (a kind of Mother Jones) faintly suggests hope for David and Lucy, just as Naomi grudgingly takes Ruth under her wing. Then, like Ruth, Lucy becomes a mother herself, apparently on her own terms. Ruth and Lucy both submit to a kind of self-sacrifice within a broad ethnic and religious conflict, but both emerge somehow intact and even, within certain parameters, self-determined.

The self-determination and self-sacrifice of Ruth and Lucy are tied to agriculture. Ruth's decision to follow Naomi coincides with the end of famine and the feast of the barley harvest. Lucy's decision to stay on the farm and bring her child to term suggest an antimodernist (i.e., antipatriarchal and antiracist) affirmation of life on the land. Both women become mothers away from their parents but close to a land they have chosen on their own terms. Noting this fact about Lucy, Lurie muses to himself, "Curious that he and her mother, cityfolk, intellectuals, should have produced this throwback, this sturdy young settler. But perhaps it was not they who produced her: perhaps history had the larger share" (Coetzee 1999, 61).

Conclusion

If Girard shows how sacrifice often concerns conflict between ethnic groups, Bal and Jay show the link between patriarchy and sacrifice even in literary texts that do not narrate acts of ritualized killing. If the book of Ruth illuminates *Disgrace* by showing the importance of mothers and sacrifice motifs in the novel, *Disgrace* suggests a reading of Ruth's relationship to Boaz as an analogy to that of Petrus and Lucy, a dispassionate calculation to gain protection and preserve order. Lucy and Ruth stand at the center of dangerous conflict between groups, but neither woman submits to the role of sacrificial victim. Ruth and Lucy redeem themselves against long odds, transforming themselves from victims to self-defining agents. While both Ruth and *Disgrace* are ostensibly patriarchal texts, one can read Ruth and Lucy as agents of self-determination who move their own stories forward. Without their biological mothers (of either the Mother Goose or Mommie Dearest variety), both take surrogate mothers, Naomi and Bev Shaw, who, like Mother Jones, model strength and independence on the way to becoming mothers themselves. In a system where mothers are displaced and daughters are sacrificed to the conflict between opposing groups, the daughters can be saved only through extraordinary steps on their own behalf.

But in *Disgrace*, it is David, not Lucy, who needs redeeming. (One could read Boaz, and the entire patriarchal system of ancient Israel, in a similar light; see Bal and Ruth 4:1–10, which depicts an odd system of exchange distant from the narrator's time and arguably secondary to the initiative taken by Ruth.) In that sense, Coetzee's book directs attention to the patriarchal source of the problem, just as feminist readings of Boaz have done. In Ruth and Lucy, therefore, we can find women who manage, albeit through a kind of self-sacrifice (giving themselves to men), to overcome a patriarchal culture that gives them up. Do they redeem the men as well? Not automatically, to be sure, for Boaz and Lurie are agents of the patriarchal systems that put these daughters in peril. Yet Lurie seems to accept his fate and even to take solace in giving comfort to animals, while Boaz and the men of Bethlehem are put in their place by the women who proclaim Ruth to be better to Naomi than seven sons (Ruth 4:15). Whether Ruth and Lucy salvage these men or transform the patriarchies they inhabit is ultimately a literary and religious question, but the terms of such a question must extend to the cultural institutions that would routinely displace mothers and sacrifice daughters. To limit the significance of Ruth and *Disgrace* to individual characters apart from larger institutions and conflicts would mean that Ruth and Lucy only reinforce the patriarchy that nearly destroys them.

Works Cited

Bal, Mieke. 1987. *Lethal Love: Feminist Literary Readings of Biblical Love Stories*. Bloomington: Indiana University Press.

———. 1988. *Death and Dissymetry: The Politics of Coherence in the Book of Judges*. Chicago: University of Chicago Press.

Britt, Brian. 2003. Unexpected Attachments: A Literary Approach to the Term dsx in the Hebrew Bible. *JSOT* 27:289–307.

———. 2005. Death, Social Conflict, and the Barley Harvest in the Hebrew Bible. *Journal of Hebrew Scriptures* 5. Online: http://www.arts.ualberta.ca/JHS/Articles/article_45.pdf.

Campbell, Edward E. Jr. 1975. *Ruth*. AB 7. New York: Doubleday.

Coetzee, J. M. 1999. *Disgrace*. New York: Viking.

———. 2003. *Elizabeth Costello*. New York: Penguin.

Delaney, Carol. 1998. *Abraham on Trial: The Social Legacy of Biblical Myth*. Princeton: Princeton University Press.

Exum, J. Cheryl. 1993. *Fragmented Women: Feminist (Sub)versions of Biblical Narratives*. Valley Forge, Pa.: Trinity Press International.

Freud, Sigmund. 1965. *The Interpretation of Dreams*. Translated by James Strachey. New York: Avon.

———. 1975. Obsessive Actions and Religious Practices. Pages 117–27 in vol. 9 of *Standard Edition of the Complete Psychological Works of Sigmund Freud*. Edited by James Strachey. London: Hogarth. (orig. 1907).

Girard, René. 1977. *Violence and the Sacred*. Translated by Patrick Gregory. Baltimore: Johns Hopkins University Press.

———. 1999. Violence in Biblical Narrative. *Philosophy and Literature* 23:387–92.

Gosse, Bernard. 1996. Le Livre de Ruth et ses liens avec II Samuel 21:1–14. *ZAW* 108:430–33.

Gunn, David M. 2005. *Judges*. Blackwell Bible Commentaries. Malden, Mass.: Blackwell.

Hubert, Henri, and Marcel Mauss. 1964. *Sacrifice: Its Nature and Function*. Translated by W. D. Halls. Chicago: University of Chicago Press. (orig. 1898)

Jay, Nancy. 1992. *Throughout Your Generations Forever: Sacrifice, Religion, and Paternity*. Chicago: University of Chicago Press.

Kirk-Duggan, Cheryl A. 1999. Black Mother Women and Daughters: Signifying Female-Divine Relationships in the Hebrew Bible and African-American Mother-Daughter Short Stories. Pages 192–210 in *Ruth and Esther: A Feminist Companion to the Bible*. Second Series: 3. Edited by Athalya Brenner. Sheffield: Sheffield Academic Press.

LaCocque, André. 1990. *The Feminine Unconventional: Four Subversive Figures in Israel's Tradition*. Minneapolis: Fortress.

Levenson, Jon. 1993. *The Death and Resurrection of the Beloved Son: The Transformation of Child Sacrifice in Judaism and Christianity*. New Haven: Yale University Press.

Trible, Phyllis. 1978. *God and the Rhetoric of Sexuality*. Philadelphia: Fortress.

4

Of Virtue and of Eating Shorts

Breaking Down the Configuration of Faithful Mother and
Wayward Son in Judges and *The Simpsons*

Frank M. Yamada

Introduction: Writing Scripts for Mothers and Sons

The mother-son relationship is a common configuration throughout the
history of literature and modern American media. The dynamic tension
between these two character-types takes various forms. From Jocasta and
Oedipus to Clytemnestra and Orestes, from Prince Hamlet and Gertrude
to Norman Bates and "Mother," the relationships of mothers to their sons
has provoked the imagination of authors, playwrights, philosophers, psychologists, and directors in cultures present and past.[1]

The biblical writers of both the Jewish and Christian scriptures also
used the mother-son configuration in order to explain significant moments
in the respective traditions. Sarah plays a key role in securing Isaac's future
as Abraham's heir. Similarly, Rebekah aids her son Jacob in order to deceive
Isaac into blessing their younger son rather than Esau. In the New Testament, the miraculous conceptions of both Elizabeth and Mary provide
the dramatic opening scene out of which the stories of John the Baptist
and Jesus emerge in Luke's Gospel. A consistent theme within three of the
biblical stories above is the woman's barrenness. This motif is usually associated with both divine intervention and the exceptional destiny of the
child who will be born.

The abundance of the mother-son configuration within literature
points to its importance within the cultures out of which these writings
emerge. As feminist scholars have noted, however, this characterization

---

1. For discussion of the representations of mothers in literature and contemporary popular culture, see Kaplan 1992; Daly and Reddy 1991; Thurer 1994; and
Luna 2004.

of women and their male children is not without problems. A woman's fate in literature is often tied to the scripts of men, including their male sons. Similarly, the mother's virtue is often a significant theme that helps determine the fate of her son. These limiting narrative plots point to larger cultural scripts within patriarchal societies that would seek to confine a woman's place to childbearing and the continuation of patralineal histories (Fuchs 2000, 44–90). Characterizations of motherhood, which some contemporary readers might evaluate positively by modern standards, often function in ways that ultimately seek to reinforce male-dominated cultural scripts.

This essay will explore a particular configuration of this mother-son characterization, namely, the virtuous mother and the wayward son. The prime example for this narrative theme occurs in the Samson saga, beginning with the announcement of the protagonist's birth in Judg 13. I will argue that this mother-son dyad serves a particular literary and cultural function in the book of Judges through a well-known biblical story form known as the annunciation type-scene. In patriarchal scripts, when cherished plots with predictable character-types are disrupted, the resulting tension serves particular ideological purposes. My analysis will not be limited to the biblical material. In order to illustrate and expose the subtleties in this cultural-textual dynamic in Judges, I will use another mother-son relationship from a different historical period that nevertheless contains strikingly similar patterns of configuration between two patriarchal cultures—ancient Israel and the United States. This contemporary example, Marge and Bart Simpson, reflects the postmodern complexities and anxieties that characterize the latter half of the twentieth century in North America. However, the embodiment of the virtuous mother–wayward son in *The Simpsons* is a satirical gesture that ultimately reinforces traditional relational structures within a contemporary American society, particularly in its valuing of the so-called nuclear family. The end result is the same. Both biblical and contemporary embodiments of this mother-son configuration serve the ends of the patriarchal scripts within their respective cultures.

The Simpsons: Parody, the Sitcom,
and the Traditional American Family

Upon first blush, *The Simpsons* do not appear to be a good dialogue partner with the biblical text. The show often tackles themes about religion satirically and humorously as part of its broader lampooning of suburban American values.[2] I will argue that this enormously popular show, while seeking to subvert the stereotypical suburban family made popular in situation comedies such as *Leave It to Beaver* and *The Cosby Show*, actually

---

2. For a more complete discussion of *The Simpsons* and religion, see Pinsky 2001.

reinforces the centrality of the nuclear family. Gendered relationships, including the faithful mother–wayward son dynamic, are critical for the development of narrative scripts, which move toward eventual resolution within an episode's half-hour time slot.

For those unfamiliar with *The Simpsons*, the show is an animated parody of the sitcom and focuses on the lives of one particular family in Springfield, U.S.A.[3] Written and created by Matt Groening, the original cartoon shorts were regularly played on *The Tracey Ullman Show* in the late 1980s. Fox Network aired *The Simpsons* as a half-hour show in 1989 with great success. In fact, as others have noted, "the show has become the longest-running cartoon (surpassing *The Flintstones*) and the most successful 'situation comedy' in American history" (Singh 2002, 209). *The Simpsons* has been enormously successful, to the point of being an icon of American culture (Gray 2006, 6–7). In December 1999, *Time* magazine awarded the animated series with the designation, "Best TV Show" in its "Best of the Century" list. It is hard to argue with the impact that this animated show has had on American culture for better or for worse.

Within the show itself, the very structure of the family unit is laughably stereotypical and "traditional." The cast includes a working father (Homer), a stay-at-home mother (Marge), two and half children (Bart, Lisa, and the perpetual infant, Maggie), and a dog and cat. As scholars, cultural critics, and the media have suggested, *The Simpsons* thrives on contradiction and caricature as the basis for its humor. The characters themselves are "*hyper*-stereotypes" (Gray 2006, 64) or, in some cases, are antitypes to the unrealistic "beauty" that one finds on most of mainstream television. For example, Marge sports a blue, beehive hairdo to complement her skin tone of bright yellow—a color that is typical for most of Springfield's cast of characters. In spite of the visually grotesque quality of her characterization, within the Springfield universe, Marge is considered to be a typical mother in both function and appearance. Such visual cues, combined with the overly stereotypical characterizations of the entire cast, are key elements of what makes *The Simpsons* work as an animated spoof of the domesticon.

In spite of the obvious parody within the show, *The Simpsons* betrays a surprisingly traditional message within its nonconventional disguise. In an influential essay, Paul Cantor explains:

> What makes *The Simpsons* so interesting is the way it combines traditionalism with antitraditionalism. It continually makes fun of the traditional American family. But it continually offers an enduring image of the nuclear family in the very act of satirizing it. Many of the traditional values of

---

3. Jonathan Gray, in his excellent study on *The Simpsons* as a discursive form of intertextual parody, compares the show to the "domesticon," or family oriented situation comedy (2006, 52–55).

> the American family survive this satire, above all the value of the nuclear
> family itself. (Cantor 1999, 737)

Thus, *The Simpsons*, though a parody of the situation comedy, mirrors
precisely the aims and function of the domesticon in its persistent reaffirmation of the nuclear family. As scholars and television critics have well
noted, the genre of the situation comedy sought to reinforce "traditional"
family values. Appearing in primetime, such shows offered images of the
family at hours when the entire family could gather to watch television.
In their plot lines, sitcoms provided happy resolutions within a single episode, which further reinforce the resilience of the nuclear family (Gray
2006, 54). Though *The Simpsons* provide a parody of this type of television
program, it subverts and disrupts the genre while affirming some of its
major components and themes. The recurring opening scene of the show
illustrates this point. After displaying a dizzying barrage of individual
character portraits—Bart writing the same sentence on the chalkboard as
punishment, Lisa playing a saxophone in class, and Marge shopping with
baby Maggie—the family meets up at home to gather around the TV upon
Homer's return from work. Hence, right from the start, the show gathers
these different character-types into their proper place within the sitcom
world. They are at home with each other, doing what any traditional nuclear family would be doing at primetime—watching a television show
about the nuclear family. In this way, the show reflects its own biting self-
consciousness in that it provides satirical commentary on the very genre
within which it participates.

Within *The Simpsons* weekly narrative scripts, the plot plays out among
various stereotypical character dyads: working father–stay-at-home
mother; slacker, beer-drinking husband–moralistic mother; rebellious
son–academically overachieving daughter, and so on. The faithful mother–
wayward son dynamic is one of the many character configurations that
are at play in the show. Hence, in order to understand Marge's unwaver-
ing care and devotion for "her little guy," one must first recognize what
is at work within these larger relational structures and what is at stake in
evoking and sustaining them. One way to illustrate the function of the
faithful mother–wayward son component in *The Simpsons* is to find out
what happens when Marge or Bart fails to live up to their assigned roles.
In other words, what happens when Marge is not a virtuous mother and/
or Bart is not a rebellious child? As one would expect within the genre of
the domesticon, when a character ventures beyond his or her given role,
the resulting effect upon the family is perceived within the show's world
as chaos. Gerard Jones notes, "Domestic harmony is threatened when a
character develops a desire that runs counter to the group's welfare, or
misunderstands a situation because of poor communication, or contacts a
disruptive outside element" (Jones 1992, 4, cited in Gray 2006, 52). Hence,
dramatic tension within this genre relies on an assumed equilibrium in

the family unit or social group. An episode achieves resolution when a character's initial disruption is reconciled within the larger group, resulting in a reaffirmation of the nuclear family and the individual's proper place in the social order.

Marge and Bart represent a certain character balance within the show (as do Homer and Lisa).[4] Marge is both a domestic goddess in the home and a feminist on most social and political issues. That is, she is a conflicted stereotypical representation and parody of female virtue in the United States. Bart, by contrast, is the personification of youthful, if not naïve, rebellion. His characteristic phrases include the well-known "Eat my shorts" and "Don't have a cow, man." His name is an anagram for "brat." Bart's playful rebellion is the antithesis to Marge's sometimes overserious morality. This not-so-subtle balance among and between the characters is part of *The Simpsons'* formula. However, within the show's almost twenty-year history, there are many examples of how the writers transgress these simplistic characterizations in order to create the plot lines for different episodes.

Though Marge and Lisa are the closest things to role models in *The Simpsons*, the former has often digressed into morally questionable behavior. Marge has dealt with being a compulsive gambler, was arrested for shoplifting, was diagnosed with road rage, and used steroids to bulk up her physical appearance. In these episodes Marge breaks out of her stereotypical role as faithful mother and explores her morally questionable side. The resulting plot progression within such episodes is predictable and telling. For example, in "$pringfield (Or How I Learned to Stop Worrying and Love Legalized Gambling)," Marge becomes addicted to slot machines after a casino is built in Springfield. She neglects her family with disastrous results. Bart begins to run his own child version of a casino in his treehouse. After Lisa has a bad dream about the boogeyman, a rifle-wielding Homer barricades himself and the children indoors for protection. In other words, all hell has broken loose in the Simpsons' household. The crowning scene has Lisa receiving an underachiever's award on her state project since it was obvious that she received no help from her parents (she was wearing a California-shaped paper bag that read "Floreda" on it, courtesy of Homer). The lesson is simple: the family unit becomes chaotic when Marge digresses from her role as a virtuous stay-at-home mother.

Similarly, Bart, the stereotypical wild child, has on occasion stumbled

---

4. In the father-daughter example, Lisa is a smart, overachieving intellectual who "is *politically correct* across the spectrum" (Cantor 1999, 738, emphasis added). Homer, on the other hand, represents everything that is wrong with men. He drinks too much. He takes his wife and children for granted. He beats and yells at his son. He is selfish, stupid, and ignorant about socially relevant and political issues. In a word, he is the epitome of someone who is *politically incorrect*.

on to the straight and narrow. In one particular episode, "The Father, the Son, and the Holy Guest Star," Bart and Homer contemplate converting to Roman Catholicism. Bart is intrigued with the religion after reading a comic-book version of the saints, which he receives from a hip, young priest. Within the episode, Bart's potential conversion is a point of crisis for the family, especially Marge, since the family attends a Protestant church. In the end, Bart decides not to convert after attending a Protestant youth festival in which he is allowed to play paint ball. In a moment of rare insight, Bart declares to the gathered group how silly it is for different denominations to be fighting. The closing scene looks forward into the distant future, where two parties are warring in an apocalyptic battle over whether Bart's teachings emphasized love or peace. While this episode is certainly a satirical look at Western Christianity, there is another implicit message that helps to drive the script. *The Simpsons*, indeed the fate of religion, are better off when Bart is not a saint.

From these examples, one can see how the mother-son balance works within *The Simpsons*. Each character has his or her place, and the family unit as a whole is better off when the different members of the family remain in step with their assigned roles. While the individual characters' digressions are certainly part of what drives the plot forward, the resolution at the end of each episode relies on relational balance between the characters in order to maintain the nuclear family unit. Marge, in some strange way, needs Bart's bad-boy image to balance her virtue, and Bart needs his mother's moral authority to counteract his rebellious nature. This delicate family balance within *The Simpsons* suggests at least two things about the show's function within American culture: (1) though a parody of the situation comedy, the show affirms the centrality of the nuclear family; and (2) the narrative scripts of the different episodes rely on the characters fulfilling specific roles within the family unit. Hence, any character's digression from his or her character-type is perceived as chaos. The larger social message is clear. Even if *The Simpsons* teaches us to look at the traditional suburban family more ironically and satirically, it nevertheless affirms the centrality of the family unit with affection. Moreover, the characters live into their true selves only so far as they fulfill their designated role within the larger group. In this way, the show, ironically, serves to affirm the stereotypical roles of mother/father and parent/child, even as it attempts to subvert such configurations through parody.

The plot movement also suggests something about the psyche of *The Simpsons'* assumed audience. The show reflects a particular anxiety that exists within contemporary culture. The show's popularity can be attributed to American society's nostalgia for the nuclear family, but it also depends on the social currency of certain stereotypical gender roles. Each episode's predictable story line mirrors the assumed culture's anxiety over the disruption of traditional roles for mothers, fathers, sons, and daughters. The early reaction to the show was very negative. The language of the critics evoked themes of social disintegration and eroding values, charging that *The Simpsons* represented a threat to the modern American family.[5] Tellingly, the show generated a discourse from its detractors that mirrored the movement toward social chaos within *The Simpson's* own narrative plots. When the show transgressed "accepted" roles for men, women, and children, the culture perceived such movements as threatening, disruptive, and in need of resolution.[6]

Judges 13: Giving Birth to Another Gendered Script

Commentators have long noted the importance of the Judg 13 to the overall shape and literary meaning of the Samson cycle.[7] This initial chapter sets the tone for the rest of the story and provides the reader with important motifs that propel the plot forward toward its dramatic conclusion (Exum 1983). The miraculous opening of a barren woman's womb, along with the divine announcement of the child's birth, provides a recognizable script within the Hebrew Bible. In such stories, the child will be destined for great things. Samson's failure to live up to this ideal, and the ironic way that he ends up avoiding and fulfilling his announced fate, are key characteristics within the story's literary artistry (Bal 1988, 200; Gros Louis 1974, 158; Reinhartz 1993, 157). While much has been written on both the Samson cycle in general and on his nameless mother in particular, I will focus my attention on the ways in which this annunciation story constructs gender within its assumed culture, particularly in the faithful

---

5. At the heart of the so-called culture wars, critics often pointed to *The Simpsons* as an example of eroding American traditions and values, particularly in its portrayal of the family unit. In 1992, while in the midst of a re-election campaign, George Bush Sr. said, "We're going to keep on trying to strengthen the American family. To make the American family more like the Waltons and less like the Simpsons" (cited in Singh 2002, 210). Singh notes that Bart responded to the president in the episode immediately following the President's comments by saying, "we're just like the Waltons. We're praying for an end to the depression too" (210).

6. Most of the show's critics are social conservatives. However, Singh notes that social progressives have been slow to criticize *The Simpsons*, though its content tends to mock equally both liberal and conservative positions on social issues (Singh 2002, 212, 223–25). For example, critics have been slow to point out the lack of racially diverse characters in *The Simpsons*. Apu, the minimart owner, is the only regular person of color on the show. He is a crude stereotype of the perpetually foreign South Asian. Moreover, as I will argue below, part of *The Simpsons'* formula relies heavily on resolutions that restore social order, including the reinforcement of predictable gender roles for each of the family's characters.

7. Exum rightly notes that scholars are in agreement that chapter 13 was appended to the Samson cycle at a later time. Nevertheless, this chapter "provides an indispensable introduction to the following stories, giving them direction and context, and presenting and expounding what will become the major motifs of the saga" (Exum 1983, 35).

mother–wayward son motif.[8] More precisely, I will examine the ways that this embodiment of the type-scene overturns its assumed audience's expectations about genre while reinforcing certain representations of gender within a culture of patriarchy.

A quick glance at the entire book of Judges reveals an identifiable pattern of events. The narrator provides this sequence in 2:11–21. The structure is also illustrated briefly in the life of the first judge, Othniel (3:7–11). The characteristic movement can be summarized as follows: (1) Israel does evil in the sight of the LORD; (2) the LORD's anger is kindled against Israel, and the LORD hands them over to their enemies; (3) the people cry out to the LORD; (4) the LORD raises up a judge as deliverer; and (5) there is a brief peace, after which the cycle starts again (Gros Louis 1974, 143–44; Olson 1988, 725–26, 755–57; McCann 2002, 9–10, 34–40; and Soggin 1981, 43–44). This ordered structure of events gives way increasingly to a more disorderly narrative script toward the end of the book. The conclusion in chapters 17–21 ends with Israel in social, moral, and religious collapse. The narrator characterizes this period of decline as a time when "there was no king in Israel; every man did what was right in his own eyes" (17:6 and 21:25).[9] In Judg 17–21, the people and their leadership again return to the worship of idols. Priests and their families have become corrupted by tribal politics. A Sodom-and-Gomorrah-like mob in Gibeah gang rapes a woman, after which her Levite husband chops up her body into pieces and distributes them to the various tribes. In retaliation for this crime, Israel commits an act of holy war against itself, almost extinguishing the tribe of Benjamin. Ridiculously, the remaining tribes decide to help repopulate Benjamin by slaying the inhabitants of Jabesh-gilead, giving the young women who were left to the decimated tribe. When this plan does not provide enough wives, the inhabitants of Benjamin are encouraged to abduct another group of young women who are processing out from a festival in Shiloh. Hence, the book of Judges ends in complete moral and social decline, evoking the refrain of the editor, who looks forward to a time when a king might be able to bring order to this chaotic situation.

The cyclical pattern at the beginning of Judges is disrupted with the Samson saga. Though the people once again do evil (Judg 13:1), they do not follow their apostasy by returning to the LORD, crying out for the deity's help. Moreover, though the announcement of Samson's birth provides the expected promise of a deliverer, this judge ends up falling far short of his expected role. Throughout this cycle of stories, Samson fails to live into his hero's role. He violates every aspect of his Nazirite vow, an oath to which

---

8. By "gender construction" I mean that the texts themselves produce configurations of gender that reinforce ideas of male and female within their assumed culture. For a discussion of the construction of gender, see Anderson 2004, 7–9.

9. The refrain also occurs in abbreviated form ("In those days, there was no king in Israel") in Judg 18:1 and 19:1.

he is bound from his birth.[10] Though he kills many of Israel's enemies, he does so usually in the midst of one of his quests for different women. In the end, while he is imprisoned and his captors humiliate him publicly, he commits one last act of great strength, killing more Philistines in his death than he did in his life (16:30). He is a deliverer who does not deliver Israel, and, in this way, he provides an appropriate transition to the eventual chaos that marks the end of the book. The overall effect of the plot and narration is clear. Samson is a symbolic antihero whose faults anticipate the collapse of social order in Israel during this period.

In terms of genre or form, scholars have long recognized Judg 13 as an annunciation type-scene (Alter 1983; Fuchs 1989; Exum 1980; and Ackerman 1998, 186–93).[11] Three elements characterize this kind of story: (1) the woman's initial barrenness; (2) a word of divine promise that predicts the birth of a male child; and (3) the birth of the child, who will be destined to accomplish great things (Alter 1983, 119–20).[12] The birth is considered miraculous—a site of divine intervention—because of the woman's initially barren state. The oracle of promise, which God or an angel delivers, serves to emphasize the supernatural character of this birth and creates the expectation in the audience that the child is destined to be a hero. At every point, Samson frustrates this presumed outcome, since he fails as a deliverer. Hence, the opening chapter sets up the reader in such a way that his or her expectations will be overturned in the story's telling. Irony runs thick throughout Judg 13–16.[13] Samson's virtuous mother, who receives the characteristic announcement for a child born to do great things,

---

10. There is some debate about how much the Nazirite theme is evoked within this narrative. The conditions for the vow can be found in Num 6:1–21. The word itself, *nāzîr*, which means "consecrated one," plays a significant role in the plot. Moreover, Samson's narrated behavior within this cycle of stories suggests that the final editors were aware of the Nazirite vow and used it intentionally to frame his disobedience. For another perspective, however, see Niditch's discussion (1990, 612–13). Ackerman sees the Nazirite vow, which is also found in the story of Samuel's miraculous birth (1 Sam 1:1–28), as functioning in a similar way to the near-death episodes found in some of the other annunciation type-scenes. She interprets both the vow and the near-death experience as signs that the child belongs to the LORD (Ackerman 1998, 186–93).

11. Alter (1983) recognizes six annunciation type-scenes: Sarah (Gen 18:9–15; 21:1–7); Rebekah (Gen 25:19–25); Rachel (Gen 30:1–8, 22–24); Judg 13:1–11; Hannah (1 Sam 1:1–28); and the Shunammite woman (2 Kgs 4:8–17).

12. See, however, Fuchs, who argues persuasively that the annunciation scene, with its characteristic depiction of faithful mothers, ultimately serves the ends of patriarchal culture, since it ties the woman's biological function to her character in problematic ways (1983; 2000, 44–90, esp. 83–90).

13. Exum and Whedbee argue that the Samson stories fit within the genre of classic comedy (as opposed to tragedy). For a discussion of Samson as comedy, including the use of comic irony, see Exum and Whedbee 1984.

ends up giving birth to a comic hero (Exum and Whedbee 1984, 32–33). This wayward son is charismatically gifted, as is evident in his tremendous physical strength. His might, however, serves only to further his selfish exploits or to settle personal disputes. A character whose beginnings are the most celebrated in the book of Judges ends up being the epitome of a failed form of leadership. As Olson rightly notes, "In short, Samson represents the implosion of the whole judge system" (1998, 842). Hence, the narrator uses the well-known annunciation type-scene within the Samson saga in order to dramatize the contrast between a promised son's miraculous birth and his moral wanderings that lead to eventual death.

The ironic juxtaposition between hero and fool provides the perfect ideological setup for Judg 17–21. As stated above, the narrator of Judges subverts the expectations of genre in order to evoke a story world that moves increasingly toward chaos. As one would expect, the Deuteronomistic editors do not leave the audience with this unresolved dramatic tension, pointing to the possibility of resolving the chaos within the refrain in Judg 17–21, that is, in the hope of a better world under a king. However, it is with another annunciation scene in 1 Sam 1:1–11 that the faithful mother–heroic son motif is reestablished in the characters of Hannah and Samuel.[14] Order is restored to the mother-son paradigm in the biblical tradition through another faithful woman and a male character who represents the transition from judge to king. The narrator of Judges evokes chaos in the Samson cycle at the end of the book in order to propose a particular resolution—one that finds fulfillment in the person of Samuel and the imminent monarchy. Thus, in Judg 13 the faithful mother–wayward son relational dyad contributes to a satirical look at the end of this period when judges ruled. It also serves the ideological purposes of the Deuteronomistic editors who would seek to find order in a king.

Though the Samson cycle subverts the reader's expectations through irony and satire, the story continues to construct gender in ways that reinforce a culture of patriarchy. Certainly, Samson's mother is portrayed in a humorously positive light, especially when contrasted with her husband Manoah, a Danite from Zorah.[15] In the story, the mother's role is primary and the father's secondary (Exum 1980, 58). This can be seen in a few ways. First, the woman is the preferred recipient of divine revela-

---

14. The Christian canon, following the Septuagint, places the book of Judges before the book of Ruth. In this way, the Deuteronomistic arrangement from Judges to Samuel is interrupted in both Protestant and Roman Catholic traditions, but not in the Tanak. The story of Ruth and Naomi, however, provides another type of resolution to the chaos in Judg 17–21. The two women represent complementary images of faithfulness in a storyline that reinforces the theme of hope and social order albeit within a patriarchal world (see Trible 1984, 84–85; Fuchs 2000, 73–82).

15. However, see Boling, who views the woman as "speaking better than she knew" (1975, 221).

tion. The angel of the LORD appears first to the woman (Judg 13:3). After the wife conveys the oracle to her husband, Manoah prays to the LORD for more information about how to raise this promised son in verse 8.[16] The angel of God, however, returns not to Manoah but *'el-h 'iššâ*, "to the woman" (v. 9). The end of the verse emphasizes the husband's lesser role when the narrator adds, "but Manoah, her husband, was not with her." Secondly, the woman is more perceptive. In contrast to her husband, she recognizes early on in the narrative that the visitor is a divine being (v. 6). Manoah is oblivious to this fact (v. 16) until the angel ascends in a fiery flame from the altar (vv. 20–21). Lastly, the woman is theologically more astute. The husband is suspicious of the divine promise, questioning the angel repeatedly and eventually asking for the messenger's name (v. 17). Manoah is also fearful of the divine. After seeing the flames from heaven, he declares, "we will surely die for we have seen God." The woman, on the other hand, provides the more rational response, pointing out that if the LORD had wanted to kill them, their offering would not have been accepted nor would they have received a divine word of promise about their forthcoming child (v. 23). Thus, the woman is the "better theologian" in that she appears to trust God's promise and the divine will (Exum 1980, 59). She is faithful and levelheaded in contrast to her husband's suspicion and fear. Susan Niditch appropriately observes: "Manoah plays the timid uncomprehending fool to his wife, who is featured in the most important scene with the divine messenger and who is more able than her husband to comprehend his message and true identity" (Niditch 1990, 611).

Beyond the comparison between husband and wife, this unnamed woman provides insight into the divine messenger's words that prove to be prophetic in determining the fate of her unborn son.[17] In Judg 13:3–5, the angel gives the birth announcement and instructions concerning the child. The wife repeats these words to her husband but with significant changes. She omits both the prohibition against a razor touching the child's head and the phrase "he shall begin to deliver Israel from the hand

---

16. Gunn and Fewell point out that in Judg 13:8 Manoah seeks to include himself in the human/divine discussions through first-person plural forms: "come again to *us*, and teach *us* what *we* are to do" (1993, 129).

17. Anonymous women play important roles within the book of Judges. Jephthah's daughter (Judg 11) and a Levite's concubine (Judg 19) are both victims of violence at the hands of men. Reinhartz notes that their anonymity is not a reflection of their minor status as characters but "is symbolic of a victimized state" (1993, 159). Reinhartz goes on to argue that Manoah's wife is assigned greater importance since her anonymity is connected to the other nameless character in Judg 13, the angel of the LORD (see Reinhartz 1993). I find Fuchs's analysis more compelling. She argues that nameless mothers such as Manoah's wife and the Shunammite woman (2 Kgs 4:8–37) are blessed with virtue precisely because they are nameless. Important named mothers in Israel are characterized in a much more critical light because they have relatively more social power (Fuchs 2000, 61–62).

of the Philistines" (v. 5). Thus, liberation is absent from the future mother's retelling of the incident (Alter 1981, 101). Instead, she includes an allusion to her son's death: "the boy shall be a Nazirite of God from birth until the day of his death." By inserting the last phrase, *'ad-yôm môtô*, to the angel's original statement about the Nazirite vow, she includes an element to the promise that provides an ominous tone for the rest of the narrative.[18] Her words, both in what she adds and what she excludes, prove to be illuminating when seen within the context of the full story. This son, whose birth announcement suggests his future heroic status, will not deliver Israel from the Philistines. Rather, he will face his death, in large part, because he failed to keep his vow by allowing a razor to touch his head.

The positive assessment of Manoah's wife has led some commentators to assume that Judg 13 runs counter to limiting patriarchal notions of motherhood (Amit 1993; Reinhartz 1993; McCann 2002, 94–101).[19] Exum and Fuchs, however, have rightly noted that one must observe how this story relates to other configurations of female characterization in the biblical text,[20] while being cognizant of how patriarchal cultures construe both positive and negative images of mothers (see Exum 1993; Fuchs 1989; 2000). Exum, while acknowledging that this wife/mother is painted in a positive light, argues that her characterization still serves the ends of patriarchy. Though the image of this woman is a positive one, she is, nevertheless, a character who is limited to her role of motherhood without the benefits of female sexuality—a separation of function and being that patriarchy uses to control the female body. The erotic aspect of womanhood is reserved for a different negative stereotype in the biblical literature: the whore (Exum 1993, 65–66). The female character of Judg 13 can be portrayed positively because she does not represent a threat to the status quo. She is anonymous, and the audience knows relatively little about her, unlike the long traditions associated with the more powerful named matriarchs of Israel's lineage. Biblical narrative allows this relatively minor character to be an example of virtue and faithfulness precisely because she is a minor character. Fuchs states:

> Why does the biblical narrative let relatively unimportant mother-figures outshine the "mothers" of the nation? I would like to suggest that

---

18. The phrase "from birth … until the day of his death" is an idiom that means "his entire life," as Reinhartz correctly notes (1993, 163). However, Bal has proposed a more radical interpretation of the woman's comments, arguing that "[h]er knowledge, moreover, is fatal, in the double sense of the word. It predicts Samson's' fate, and produces it, thus producing his death" (1988, 74).

19. McCann goes so far as to suggest that Samson's mother is the true hero of the story (2002, 95). His interpretation, while attractive in some respects, fails to understand this text's function as parody.

20. For a survey of the different women characters in the book of Judges, see Klein 1993a; 1993b (reprinted in Klein 2003, 9–32); and Ackerman 1998.

> it is precisely because the latter characters are accorded the high status
> of national progenitrices that they are deprived of the more impressive
> characterization of their counterparts. (Fuchs 2000, 61)

Thus, a positive role model actually functions within patriarchal culture to
create negative effects for women. Though the woman of Judg 13 is virtuous, she is limited to the role of an anonymous mother who will fade into
the background of her wayward son. Her fate, like her words, will always
be tied to his nondeliverance of Israel; hence, her legacy will be bound to
this last judge whose life symbolizes the decline of a nation into chaos.
Though her faithfulness is contrasted with her inept husband, it is Manoah's lack of understanding about God's ways that will forever characterize
her son. Moreover, her virtue in this story, like all women in annunciation type-scenes, is forever linked with her role as mother. This nameless
woman's faithfulness and theological insight are extolled only to the extent that she fulfills her duty within this patralineal script—a plot line that
progresses from the promise of a son to an unexpected fulfillment, from a
failed judge to a nation's collapse, and from social chaos to the promise of
order in a king. What was in the beginning will be in the end … a narrated
history of men replacing men.

Cracking the Ideological Code:
The Subversion of Form and the Maintenance of Culture

How are the Simpsons related to Samson? What does Springfield have to
do with Zorah? The preceding analysis of two different "texts"—one from
biblical literature and one from television—has revealed a similar conclusion. Both subvert or play with well-known forms within their culture in
order to create different types of parody. The Simpsons provide a satirical
look at the domesticon or family-based situation comedy. Judges 13 uses
the annunciation scene in order to create expectations of a hero that will
be disappointed throughout the rest of the Samson saga. One could argue
that the popularity of both pieces has much to do with this subversion of
form—the subtle interplay between continuity and discontinuity in literature and the arts.

Literature, however, always serves a particular end. In this respect,
both pieces evoke chaos as a theme in order to put forward their respective
visions of the world. In *The Simpsons*, the chaos is tied directly to the genre
of situation comedy. Whether this animated family from Springfield is facing a serious sociopolitical issue, individual crises, or the breakdown of
modern Western civilization, they will face the problem and resolve it as a
happy nuclear family (of course, all within a half hour, including commer-
cials). Similarly, the narrator of Judges uses the Samson cycle to signal the
end of an era—the decline of the period of the judges. In this topsy-turvy
world, a hero's birth announcement gives way to the exploits of a comic
fool. Israel is not delivered from the hands of the surrounding nations but

becomes its own worst enemy (see Judg 20). Eventually, the descent of this one judge is symbolic of a world that moves toward increasing social, religious, and moral disintegration in Judg 17–21. The resolution to this chaos is found in the hope for a king. Thus, both *The Simpsons* and the book of Judges betray their ideological leaning. By evoking chaos as a theme, these modern and ancient writers put forward their agendas through the promise of an ordered resolution.

In the service of ideology, both texts use gendered scripts that rely on the balance between mother and son. In *The Simpsons* and Judg 13, the dyad of faithful mother–wayward son is evoked, albeit in ways that are unique to their respective contexts. Both rely on the delicate equilibrium that exists between the two stereotypes. The virtue of Samson's mother is tied to the fate of her son in complicated ways. Her faithful reception of the angel's announcement stands in narrative tension with her son's continual failure as a deliverer. Indeed, her prophetic reinterpretation of the divine promise seals his fate from birth to death. Ultimately, however, the script within Judges confines this faithful unnamed woman to the role of mother. She, like all mothers in annunciation type-scenes, will fade into the background as the story continues through the life of her son. In this way, her virtue is always evaluated in terms of how well or, in this case, how ironically she continues the patrilineal storyline. Her wayward son will forever dominate her legacy.

Marge and Bart Simpson provide another example of the faithful mother–wayward son. In this embodiment of the dyad, both characters are allowed to be iconoclastic of the stereotype that they represent. Marge is allowed to venture outside the realm of motherly domesticity in order to explore humorously her moral digressions. Similarly, Bart occasionally wanders onto the straight and narrow, wading in the shallow water of his more intelligent and socially responsible self. However, usually by the end of each episode, the family finds its resolution with each member securely placed within his or her given role. In fact, chaos results when the characters stray too far from their stereotypical script. The social message of *The Simpsons* is clear: the world is a more ordered place when each of the characters stays true to form.

The preceding analysis has revealed an important lesson about literature, media, and the construction of gender within patriarchal cultures. While certain shows like *The Simpsons* might be hailed as groundbreaking and satirically edgy, they can remain remarkably conservative in their affirmation of "traditional" patriarchal values about family and gender (Singh 2002). Subversive interpretation of form does not necessarily lead to the dismantling of oppressive social structures.[21] Likewise, Judg 13 pres-

---

21. I have argued elsewhere that deconstruction, another type of subversive reading, while having the potential to be ethically responsible, does not necessarily lead to social advocacy. See Yamada 2000.

ents readers with a positive female character in Manoah's wife. However, this particular image of a woman ultimately ends up reinforcing the faithful mother stereotype—an image that has served patriarchal culture well, since it ties woman's virtue to the task of childbearing. E. Ann Kaplan's comments about motherhood and representation are a fitting conclusion to this intertextual discussion:

> For women, one of the most subordinated *and* fetishized positions has been that of "mother." Once this position is opened up as only a part of any specific woman's subjectivity, not the all-consuming entirety of it; once any specific woman is seen to be constituted "mother" only when interacting with her child; once "mother" is no longer a fixed, essentialized quality, then women may be freed from the kind of discursive constraints and burdens studied in this *or any other* book. (Kaplan 1992, 219, emphasis added)

Works Cited

Ackerman, Susan. 1998. *Warrior, Dancer, Seductress, Queen: Women in Judges and Biblical Israel*. ABRL. New York: Doubleday.

Alter, Robert. 1981. *The Art of Biblical Narrative*. New York: Basic Books.

———. 1983. How Convention Helps Us Read: The Case of the Bible's Annunciation Type-Scene. *Prooftexts* 3:115–30.

Amit, Yairah. 1993. "Manoah Promptly Followed His Wife" (Judges 13.1): On the Place of the Woman in Birth Narratives. Pages 146–56 in *A Feminist Companion to Judges*. Edited by Athalya Brenner. The Feminist Companion to the Bible 4. Sheffield: Sheffield Academic Press.

Anderson, Cheryl B. 2004. *Women, Ideology, and Violence: Critical Theory and the Construction of Gender in the Book of the Covenant and the Deuteronomic Law*. JSOTSup 394. London: T&T Clark.

Bal, Mieke. 1988. *Death and Dissymmetry: The Politics of Coherence in the Book of Judges*. CSJH. Chicago: University of Chicago Press.

Boling, Robert C. 1975. *Judges: Introduction, Translation, and Commentary*. AB 6A. New York: Doubleday.

Cantor, Paul A. 1999. The Simpsons: Atomistic Politics and the Nuclear Family. *Political Theory* 27:734–49.

Daly, Brenda O., and Maureen T. Reddy, eds. 1991. *Narrating Mothers: Theorizing Maternal Subjectivities*. Knoxville: University of Tennessee Press.

Exum, J. Cheryl. 1980. Promise and Fulfillment: Narrative Art in Judges 13. *JBL* 99:43–59.

———. 1983. The Theological Dimension of the Samson Saga. *VT* 33:30–45.

———. 1993. *Fragmented Women: Feminist (Sub)versions of Biblical Narratives*. Valley Forge, Pa.: Trinity Press International.

Exum, J. Cheryl, and J. William Whedbee. 1984. Isaac, Samson, and Saul: Reflections on the Comic and Tragic Visions. *Semeia* 32:5–40.

Fewell, Danna Nolan, and David M. Gunn. 1993. *Gender, Power, and Promise: The Subject of the Bible's First Story*. Nashville: Abingdon.

Fuchs, Esther. 1989. The Literary Characterizations of Mothers and Sexual Politics in the Hebrew Bible. *Semeia* 46:151–66.

———. 2000. *Sexual Politics in the Biblical Narrative: Reading the Hebrew Bible as a Woman*. JSOTSup 310. Sheffield: Sheffield Academic.

Gray, Jonathan. 2006. *Watching with the Simpsons: Television, Parody, and Intertextuality*. Comedia. London: Routledge.

Gros Louis, Kenneth R. R. 1974. The Book of Judges. Pages 141–62 in *Literary Interpretations of Biblical Narratives*. Edited by Kenneth R. R. Gros Louis, James S. Ackerman, and Thayer S. Warshaw. Nashville: Abingdon.

Jones, Gerard. 1992. *Honey, I'm Home! Sitcoms: Selling the American Dream*. New York: Grove Weidenfeld.

Kaplan, E. Ann. 1992. *Motherhood and Representation: The Mother in Popular Culture and Melodrama*. London: Routledge.

Klein, Lillian R. 1993a. The Book of Judges: Paradigm and Deviation in Images of Women. Pages 55–71 in *A Feminist Companion to Judges*. Edited by Athalya Brenner. The Feminist Companion to the Bible 4. Sheffield: Sheffield Academic Press.

———. 1993b. A Spectrum of Female Characters. Pages 24–33 in *A Feminist Companion to Judges*. Edited by Athalya Brenner. The Feminist Companion to the Bible 4. Sheffield: Sheffield Academic Press.

———. 2003. *Deborah to Esther: Sexual Politics in the Hebrew Bible*. Minneapolis: Fortress.

Luna, Alice M. 2004. *Visual Perversity: A Re-articulation of Maternal Instinct*. Lanham, Md.: Lexington Books.

McCann, J. Clinton. 2002. *Judges*. IBC. Louisville: Westminster John Knox.

Niditch, Susan. 1990. Samson as Culture Hero, Trickster, and Bandit: The Empowerment of the Weak. *CBQ* 52:608–24.

Olson, Dennis T. 1998. The Book of Judges: Introduction, Commentary, and Reflections. *NIB* 2L722–888. Edited by Leander E. Keck. Nashville: Abingdon.

Pinsky, Mark I. 2001. *The Gospel according to the Simpsons: The Spiritual Life of the World's Most Animated Family*. Louisville: Westminster John Knox.

Reinhartz, Adele. 1993. Samson's Mother: An Unnamed Protagonist. Pages 157–70 in *A Feminist Companion to Judges*. Edited by Athalya Brenner. The Feminist Companion to the Bible 4. Sheffield: Sheffield Academic Press.

Singh, Robert. 2002. Subverting American Values?: The Simpsons, South Park and the Cartoon Culture War. Pages 206–29 in *American Politics and Society Today*. Edited by Robert Singh. Cambridge: Polity.

Soggin, J. Alberto. 1981. *Judges: A Commentary*. Translated by J. S. Bowden. Philadelphia: Westminster.

Thurer, Shari L. 1994. *The Myths of Motherhood: How Culture Reinvents the Good Mother*. Boston: Houghton Mifflin.

Trible, Phyllis. 1984. *Texts of Terror: Literary-Feminist Readings of Biblical Narratives*. OBT. Philadelphia: Fortress.

Yamada, Frank M. 2000. Ethics. Pages 76–84 in *Handbook of Postmodern Biblical Interpretation*. Edited by A. K. M. Adam. St. Louis: Chalice.

5

Mothering a Leader
BATHSHEBA'S RELATIONAL AND FUNCTIONAL IDENTITIES

Mignon R. Jacobs

Introduction

The images of mothers encompass the ideal and atrocities of the real and through modern media have become a normative part of modern sensibilities. Nowhere is this more evident than the mother who gives her organ to save her child and the economically challenged woman who mothered a president of the United States juxtaposed against mothers who abandon and murder their children. These modern images of mothers do not represent new portraits of motherhood or the various characteristics of the women who embody them. Rather, the biblical text is an ancient version of the modern media bearing witness to many manifestations of motherhood and women's embodiment of their relational and functional identities. The discussion of a leader's mother (one manifestation of motherhood) may identify various leaders and their mothers. This essay identifies and examines the mothers of kings and builds on the following two assertions. First, leadership is domain-specific and includes the private (family) and public (religious and political) dimensions. Second, overlaps between the private (family) and public (political) domains are inevitable for the persons involved. Consequently, to the extent that she influences her son, the king's mother is a leader within the family and the political domains. Using the mother-leaders within the family-political domain as a part of the investigational framework, I focus on 1 Kgs's 1–2 portrayal of Bathsheba and propose that Bathsheba demonstrates the inevitable interplay of her role as mother (*'ēm*–relational) and functions strategically as the king's mother (*'ēm hammelek*–functional). This essay includes four sections: (1) "Delineating the Parameters of the Investigation"; (2) "Family Dynamics of a Mother-Leader"; (3) "A Mother's Counterstrategy"; and (4) Use of a Mother's Influence and Discernment."

1. Delineating the Parameters of the Investigation

Regarding the availability of data in the Old Testament about mothers, the issue is the specificity of that data regarding the mothers of kings. Because Bathsheba is often discussed as a *gəbîrâ* (typically translated "queen mother"), this essay engages discussions about the *gəbîrâ* (e.g., Andreasen 1983; Ben-Barak 1991; Ackerman 1993; Bowen 2001). First, I contend that *gəbîrâ* designates functional identity but is not identical to the king's mother (*'ēm hammelek*) or mothers named in the succession formulae—"and his mother's name..." (*wəšēm 'immô*). Table 1 illustrates the infrequent occurrence of queen mother (*gəbîrâ*) and king's mother (*'ēm hammelek*) as indicators of functional identity.

Second, the terms used to identify a ruler's mother are part of the construction of the model of mothering. Regarding *gəbîrâ*, the desire to construct a particular model of the mothers' functional identity shapes the choice of texts and often results in a clearer picture than the limited and multivalent data may allow (see de Vaux 1965; Andreasen 1983; Ackerman 1993; contrast Ben-Barak 1991; Bowen 2001). "Queen mother" is one meaning of *gəbîrâ*, but the term is rarely used of the mothers of Judean kings. Only Maacah (1 Kgs 15:13) is explicitly identified as *gəbîrâ* and Nehushta identified by her connection to Jehoiachin (Jer 29:2). The term *gəbîrâ* also designates a female functional superior (mistress) over her female subordinate (maidservant *šipḥâ*), such as Sarai over Hagar (Gen 16:4, 8, 9); Naaman's wife (2 Kgs 5:3). It is also used in a general sense of the mistress-maid relationship (Ps 123:2; Prov 30:23; Isa 24:2).

In Isa 47:5, 7 *gəbîrâ* is used of Babylon, the female ruler or queen. When *gəbîrâ* is translated "queen," it may refer to the mother or the wife of the king—of mother (1 Kgs 15:13//2 Chr 15:16; 2 Kgs 10:13; Jer 13:18; 29:2);[1] of wife (Tahpenes, Pharaoh's wife—1 Kgs 11:19; see also Ahlström 1963, 57–88; de Vaux 1965, 117–18). The occurrence of the term in 1 Kgs 11:19; 15:13; 2 Kgs 10:13; Jer 13:18; 29:2; and 2 Chr 15:16 suggests that *gəbîrâ* designates a woman of status but not necessarily the mother who automatically acquires the status when her son becomes king (see Bowen 2001, 598–99; contrast de Vaux 1965, 117–18; Ackerman 1993). The tendency is to assign the label to all mothers of kings and to emphasize those whose influence is depicted—particularly Bathsheba, Hamutal, and Nehushta (see table 1). Neither Bathsheba or Athaliah are designated as *gəbîrâ*, but both play a significant role in addressing their son's reign (1 Kgs 1–2; 2 Kgs 11). The issue regarding *gəbîrâ* is about female leadership in the public domain, and some propose that the *gəbîrâ* may be equal to the king (see Ahlström

---

1. There are several discussions regarding the identity of the *gəbîrâ* in 2 Kgs 10:13. Most believe that Jezebel is the woman (see de Vaux 1965, 118; Andreasen 1983, 186). Ben-Barak (1991, 27) inquires about why a woman of the northern kingdom (Israel) is referred to as *gəbîrâ*, a term used mostly for women in the southern kingdom (Judah).

Table 1: Designation of Mothers in Relation to Kings

Mother's name	King's name	Designation	Reference
Bathsheba	Solomon	Solomon's mother (ʾēm-šəlōmō) The king's mother (ʾēm hammelek)	1 Kgs 1:11; 2:13 1 Kgs 2:19
Naamah	Rehoboam	And his mother's name (wəšēm ʾimmô)	1 Kgs 14:21, 31
Maacah	Abijam	And his mother's name (wəšēm ʾimmô)	1 Kgs 15:1–2
Maacah (or grandmother)	Asa	And his mother's name (wəšēm ʾimmô) Queen mother (gəbîrâ)	1 Kgs 15:9–10 15:13
Azubah	Jehoshaphat	And his mother's name (wəšēm ʾimmô)	1 Kgs 22:42
—	Jehoram	—	2 Kgs 8:16–18
Athaliah	Ahaziah	And his mother's name (wəšēm ʾimmô)	2 Kgs 8:26
Zibiah	Joash	And his mother's name (wəšēm ʾimmô)	2 Kgs 12:1
Jehoaddin	Amaziah	And his mother's name (wəšēm ʾimmô)	2 Kgs 14:1–2
Jecoliah	Azariah	And his mother's name (wəšēm ʾimmô)	2 Kgs 15:1–2
Jeusha	Jotham	And his mother's name (wəšēm ʾimmô)	2 Kgs 15:32–33
—	Ahaz	—	2 Kgs 16:1–2
Abi	Hezekiah	And his mother's name (wəšēm ʾimmô)	2 Kgs 18:1–2
Hephzibah	Manasseh	And his mother's name (wəšēm ʾimmô)	2 Kgs 21:1–2
Meshullemeth	Amon	And his mother's name (wəšēm ʾimmô)	2 Kgs 21:19
Jedidah	Josiah	And his mother's name (wəšēm ʾimmô)	2 Kgs 22:1
Hamutal	Jehoahaz	And his mother's name (wəšēm ʾimmô)	2 Kgs 23:31
Zebidah	Jehoiakim	And his mother's name (wəšēm ʾimmô)	2 Kgs 23:36
Nehushta	Jehoiachin	And his mother's name (wəšēm ʾimmô) King's mother (ʾēm hammelek)	2 Kgs 24:8 24:15
Hamutal	Zedekiah	And his mother's name (wəšēm ʾimmô)	2 Kgs 24:18

1963, 61–63). Perhaps it is the exception rather than the norm that a king's mother is identified as *gəbîrâ*. For this reason the mother's status should be reconstructed on the basis of the particular depictions rather than generalizations regarding a perceived role.

Third, it is noteworthy that the names of the kings' mothers are included only in the succession formulae of the kings of the southern kingdom (Judah), with the exception of Jehoram (2 Kgs 8:16–18) and Ahaz (2 Kgs 16:1–2) (see table 1). Even so, the label "king's mother" (*'ēm hammelek*) is used a few times when referring to the mothers—that is, Bathsheba (1 Kgs 2:19) and Nehushta (2 Kgs 24:15). When present, the typical formulation is *wəšēm 'immô* plus the patronymic—for example, "and his mother's name is Naamah, the Ammonite" (*wəšēm 'immô na'ămâ hā'ammōnît*; 1 Kgs 14:21). Apparently, the mothers' names are mentioned for at least two reasons.[2] The first reason is to clarify which of the kings' wives mothered the heir to the throne. This assumes a polygamous system and perhaps the order of primogeniture, which includes ranking of the mother among the other wives and concubines (see Bowen 2001, 603).

The second reason for mentioning the mothers' names may be an insidious ideology or bias. While this bias may be based on the status of the son's mother (loved vis-à-vis unloved; wife or concubine), the pairing of the mother's name with her place of origin and evaluation of her son's reign gives further insights regarding the historian's perspective about the kings' mothers. Nancy Bowen notes that a negative evaluation is a by-product of the Deuteronomistic religious agenda, such that "when the mothers are foreign or engage in non-Yahwistic practices, the reigns of their sons are condemned" (2001, 602). On the other hand, when the mothers are from the southern kingdom (Judah), their sons usually receive a positive evaluation (e.g., Amaziah, Azariah). All the kings after Josiah receive a negative evaluation, including Jehoiachin, whose mother (Nehushta) is from Jerusalem (2 Kgs 28:8–9). While the pattern is not as simple as Bowen suggests, it sheds light on the negative critique of Solomon because of his marriage to foreign women (1 Kgs 11:1–13). Even David receives a positive evaluation with a qualification regarding the "matter of Uriah the Hittite"; Bathsheba is not mentioned (1 Kgs 15:5). The narrative perpetuates the antiforeign sentiment evident in 1 Kgs 11, namely, that foreign wives influence their husbands to follow deities other than YHWH (see Deut 7:1–4). Even with this antiforeigner bias, the text reflects the significance of mothers for the sons' reigns.

This essay examines Bathsheba as a model of the relational and functional roles of mothering a ruler. As the mother of Solomon, the first

---

2. This does not include Ackerman's proposal regarding the divine sonship where the mother of the king would be the human representative of the deity Asherah, who in turn was the "consort of YHWH" (Ackerman 1998, 153–54).

designated king-successor and a king of the united monarchy, Bathsheba does not fit the pattern of being named in the succession formulae; she is identified as "the king's mother" (1 Kgs 2:19; see also 1:11; 2:13; table 1). I argue that the effectiveness of Bathsheba's strategy in the contested succession ensues from the family dynamics and David's history of being distracted. Accordingly, Bathsheba is a mother-leader speaking to King David (her husband) on behalf of Solomon (her son) and then to Solomon (the king) about Adonijah, her stepson.

2. Family Dynamics of a Mother-Leader (Bathsheba)

Mothers function according to the dynamics of the family, and their presence defines the family dynamics (see Matthews and Benjamin 1993, 27–29). Bathsheba is part of the family history of David (private domain) and the added dimension of drama within his reign (public domain).

2.1. Wife and Mother

In this portrait, David is distracted by Bathsheba as an object of his desire, and he takes her when she was another man's wife (2 Sam 11:1–3). As a leader of an army, David was at home on the roof in the afternoon while his men were at war. Taking Bathsheba as his wife was not part of the first plan; because she became pregnant, the sexual encounter took on a whole new dimension. After failing to conceal her pregnancy, David sought after and secured her as his wife by killing her husband Uriah. So rather than planning military strategies to secure victory for his army, David left that to Joab (his chief commander), while he devised a strategy to kill Uriah, one of his soldiers and the husband of his newest conquest (another part of his distraction).

Bathsheba enters David's household as a pregnant widow. The tentacles of her past with David would inevitably affect the family system. The narrative depicts the impact through Nathan's critique of David's actions of killing Uriah and taking Bathsheba (2 Sam 12). While David was already married to Nabal's wife Abigail (Carmelite) and Ahinoam (Jezreelite), he was insatiable (2 Sam 12:8; see table 2). Apart from Michal his first wife, whom his father-in-law (Saul) gave to another man, his second wife came to him after the death her husband.

As mother, Bathsheba's entry into David's family was also marked by trouble. She had already given birth to their son (*bēn*), yet the narrative reports the child's (*yeled*) illness identifying the child of Uriah's wife and thus distancing the child from David, the father (2 Sam 12:15). It also depicts David's fasting and intercession for the child but not Bathsheba's (2 Sam 12:16–18). After the death of the unnamed child, David resumes his daily activity and subsequently visits Bathsheba. Her grief is reported only in connection with David's visit. The narrative reports that David comforted her, had sex with her, and in the process she conceived and

Table 2: David's Sons and Their Mothers (2 Samuel 3 and 5)

Son	Son's Mother	Son's Birthplace	Kingship	Reported Demise
Amnon	Ahinoam	Hebron	none	2 Sam 13:32
Chileab	Abigail	Hebron	none	???
Absalom	Maacah	Hebron	attempted	2 Sam 18:32–33; 19:10
Adonijah	Haggith	Hebron	attempted	1 Kgs 2:24–25
Shephatiah	Abital	Hebron	none	?
Ithream	Eglah	Hebron	none	?
Shammua, Shobab, Nathan	Wives and concubines	Jerusalem	none	?
Solomon	Bathsheba	Jerusalem	reigned	1 Kgs 11:43
Ibhar, Elishua, Nepheg, Japhia, Elishama, Eliada, and Eliphelet	Wives and concubines	Jerusalem	none	?

eventually gave birth to Solomon (2 Sam 12:24). Bathsheba's existence would be tumultuous because of her place in David's life. YHWH rejected her first son born to David but loved (*āhēb*) her second son, Solomon, also named Jedidiah (2 Sam 12:25). Thus Bathsheba was part of the distractions that would affect David's public life extending into the last stages of his life and the lives of future generations.

2.2. *Mother in Tumultuous Family System*

A few aspects define the turmoil in David's family and hence the context of Bathsheba's life: the polygamous system; the presumed order of primogeniture; and a distracted father and king. Table 2 identifies David's sons and their mothers and serves as an illustration of the latent conflict of an unclear order of succession.

2.2.1. *Polygamous System*

Apparently David's relationship with his wives (Michal, Abigail, Ahinoam, and Bathsheba) started out on tenuous grounds. Michal had no children with David, but the other wives and concubines had children, including the firstborn Amnon (Ahinoam), Absalom and Tamar (Maacah), Adonijah (Haggith), and Solomon (Bathsheba; see table 2). Ahinoam, Abigail, Englah, and Bathsheba are identified as wives; Maacah, Haggith, and Abital are presumed to be his wives but are not labeled as such (see 1 Chr 3:1–9).

2.2.2. Order of Succession: Father's Status in the Leadership Transition

Several events highlight the family dynamics and the challenging leadership transition. David was distracted from punishing Amnon for Tamar's rape because David loved Amnon his firstborn (2 Sam 13:21) presumably more than he loved Tamar, his daughter. By mentioning the length of time between events, the narrative may indicate David's inattention to important matters. Two years after Tamar's rape, David had not addressed it, so his son Absalom avenged Tamar's honor by killing Amnon. Absalom, his second son and heir apparent, fled to Geshur, where he lived for three years. Upon the advice of Joab, which he communicated through a "wise woman" ('iššâ ḥăkāmâ) of Tekoa, David brought Absalom back to Jerusalem. When he returned, Absalom lived in Jerusalem two years before entering King David's presence. Even then David saw Absalom only after Joab prompted him to do so (2 Sam 14). Absalom schemed for four years to win the people's loyalty before declaring himself king at Hebron and leading a revolt against his father (2 Sam 15, esp. vv. 6, 11–12).

As with his mourning for Amnon, David's attention was captured by the death of his son Absalom. David had lost the confidence of the people, who vacillated about reaffirming him as king (2 Sam 18; 19). Yet David was unaware of the magnitude of the situation until Joab interpreted it and advised him about how to take control (2 Sam 19:1–8). But even after Absalom's attempted usurpation, David did not clarify the order of succession, perhaps presuming the order of primogeniture. In the overall construction of the narrative, David's problems with his sons illustrate the tumultuous family system that Nathan prophesied (2 Sam 12:10–12). David seemed dependent on others to inform him about the significance of events in his life and what he ought to do about them (that is, Nathan, Joab, and the wise woman of Tekoa).

2.2.3. Final Stages of a Leadership Transition

Against the backdrop of the tumultuous history with Absalom, David dealt with Sheba's attempted usurpation and the loss of the people's support (2 Sam 20). In this revolt, David was aware of the magnitude of the situation, perceiving that Sheba's actions had greater consequences than Absalom's (2 Sam 20:6). Here a wise woman (of Abel) intervened and assisted Joab to squelch the revolt (2 Sam 20:16–22). Nathan's and Bathsheba's actions are to be understood as a strategy constructed in light of this history (see Long 1984, 20–21, 34).

2.2.3.1. *David's age and physical condition.* Even in the last stage, his servants offered the aged and ailing David a distraction—a beautiful young woman (*na'ărâ bətûlâ*) to be his "attendant" (*sōkenet*) and to warm (*ḥam*) him (1 Kgs 1:1–4). The narrative introduces Abishag, the Shunammite attendant, and Adonijah, the heir apparent, in sequence, thus contrasting David the ailing old man (*zāqēn*), Abishag, the young, viral, "beautiful" (*yāpâ*) woman, and Adonijah the "very handsome" (*ṭôb-tō'ar mə'ōd*) son. Clearly, beauty was a significant trait in describing the early kings of Israel: Saul (1 Sam 9:2) and David (1 Sam 16:12; 17:42). Both of David's sons who attempted usurpation are identified as handsome: Absalom (2 Sam 14:25) and Adonijah (1 Kgs 1:6). Perhaps after Saul and David, being handsome was not regarded as a good trait for a king. Solomon is not described as handsome but as wise (*ḥākām*—1 Kgs 2:9; 5:7). That difference may indicate the break in the pattern.

The 1 Kgs 1 narrative juxtaposes the information about Abishag and Adonijah at the beginning of its account regarding David's final stage of life and career. David, the handsome man, has been enticed by Bathsheba's beauty—she was "very good to look at" (2 Sam 11:2). Abishag was young and beautiful, yet the narrative denies any sexual relationship between David and Abishag, indicating that David "did not know her" (*lō' yədā'âh*; 1 Kgs 1:4; cf. Gen 4:1, 17; 1 Sam 1:19). The denial sounds like Gen 20, where the narrative denies a sexual relationship between Abimelech and Sarah by claiming that "he did not approach her" (*lō' qārab 'ēlêhā*) and that God did not allow him "to touch her" (*lingōa' 'ēlêhā*; Gen 20:4, 6). Here in 1 Kgs 1 the denial itself calls attention to the possibility of its occurrence. On the one hand, lack of physical ability may not be the reason that David locked away his concubines and did not have sex with them (2 Sam 20:3). On the other hand, if he did not "know" Abishag, it was because David was too physically frail to engage in sexual activity (House 1995, 87–88; Camp 2000, 161; see also Fritz 2003, 14; De Vries 1985, 13; Provan 1995, 24). While the narrative uses David's advanced age to account for his unawareness of Adonijah's usurpation, his age does not account for his tendency to be distracted or to be irresponsible with important matters (e.g., Uriah, Amnon-Tamar situation, Absalom, and Sheba). In 1 Kgs 1, the sexual inactivity plus advanced age may indicate differences between David's typical distractions and his current inability to function.

2.2.3.2. Issues of power succession. Several elements converge to create a potentially volatile situation and a repeat of the Absalom and Sheba incidents: David's indecision about matters of succession; the fact that he had multiple sons; and the lack of precedence but assumptions regarding the order of primogeniture. Of the six sons born to David at Hebron, Amnon and Absalom and perhaps Chileab were dead; this left Adonijah as the oldest son (see table 2). Adonijah assumes that he is the rightful heir, and apparently the people shared that perception (1 Kgs 2:15). In other cases of contested succession, the people (*'am*) or people of the land (*'am hā'āreṣ*) are decisive, as with Joash (2 Kgs 11–12), Azariah (2 Kgs 15), Josiah (2 Kgs 21–22), and Jehoahaz (2 Kgs 23; see also Bowen 2001, 603–4). Likewise, the alignment of the people with the potential king is also true for Absalom (2 Sam 15) and Sheba (2 Sam 20).

Adonijah raised himself to the status of king (1 Kgs 1:5) with a strategy that parallels Absalom's but perhaps without the underlying negative motivation that Absalom had toward his father. Intimating that the son's bid for the throne was unwarranted, the text reports that there was no unpleasantness between David and Adonijah (1 Kgs 1:6; see also Long 1984, 37). Nonetheless, Adonijah's strategy mirrors Absalom's in the following ways: (1) he prepared horses and chariot; (2) he hired fifty men to run in front of him; (3) he secured the loyalty of David's key personnel (Joab, the chief commander; Abiathar, priest); (4) he divided the loyalties by inviting the kings' sons and other key persons; (6) he excluded some of the key persons; and (7) he performed sacrifices. Yet, with such a thorough and clear strategy, David and his servants were clueless. Clearly, the narrative makes a case for David's incapacity. The question is the extent of that incapacity and how it is used in the succession drama. Isaac was old (*zāqēn*) and visually impaired and succumbed to a scheme that his wife (Rebekah) and son (Jacob) orchestrated and carried out (Gen 27). David is also a pawn in a scheme that his wife (Bathsheba) carried out to benefit her son (Solomon) with the help of the prophet Nathan.

3. A Mother's Counterstrategy for Securing Her Son's Reign

In today's context, a strategist is a part of the political process for those seeking public office. The successes and failures of these strategists usually determine whether or not a political candidate wins an office. Such strategies are also seen in David's reign and the succession process. In 2 Sam 20, Sheba took Israel and rebelled against David; likewise, Adonijah's effort drew lines between the old regime (with Adonijah) and the new regime (with Solomon). Later, Jeroboam ruled over Israel (north) while Rehoboam ruled over Judah (south) (1 Kgs 12; see also Long 1984, 134–36; Provan 1995, 25).

3.1. Anatomy of the Leadership Transition

Nathan (the prophet who had condemned David for his adultery) and Bathsheba (the woman with whom David had committed adultery) joined forces to facilitate a leadership transition (2 Sam 12; 1 Kgs 1). Bathsheba and Nathan faced off with highly influential men: Joab (chief commander), who executed David's order to have Uriah killed; and Abiathar (the priest).

3.1.1. The Key Players

There are at least four key persons in the counterstrategy to secure the throne: Nathan (prophet); Bathsheba (mother and wife); Solomon (son);

and Abishag (attendant). One cannot help but wonder what they have in common and how the Mother Goose rhyme about the "Crooked Man"[3] serves as a vehicle for illustrating the association. People will gravitate toward those who resemble them; there is no surprise that like attract like. All of the players have David and the ensuing challenges in common.

Nathan influenced David earlier in his reign but is noticeably absent after naming Solomon until he returns to the scene to update Bathsheba about Solomon becoming king (2 Sam 7; 12). In the interim, David's key advisor is Joab, who has sided with Adonijah. Nathan and Solomon were not invited to join Adonijah's effort (1 Kgs 1:10), so it appears that Adonijah perceived Solomon as a threat. Nathan alerts Bathsheba of Adonijah's action and outlines a counterstrategy (1 Kgs 1:11–14).

Bathsheba, Eliam's daughter and the former wife of Uriah, was once the object of desire taken as a wife (2 Sam 11). Now she strategizes to acquire the throne for her son Solomon. Nathan contacted her as Solomon's mother ('ēm-šalōmō) rather than David's wife ('ēšet dāwid), though she is both. The emphasis is on saving her life and the life of Solomon after David's death (1 Kgs 1:12).

Bathsheba functions like each wise woman ('iššâ ḥăkāmâ) whom Joab utilizes to bring about positive outcomes for David. The wise woman of Tekoa counseled David regarding Absalom, and David brought Absalom back to Jerusalem (2 Sam 14). She and Bathsheba fulfilled someone else's agenda, and David responded to the script designed for him (2 Sam 14; 1 Kgs 1:15–21). Unlike the woman of Tekoa, Bathsheba does not disclose the source of her instruction. The wise woman of Abel deterred Joab and convinced him that she and her people could stop Sheba (2 Sam 20:16–21). Like both wise women, Bathsheba also exemplified her own agenda and skillfully executed a plan.

Solomon, another key player, represented a threat to Adonijah's reign. That Adonijah invited all of his brothers (kol-'eḥāyw), the king's sons (banê hammelek), except for Solomon, indicates his awareness of the threat (1 Kgs 1:9–10). How he became aware of the threat is not mentioned. The promise in 2 Sam 7:12–17 speaks of an offspring but does not identify the offspring (see Knoppers: 88–89).

To the extent that her presence allowed David to function, Abishag, the belly-warming attendant, must also be mentioned. She is not a concubine (pîlegeš), a wife ('iššâ), or a mother ('ēm), but perhaps a rival to Bathsheba. Abishag is present at crucial moments, and her presence and youth are reminders of David's advanced age and imminent death. Thus Camp notes that David's inability to perform sexually with Abishag indicates his inability to function politically (Camp 2000, 161).

---

3. Mother Goose: "There was a crooked man, and he went a crooked mile, And found a crooked sixpence against a crooked stile, He bought a crooked cat, which caught a crooked mouse, And they all lived together in a little crooked house."

3.1.2. Motives and Methods

Whatever Nathan's motive, his goal is to acquire the throne for Solomon. Nonetheless, his approach raises questions concerning the use of deception to manipulate David. The succession narrative sets up the scenario where the basic claims are unconfirmed. When did David promise to make Solomon king? More than likely, Nathan uses a ruse to manipulate Bathsheba and does not mention the oath to David (House 1995, 90; Fritz 2003, 19; contrast Wiseman 1993, 70). If David promised Bathsheba, would she not know the promise? Or is her willing participation motivated by survival and the prospect of status elevation and less by her knowledge of a promise?

3.2. Counterstrategy

There is no record of David's promise to Bathsheba, Nathan, or any other person. Adonijah's attempt to seize the throne and exclude Solomon leaves open the possibility of indicators (however subtle) that Solomon was a viable candidate for the kingship. Nathan's counterstrategy is a model of skillful orchestration. Nathan may first appear to be the master player in this strategy, but a closer reading reveals that Bathsheba is the master strategist. Likewise, Bathsheba is not disoriented in her approach to the challenge of securing the throne for her son.[4]

3.2.1. The Phases of the Strategy

Nathan's strategy to put Solomon on the throne, and the fact that he was excluded from Adonijah's invitation list, highlights his waning influence in the kingdom. Clearly, if Adonijah was confirmed as king, Nathan would not be part of the inner circle of that reign. It was therefore in Nathan's best interest to ensure that Adonijah did not rule after David. Nathan's three-part strategy was to use Bathsheba and David to ensure the desired result.

3.2.1.1. Phase 1: Nathan recruits Bathsheba (1 Kgs 1:11–14). In Nathan's plan, Bathsheba's role is to set the stage for Nathan by heightening David's need to act. (a) *Nathan's Questions.* He draws Bathsheba into his scheme by asking her if she knew about Adonijah's bid for the throne and about David's ignorance of the bid. (b) *Nathan's Response.* He assumes Bathsheba's unawareness of the usurpation and proceeds to give her ad-

---

4. Contrast this to the image of "Little Bo-Peep" who lost her sheep. In that image she is disoriented because she lost valuable possessions or perhaps commodity placed in her care. In her disorientation, she applies ineffective strategies to secure her lost possession. To further compound the situation, the repossession of the property revealed that the property had been altered. What was found was not in the same condition as when it was lost. This is a contrasting image to Bathsheba—the narrative in no way depicts her as disoriented.

vice. (i) *Heightened Risk.* Next he highlights the potential risk to Bathsheba
and Solomon and through this may have heightened the urgency for her
to act. (ii) *Proposed solution.* Nathan outlines a plan to remedy the situation.
He tells Bathsheba to go and speak with King David and to remind David
of his oath to give Solomon the throne (1:13). Nathan tells Bathsheba to
ask David if David made the oath. He gives Bathsheba the question that
she should ask, but in posing the question Nathan only implies that David
made the oath. Apparently, Nathan's strategy is to make Bathsheba believe that David swore (*šāba'*) to her. Adonijah's self-proclamation as king
and the people's approval would not nullify the oath and would be a vain
grasp for power. (iii) *Confirming the information.* Nathan also planned the
timing to interrupt Bathsheba while she was speaking to the king (1:14). So
while the narrative shows the clear lines of loyalties made known publicly
by inviting or excluding persons, Nathan aligns with Bathsheba privately.
This phase brings Bathsheba into the drama while concealing the extent of
her role in it. If she is aware that Nathan is using her, she does not display
that awareness. Perhaps she also uses Nathan and David to secure her
son's place on the throne.

3.2.1.2. *Phase 2a+b: Persuading David.* (2a) *Bathsheba (mother) speaks with
David (king) (1 Kgs 1:15–21).* While Adonijah carries out the usurpation
strategy publicly, Bathsheba and Nathan carry out the counterstrategy privately. The context is David's room, a private zone but occupied
by another woman (Abishag, the attendant; 1 Kgs 1:15). The narrator is
noticeably silent about the encounter between the two women: the once-
enticing Bathsheba and the current bed companion and possible sexual
partner (see Camp 2000, 163). The narrative appears to justify Abishag's
presence again by contrasting her function of "attending to" (*məšārat*) the
aged King David (*zāqēn məʾōd*). Additionally, the narrative's silence echoes
in Bathsheba's silence toward Abishag. Whatever the nature of the relationship between the two women, Bathsheba focuses on her mission to
persuade David. She is not the focus of his sexual desire but the mother
of the future king. As if to redeem her place in history, Bathsheba, the
former distraction, becomes the instrument used to pull David out of his
latest distraction and to focus his attention on the important matters of his
kingdom's future. Whether hers is a prudent psychological manipulation,
in this strategy Bathsheba demonstrates that her entry into the family does
not dictate her eventual status in shaping the legacy of the family.

(i) *Bathsheba's Obeisance.* She shows David honor by bowing and doing
obeisance to him (*šāhah*). David invites her to voice her request (1 Kgs
1:16). (ii) *Bathsheba's speech.* Even in her speech she shows David respect by
referring to herself as his servant (*'āmâ*). She identifies Solomon as David's
son and informs David about the attempted usurpation. (iia) *Regarding*

David's oath. Bathsheba begins with David's oath, declaring it as fact rather than inquiring about it and indicating that David swore by YHWH. She cites David's words assuming that he said them. Either she believes that he said them, or she believes that she can convince him that he did. If she is aware that David did not give an oath regarding Solomon, she is audaciously manipulative. But perhaps the matter of his age is only one contributing element in her confident approach. The solemnity of the oath becomes the basis of her courage to challenge David. (iib) *Call to task.* Bathsheba informs David about Adonijah's action of becoming king and affirms David's ignorance concerning the action (1 Kgs 1:17–18). Her affirmation exculpates him of failing to keep his oath and demonstrates her confidence in this character. Next she details what Adonijah did in declaring himself king, listing the elements that the narrative presented and thus exceeding the information that Nathan gave to her. She highlights the fact that Solomon had been excluded from the political intrigue (1 Kgs 1:19).

After laying out the information, Bathsheba defines the situation with respect to the nation, thus taking the focus off herself and appearing to be concerned about David's reputation and national status. Finally, she sets out the implication of David's indecision, namely, that she and Solomon would be ostracized (1 Kgs 1:20). In her designation of Solomon as her son, Bathsheba may suggest Solomon's insignificance if David does not designate him as heir to the throne. If Adonijah was confirmed because of David's inactivity, Solomon's identity as David's son would accelerate the adverse effects on Solomon. The narrator's depiction signals that Bathsheba is not simply a pawn in Nathan's scheme but is also informed, proactive, and wisely securing what she wants for herself and for her son. Bathsheba skillfully executes her part of the counterstrategy.

(2b) *Nathan speaks with David (1 Kgs 1:22–26).* Nathan follows through with a well-timed entrance to confirm the information. (i) *His timing.* He enters just as Bathsheba is concluding her speech (1 Kgs 1:22) and before David spoke. (ii) *Nathan's obeisance.* Unlike Adonijah, who raised himself up (*mitnaśśēʾ*) as king (1 Kgs 1:5), but like Bathsheba, who bowed to David, and Solomon, who bowed to Bathsheba, Nathan bowed (*wayyištaḥû* from *šāḥah*) before the king (1:23). (iii) *Nathan's speech.* As he did with Bathsheba, Nathan started with a question regarding David's declaration. *Question.* He asked if David said (*ʾāmar*) that Adonijah would be king. Curiously, Nathan represented the matter to Bathsheba as an oath but in front of David as a simple declaration. In contrast, Bathsheba asserted that David swore by YHWH. *Assertion of facts.* Nathan follows his question with a declaration regarding Adonijah's actions and names the actions. Nathan is as detailed as Bathsheba and the narrator but adds the information that Adonijah's guests are celebrating him: "Long live King Adonijah!" Nathan also lists the people who had not been invited: himself, Solomon, and others (1 Kgs 1:25). *Question seeking clarification.* Nathan's concluding question includes two elements: whether David authorized Adonijah's proclamation as king and whether David excluded Nathan from knowing (1 Kgs 1:27). Nathan is less confrontational than Bathsheba and milder in his approach than when he critiqued David regarding Uriah and Bathsheba (2 Sam 12). Nathan's question presumes his prior influence in the king's life. But if he is so influential as to merit inclusion in the king's decision, why does he need Bathsheba's help?

3.2.1.3. Phase 3: David designates and confirms Solomon as king (1 Kgs 1:28–40). David's response demonstrates the success of Nathan's strategy. (a) *Oath to Bathsheba.* Whether he previously swore that Solomon would be king, David now swears it to Bathsheba in his room (1 Kgs 1:28; see also Provan 1995, 26). Just like the initial sexual encounter that turned into a lifetime together, so a moment of persuasion would define David's legacy. Bathsheba showed respect for him by bowing to him and affirming him as king (1 Kgs 1:28–29). (b) *Preparation for the coronation.* David summoned the people excluded from Adonijah's usurpation—the priest Zadok, the prophet Nathan, and Benaiah son of Jehoiada (1 Kgs 1:31–37)—and prepared to fulfill his oath to Bathsheba. (c) *Solomon's coronation.* Zadok anointed Solomon as king, Solomon made procession on the mule while a trumpet sounded, and all the people (*kol-hā'ām*) celebrated Solomon as king (1 Kgs 1:38–40).

Bathsheba's alignment with Nathan is central to the narrative because of the implication of the partnership. Bathsheba is a model of a proactive mother-leader who focuses on the task at hand to accomplish her goal.

4. Use of a Mother's Influence and Discernment

Other changes accompanied the transition from David to Solomon. Among them were the appointment of Nathan and other officials and the establishment of Bathsheba to her new status as King Solomon's mother (*'ēm-šəlōmō*; 2 Kgs 2:13). Like Nathan, who saw her as a key to the succession, so Adonijah saw her influence as a key to carrying out his strategy. In her compliance to his request, the narrative leaves some questions about Bathsheba's awareness of Adonijah's agenda.

4.1. Strategy to Use Bathsheba's Influence

Adonijah, like Nathan, recognizes Bathsheba as integral to his strategy, but he behaves as if Bathsheba is unaware of the potential threat that lingers after Solomon's confirmation as king. He does not bow to Bathsheba when he enters her presence, as he does to King Solomon. (1) *Preface to the request.* Adonijah claims that the kingdom was his, that all of Israel (*kol-yiśrā'ēl*) knew it, but that God gave it to Solomon (2 Kgs 2:15). As the basis of his request, this affirmation doubles as an accusation and as a demand for restitution of loss. If he comes in peace as he claims, why raise the issue of his loss of what was rightfully his? Adonijah asked Bathsheba not to refuse him, thus indicating the likelihood of refusal. (2) *Adonijah's request.* Of all that he could request, he asked for Abishag to be his wife. He affirms that Solomon will not refuse the request because it comes from Bathsheba. Even so, Adonijah's request places him in a usurpation strategy similar to Absalom, who took David's concubines (2 Sam 16:20–21). So, was he asking Bathsheba to assist him in overthrowing her son?

4.2. Exercising Influence and Discernment

At first glance, Bathsheba seems to be oblivious to the nature of the request (Fritz 2003, 28). Or perhaps she is aware, and the awareness fuels her urgency to communicate with her son, the king, to alert him of the threat to his reign (see Long 1984, 51; Provan 1995, 38; Bowen 2001, 605). Nathan already outlined the threat to Bathsheba and Solomon should Adonijah be king. As her opening question to Adonijah indicates (2 Kgs 2:13), she was not oblivious to the threat posed by her stepson.

As in her strategy with David (her husband), so with Solomon (her son) she exemplifies great skill. (1) *Bathsheba's entrance.* The narrative claims that she went to the king on behalf of Adonijah, but her execution of the request suggests an ulterior motive. The nature of her influence is highlighted in that the king, her son, rose to meet her and bowed to her as she had bowed to his father David. Solomon also set up a throne for her next to him (2 Kgs 2:19). (2) *Bathsheba's speech.* Just as she had done when sent by Nathan, here, too, Bathsheba adjusts the speech. Adonijah said he had "one request" (*šə'ēlâ 'aḥat*; 2 Kgs 2:16); Bathsheba said that she had "one small request" (*šə'ēlâ 'aḥat qəṭannâ*; 2 Kgs 2:20). Adonijah asked her not to refuse him; she asked Solomon not to refuse her. She simply invited Adonijah to speak; Solomon invited her to speak and based on the fact that she is his mother (*'ēm*), affirms that he would not refuse her request. She does not refuse Adonijah but talks to Solomon. Solomon refuses her requests and goes to kill Adonijah. So what did she miss in carrying Adonijah's request to Solomon? Was this an error in judgment or the mark of a skilled strategist? Perhaps Bathsheba was a wise mother who used her role and perceived ignorance to alert her son to get rid of the threat to his kingdom.

Bathsheba informed Solomon that a conspiracy was still alive and growing. Solomon responded by getting rid of the key conspirators: he banished Abiathar (the priest) and ordered the death of Adonijah. Solomon appointed Benaiah as the commander of the army (1 Kgs 2:19–46), thus replacing Joab (the chief commander). Through these actions and with his mother's help, Solomon wisely secured his throne.

Conclusion

Bathsheba's role in the family-political domains highlights several aspects of her influence as mother-leader. First, a mother-leader must navigate the family dynamics. Second, people may attempt to use a mother-leader as leverage even to gain advantage over her son. This requires that the mother is discerning regarding those who seek to align themselves with her (even relatives) and solicit the use of her influence. Bathsheba is integral to Solomon's becoming king and to securing the throne against rivals. Unlike David, who is often presented as being distracted from the important matters, as a model mother-leader Bathsheba appears as a skillful negotiator in the aspects of the family-public domains.

Bathsheba is the embodiment of skillfully applied strategy just like the Mother Goose rhymes. What seem like little rhymes offer perspective on reality and an underlying message. We recite these rhymes as children, but the lessons transcend childhood. The Mother Goose rhymes are so unassuming in their mode that most miss the wisdom and ideology communicated through them. The figure of Bathsheba is like Mother Goose in this way. Bathsheba seems unassuming and even pliable in the hands of Nathan and Adonijah. Nob one expects a goose to be wise, and few would study the philosophy of Mother Goose. Similarly, while many recognize Bathsheba as the object of David's sexual desires, most do not see her as a model of wisdom that is applied to benefit her son Solomon. In today's media she would be another tabloid headline: "Political Leader Seduces Woman." "Husband of Seduced Woman Turns Up Dead." Yet the tragedies of being wife to the man who murdered one's husband, the loss of a child, and being set aside did not define or limit her to the margins of life. Rather, the discussion above demonstrates Bathsheba's wisdom and profound influence in the private and public domains.

Works Consulted

Ackerman, Susan. 1990. Sacred Sex, Sacrifice and Death. *BRev* 6.1:38–44.

———. 1993. The Queen Mother and the Cult in Ancient Israel. *JBL* 112:385–401.

———. 1998. *Warrior, Dancer, Seductress, Queen: Women in Judges and Biblical Israel*. New York: Doubleday.

———. 2002. The Personal Is Political: Covenantal and Affectionate Love (*aheb, ahabâ*) in the Hebrew Bible. *VT* 52:437–58.

Ahlström, Gösta W. 1963. *Aspects of Syncretism in Israelite Religion*. Lund: Gleerup.

Andreasen, Niels-Erik. 1983. The Role of the Queen Mother in Israelite Society. *CBQ* 45:179–94.

Bach, Alice. 1999. *Women in the Hebrew Bible: A Reader*. New York: Routledge.

Ben-Barak, Zafrira. 1991. The Status and Right of the Gebîrâ. *JBL* 110:23–34.

Berlin, Adele. 1982. Characterization in Biblical Narrative: David's Wives. *JSOT* 23:69–85.

Bowen, Nancy R. 2001. The Quest for the Historical Gebîrâ. *CBQ* 63:597–618.

Brenner, Athalya. 1985. *The Israelite Woman: Social Role and Literary Type in Biblical Narrative*. Sheffield: JSOT Press.

———. 1994. *A Feminist Companion to Samuel and Kings*. Sheffield: Sheffield Academic Press.

———, ed. 2000. *Samuel and Kings*. FCB 2/7. Sheffield: Sheffield Academic Press.

Camp, Claudia V. 2000. *Wise, Strange and Holy: The Strange Woman and the Making of the Bible*. JSOTSup 302. Gender, Culture, Theory 9. Sheffield: Sheffield Academic Press.

Davis, John J. 1970. *The Birth of a Kingdom; Studies in I–II Samuel and I Kings 1–11*. Grand Rapids: Baker.

De Vries, Simon J. 1985. *1 Kings*. WBC 12. Waco, Tex: Word.

Deventer, H. J. M. van. 1999. Would the Actually "Powerful" Please Stand? The Role of the Queen (Mother) in Daniel 5." *Scriptura* 70:241–51.

———. 2000. Another Wise Queen (Mother): Woman's Wisdom in Daniel 5:10–12. *ThViat* 26:92–113.

Fritz, Volkmar. 2003. *1 and 2 Kings*. CC. Translated by Anselm Hagedorn. Minneapolis: Fortress.

Frymer-Kensky, Tikva. 1998. Virginity in the Bible. Pages 79–96 in *Gender and Law in the Hebrew Bible and the Ancient Near East*. Edited by Victor H. Matthews, Bernard M. Levinson, and Tikva Frymer-Kensky. JSOTSup 262. Sheffield: Sheffield Academic Press.

House, Paul R. 1995. *1, 2 Kings*. NAC 8. Nashville: Broadman & Holman.

Huffmon, H. B., F. A. Spina, and A. R.W. Green, eds. 1983. *The Quest for the Kingdom of God: Studies in Honor of George E. Mendenhall*. Winona Lake, Ind.: Eisenbrauns.

Jacobs, Mignon R. 2007. *Gender, Power, and Persuasion: The Genesis Narratives and Contemporary Portraits*. Grand Rapids: Baker.

Knoppers, Gary N. 1993. *Two Nations under God: The Deuteronomistic History of Solomon and the Dual Monarchies*. Volume 1. HSM 52. Atlanta: Scholars Press.

Long, Burke O. 1981. A Darkness Between Brothers: Solomon and Adonijah. *JSOT* 19:79–84.

———. 1984. *1 Kings: With an Introduction to Historical Literature*. FOTL 9. Grand Rapids: Eerdmans.

Matthews, Victor H., and Don C. Benjamin. 1993. *Social World of Ancient Israel 1250–587 B.C.E.* Peabody, Mass.: Hendrickson.

Montgomery, James A., and Henry S. Gehman. 1967. *The Books of Kings*. ICC. Edinburgh: T&T Clark.

Otwell, John H. 1977. *And Sarah Laughed: The Status of Woman in the Old Testament*. Louisville: Westminster.

Phipps, Williams E. 1992. *Assertive Biblical Women*. Contributions in Women's Studies 128. Westport, Conn.: Greenwood.

Provan, Iain W. 1995. *1 and 2 Kings*. NIBC. Peabody, Mass.: Hendrickson.

Rogers, Jeffrey S. 1992. Synchronism and Structure in 1–2 Kings and Mesopotamian Literature. Ph.D. Dissertation. Princeton Theological Seminary.

Seitz, Christopher R. 1989. *Theology in Conflict: Reactions to the Exile in the Book of Jeremiah*. BZAW 176. Berlin: de Gruyter.

Solvang, Elna K. 2003. *A Woman's Place Is in the House: Royal Women of Judah and Their Involvement in the House of David*. London: Sheffield Academic Press.

Spanier, Ktziah. 1994. The Queen Mother in the Judaean Royal Court: Maacah—A Case Study. Pages 186–95 in Brenner 1994.

———. 1998. The Northern Israelite Queen Mother in the Judaean Court: Athalia and Abi. Pages 136–49 in *Boundaries of the Ancient Near Eastern World*. Edited by Meir Lubetski, Claire Gottlieb, and Sharon Keller. JSOTSup 273. Sheffield: Sheffield Academic Press.

Trible, Phyllis. 1995. Exegesis for Storytellers and Other Strangers. *JBL* 114:3–19.

Vaux, Roland, de. 1965. *Social Institutions.* Vol. 1 of *Ancient Israel.* New York: McGraw-Hill.

Wenham, Gordon J. 1972. Bethulah: A Girl of Marriageable Age. *VT* 22:326–48.

Whybray, Roger N. 1968. *The Succession Narrative: A Study of II Samuel 9–20; and I Kings 1 and 2.* SBT 2/9. Naperville, Ill.: Allenson.

Wiseman, Donald J. 1993. *1 and 2 Kings: An Introduction and Commentary.* TOTC. Downers Grove, Ill.: InterVarsity Press.

6

Parturition (Childbirth), Pain, and Piety

Physicians and Genesis 3:16a

Linda S. Schearing

Unto the woman he said, I will greatly multiply thy sorrow and thy conception; in sorrow thou shalt bring forth children.

— Gen 3:16a (KJV)

At one point in my pains I remembered in the Bible where it said, "In sorrow she shall bring forth children." I know what that means. I said, "Thank you Jesus," when it was over! Never, never do I want to do that again! My husband said, "Well, it's your fault. You gave the apple to Adam."

— Eunice Mitchell, mother (Arms 1975, 117)

By the mid-nineteenth century, physicians could alleviate much of the pain of childbirth, yet some doctors found themselves faced with a dilemma. As physicians, their task was to restore health, preserve life, and combat suffering. With the discovery of chemical anesthesia, they *could* bring relief from the pains of childbirth. But the question remained: *Should* they?

This paper examines Anglo-American exegetical reactions to the development of obstetrical technology in the last two centuries. Of specific interest is the discovery of anesthesia and its application to obstetrics (nineteenth century) and the fear/tension/pain theory that was foundational to the painless childbirth movement (twentieth century). While both developments drew medical criticism and comment, it is the exegetical responses that will be examined.[1] Physicians who saw a connection

---

1. This is not to say, however, that scriptural objections were the most pressing. As Thatcher notes in her *History of Anesthesia*, there were three general medical responses by physicians concerning the use of anesthesia in any surgery: "(1) those who considered the dangers so inconsiderable as to justify the use of anesthesia

85

between Gen 3:16a and their work as obstetricians understood Gen 3:16a as (1) describing physical pain as a God-ordained part of childbirth; and/or (2) describing mental pain not physical pain; and/or (3) describing "toil" for women in childbirth and saying nothing about pain, and/or (4) describing childbirth as a spiritual experience that should normally be painless in spite of traditional interpretations of Gen 3:16a. To understand the context from which these responses em\erged and the reasons why medical practitioners felt obliged to become exegetes, it is necessary to look briefly at seventeenth- and eighteenth-century attitudes towards parturition (childbirth), pain, and piety.

Anglo-American treatments of Gen 3:16a in the seventeenth and eighteenth centuries argued that Eve was "cursed" to bear children painfully as punishment for her transgression. The absence of any identifiable curse formula in verse 16a did little to deter readers from this understanding. Moreover, since all women stood in vicarious solidarity with the first woman, then all women were "cursed" with painful parturition. Today, we know that the pain women feel during delivery is the result of a variety of physical, psychological, and social factors, some of which can be prevented (Wertz 1979, 110). Nevertheless, during the seventeenth and eighteenth centuries, literal readings of Gen 3:16a presented the pain of childbirth as an unavoidable divine mandate.

Some of the most popular medical literature to circulate in America from 1760 to 1840 were sex manuals bearing the name "Aristotle" (Beall 1963, 208–9). During this period at least thirty-two editions of various "Aristotle" titles were published in America (220). Although never attaining any real standing within the medical community, they were immensely successful with the general populace. As Otho T. Beall Jr. argues in his examination of American folklore, these works were "the only works on sex and gynecology . . . widely available to eighteenth-century Americans" (Beall 1963, 205).

Aristotle's Master Piece (first published in England in 1684) was neither by Aristotle nor a literary masterpiece. It provided readers with a mixture of medicine and piety that juxtaposed questions of biology with those of theology. Those who wondered why women gave birth in pain were told that such suffering was God's curse for Eve's disobedience. They were also reminded that marriage was a sacrament and birthing children its primary purpose (216).

Although the interpretation of Gen 3:16a found in *Aristotle's Master Piece* reflects folk culture, its explanation of painful childbirth as God's curse is also found in midwifery manuals and tracts of this period. In 1651,

---

prior to all operations; (2) those who wished to limit the use of anesthesia to severe operations and to discourage its general employment; and (3) those who objected altogether to the use of anesthesia as dangerous and harmful in its tendency" (1984, 17).

Nicholas Culpeper, called the "Father of English Midwifery" by some historians (Thulesius 1994, 552–56), wrote *A Directory for Midwives: Or, A Guide for Women, In their Conception, Bearing and Suckling their Children*. In it he advised women in labor that they were to "Learn, to know your first Evil, which was Pride. To be humbled for it. To look after a Spiritual Being, seeing your nature is so defective" (H. Smith 1976, 99).

Cotton Mather, a significant figure in American medical history of this period, also wrote a tract for midwives. Unlike Culpeper's manual, Mather's tract was not intended as instruction in the art of midwifery. Instead, Mather gave his tract to midwives so that they, in turn, would give it to their patients. Entitled *Elizabeth in Her Holy Retirement* (1710), it addressed expectant mothers and warned them of the pain they were about to encounter. Childbirth pain, Mather informed his readers, should "very properly lead you to Bewayl your Share in the *Sin of your first Parents*" (Mather 1972, 238). Not only was such pain punishment for Eve's sins, but Mather also saw it as useful for Eve's daughters' salvation.

After warning pregnant women that their death had entered into them and that some had, at most, only nine more months to live (maternal death was high in the seventeenth century), Mather went on to suggest that women's cries of pain were useful to their spiritual development (Mather 1972, 237–39). Mather admonished expecting mothers not to complain of their pain. "How *Unnatural* will it look in you," Mather said, "to Complain of a State, whereinto the *Laws of Nature* Established by God, have brought you" (236). Moreover, complaining of childbirth pain, might well lead to more sorrow:

> it is to be proposed unto you in the *first* place; that you do not indulge any indecent *Impatience* or discontent, at the State, which you find ordered for you. Finding yourselves in a State of Pregnancy, Froward Pangs of dissatisfaction, harboured and humoured in you, because you see that in *Sorrow you bring forth Children*, may displease Heaven and bring yett more *Sorrow* upon you. (236)

Instead of complaining, Mather argued, they should "Lett the Words of an Apostle now come into Consideration with you; 1 Tim.II,15. *She shall be Saved in Childbearing if they continue in Faith, and Charity, and Holiness, with Sobriety* (239). This salvation was possible precisely because "The Approach of their *Travails*" evoked "those Exercises of PIETY, which render them truly *Blessed*." (236)

For Mather and medical practitioners of his day, childbirth pains were both God's curse and a spiritual aid to women's salvation. Viewed in this manner, the task of a woman in delivery was to endure her God-given pains with equanimity while drawing nearer to God in repentance and prayer. The spiritual task of her midwife was to aid her patient's spiritual development by giving her Mather's tract.

While seventeenth- and eighteenth-century midwives managed the childbirth process rather than doctors, physician-managed childbirth began to dominate in the nineteenth century. One of the earliest pioneers in obstetrical education in America was Benjamin Rush, Professor of Medicine at the University of Pennsylvania and, incidentally, one of the signers of the Declaration of Independence. In an 1802 letter to Dr. Edward Miller concerning the lessening of the pains of childbirth, Rush observed that "It has generally been supposed, that a necessary and unchangeable connection exists between pain and child-bearing. Such a connection, it is true, was established between them, as part of the curse inflicted upon women after the loss of her primeval innocence" (Rush 1803, 26). Rush concluded, however, that since the curse on the earth has been partly repealed and since some women are able to have children without pain or difficulty, that "the pains of childbearing are not entailed upon the female sex by an immutable law. In our attempts, therefore, to improve and extend the means of lessening them, we do but develop the kind and benevolent disposition of the Creator of the world to the human race" (26–27).

When Peter Miller, a medical student at the University of Pennsylvania who was familiar with Rush's teachings, chose as his 1804 dissertation topic "An Essay on the Means of Lessening the Pains of Parturition," he lamented the fact that the issue of pain relief in parturition had been "almost entirely neglected" in medical literature (Miller 1804, 12). According to Miller, physicians assumed that pain was necessarily connected with childbirth. The primary reason for this association, Miller suggested, was their exegesis of Gen 3:16a (13). Thus Miller devoted five of the twenty-eight pages of his dissertation to an exegetical and theological defense of his topic. While few today would agree with Miller's medical approach to pain relief (like Rush, he advocated bloodletting to alleviate birth pains), his exegesis remains interesting.

Miller argued that the pain mentioned in Gen 3:16a should be understood as mental rather than physical. When women reflect upon the dangers attending afterbirth, the death of newborns and infants, the temptations to which youth fall prey, and the problems they bring their parents— when all this is considered, truly it can be said that in *sorrow* mothers bring forth children (14).

Miller's exegesis of Gen 3:16a is significant for two reasons. First, it assumes that it is necessary and appropriate for physicians to defend their actions exegetically. Second, it interprets Gen 3:16a in a manner that allows physicians to treat the physical pain of their patients without violating Gen 3:16's mandate. Peter Miller, however, was not the only doctor who balanced the humanitarian demands of medicine with what he saw as the scriptural demands of faith.

On December 19, 1846, ether was first used in Britain to alleviate the pain of surgery. One month later, on January 19, 1847, the Scottish physician James Young Simpson used ether in the delivery of a child (Keys 1945,

32). On November 4 of the same year, Simpson discovered the anesthetic properties of chloroform and four days later used it in a delivery. Resistance was swift and vocal. Simpson reports that in one medical school his use of anesthesia to relieve childbirth pains was denounced *"ex cathedra* as an attempt to contravene the arrangements and decrees of Providence, hence reprehensible and heretical in its characters, and anxiously to be avoided and eschewed by properly principled students and practitioners." While some opposition was public, Simpson admitted that he had also been "favoured with various earnest private communications to the same effect" as well (Simpson 1849, 110).

In answer to the opposition he encountered, Simpson, a scant one month after he used chloroform, wrote a pamphlet entitled *Answer to the Religious Objections Advanced Against the Employment of Anaesthetic Agents in Midwifery and Surgery*. In addition to other lines of argument, Simpson presented his own exegesis of Gen 3:16a.

Simpson argued that literal readings of Gen 3:16a were too selective. There were *three* curses, he insisted, in Gen 3. If it was sinful to relieve women's pain in childbirth, then it was also sinful to pull up thorns and thistles or to use a horse or ox, or water and steam power instead of the sweat of one's brow in farming. In fact, according to Simpson, a literal reading of Gen 3 called into question the whole medical profession. If humankind was destined to die, then medical skill and art should not prevent it (Simpson 1849, 111–13).

Another line of Simpson's defense involved an elaborate discussion of the Hebrew term *'eṣeb* rendered "pain" or "sorrow" in many translations. As long as *'eṣeb* referred to physical pain, verse 16a appeared problematic. Quoting Tregelles's translation of Gesenius's *Hebrew and Chaldee Lexicon,* Simpson argued semantically that the term could also mean "toil" or "labor," as it means when applied to the man in verse 17. It is at this point that Simpson's medical expertise interfaced with his exegesis. Women's labor, he argued, consisted of two elements: muscular action and effort; and the pain attendant to these contractions. While anesthesia diminished the pain of childbirth, it did not abolish muscular labor (if it had the very act of parturition would have been arrested). Thus, Simpson insisted that the term *'eṣeb* refers to the muscular action essential to birth, not the pain caused by contractions (Simpson 1849, 113–17).

Finally, to those who argued that anesthesia was "unnatural," Simpson drew attention to the first surgical operation on record: Gen 2:21. If God as surgeon could save a person unnecessary physical pain, then the concept of anesthesia was not as "unnatural" as commonly thought (Simpson 1849, 122). Apparently Simpson's pamphlet achieved its purpose in Edinburgh, for six months later Simpson could write that religious objections ceased among local doctors.

Physicians elsewhere, however, disagreed with Simpson's exegesis.

Dr. Ashwell, an obstetrician on the staff of Guy's Hospital in London, was openly critical: "Putting aside the impiety of making Jehovah an operating surgeon and the absurdity of supposing that anaesthesia would be necessary in His hands, Dr. Simpson surely forgets that the deep sleep of Adam took place before the introduction of pain into the world during his state of Innocence" (Graham 1951, 487). Simpson replied somewhat sarcastically to Ashwell: "Is it anywhere stated in your Bible that pain came in with sin, or that there was no pain endured when there was no sin? If so, then let me add, your Bible differs from mine" (Duns 1873, 256).

Simpson's mixture of Hebrew exegesis and medical expertise came under fire as well. One anonymous commentator to the medical journal *Lancet* had this to say:

> The extent of Professor Simpson's Hebrew . . . exhibited in this pamphlet, is probably as surprising to himself as to his readers. I cannot help think that, as there is at present a difficulty in filling the Hebrew chair in the University of Edinburgh. . . . the professor has an eye to this additional appointment. He need not fear a medical rival. (1848, 111)

In July, 1848, seven months after Simpson's pamphlet on religious objections to anesthesia was published, Simpson wrote a letter to Dr. Protheroe Smith. Smith, who taught midwifery at St. Bartholomew's in London, had apparently requested more information concerning Simpson's exegesis of Gen 3:16a. In referring to this previous correspondence, Simpson reports Smith's charge that "groundless allegations as to anesthesia's unscriptural character" were impeding the use of chloroform in London (Simpson 1872, 452). Simpson replied by repeating much of his earlier arguments (56–64). Soon after this, Smith wrote his own pamphlet on the subject entitled *Scriptural Authority for Mitigation of the Pains of Labour* (1848).

Another person in conversation with Dr. Simpson at this time was Dr. Walter Channing, Professor of Midwifery and Medical Jurisprudence at Harvard University and one of the first American doctors to use chemical anesthesia in childbirth. In 1848, Channing published his classic book *A Treatise on Etherization in Childbirth: Illustrated by Five Hundred and Eighty-One Cases.* Juxtaposed to the medical reports on etherization was a chapter on "Objections to Etherization" (Channing 1848, 135–58), which contained a lengthy section entitled "The Religious Objections to Etherization" (141–52). Channing had known intellectually of the problems experienced by English and Scottish doctors concerning the Gen 3:16a but had initially dismissed them as concerns confined to the clergy (142). When gathering case studies for his book, however, he was surprised to find out that some doctors would not use anesthesia for fear of its moral effects. Channing reports that when he requested from a medical friend some data concerning the friend's use of ether and chloroform in childbirth, his friend replied:

> I have never employed ether in any obstetric case, since its introduction as an agent for procuring insensibility.. . . God has said, "In sorrow shalt

thou bring forth children;" and the very suffering which a woman under-
goes in labor is one of the strongest elements in the love she bears her
offspring. I have fears for the moral effect of this discovery, both on the
patient and on the physician. (Channing 1848, 142)

To respond to such objections, Channing felt compelled to include an exegetical section in his book on etherization.

Like Peter Miller at the turn of the century, Channing defined 'eṣeb as
mental pain:

> While reading the passage from Genesis, and the context, it occurred to
> me, that the word *sorrow*, so rarely used to express a physical state, had a
> *moral* meaning; and that the first woman's "sorrow" would proceed from
> the conduct of her children. The violent death which followed in her fam-
> ily, and which was so terrible and so grievous, seemed to me to authorize
> this construction of the alleged "curse." (Channing 1848, 143)

Thus, while no "pain" is recorded in Abel and Cain's births, Channing suggests that Eve's moral anguish at the fratricide in Gen 4 more than amply
fulfills Gen 3:16a's prediction.

But Channing was not as confident of his exegetical prowess as Simpson. He submitted his interpretation to Professor G. R. Noyes, a Unitarian
clergyman holding the dual post of Professor of Hebrew and Oriental Languages and Lecturer on Biblical Literature and Theology at the Harvard
Divinity School (Farr 1983, 174). Predictably, Noyes applauded Channing's
attempt to eliminate pain but criticized his efforts at exegesis. About this
time, Channing received Simpson's pamphlet and forwarded it to Noyes
for comment. Noyes replied somewhat dryly that "the cause of science
and benevolence, in which Professor Simpson and yourself are engaged,
is not likely to be relieved by mere Hebrew philology" (Channing 1948,
146) and closed with a rather presumptuous remark that "no one" would
pretend there was anything prescriptive in Gen 3:16a (148).

Simpson reported a response from the British theological community
similar to that received by Channing in Boston. Dr. Miller, Professor of Surgery at the University of Edinburgh and one of Simpson's colleagues, was
asked to write an article on etherization for *The North British Review*. He
agreed to write the "medical" part if Dr. Chalmers (who had solicited the
article and was Moderator of the Free Church of Scotland) would write the
"theological" part. Chalmers remarked that he did not see any "theological" part to write. Finally, after a long discussion in which Miller assured
him that such ground had been taken repeatedly against etherization,
Chalmers remarked that if "small theologians" had taken such a position,
Miller was to ignore them (Gordon 1898, 259–60).

These responses by clergy and theologians, reported by both Simpson
and Miller, beg the question of exactly *how widespread* were the religious
objections to obstetrical anesthesia and exactly *who* was voicing them. A.
D. Farr in his 1982 essay "Religious Opposition to Obstetric Anaesthesia:

A Myth?" argues that "evidence of genuine religious opposition in contemporary sources has proved to be virtually non-existent." Thus, he concludes that the whole idea of a massive religious opposition to obstetrical anesthesia is an "artifact of historiography based upon a contemporary defense prepared against an attack which never materialized" (Farr 1982, 159). In other words, Simpson thought there would be religious objections and wrote a pamphlet in anticipation of the response, which, in turn, was used as proof by later writers as evidence of said objections.

While Farr is perhaps right in his assessment of the subject's lack of treatment in formal theological or denominational documents of this period, he is wrong to deduce that there were no "religious" objections. What Farr failed to realize is that it was not the formally trained theologians who were the problem; rather, it was the medically (but not theologically) trained physicians who were the issue. As obstetrical historian John Duffy notes:

> Although a few clergymen and theologians opposed obstetrical anesthesia on religious grounds, the attack from this front was never too serious despite a continued sniping for many years by some of the more fundamentalist clergymen. Surprisingly enough, the real threat to obstetrical anesthesia came from within the ranks of the medical profession itself. (Duffy 1964, 34)

As a result, physicians literally became exegetes as they struggled with understanding Gen 3:16a. Perhaps it was as Duffy suggests, that physicians "were seeking in physiology a means for rationalizing their religious convictions" (34).

Farr also ignores (or is simply not aware of) of the broader historical matrix of Gen 3:16a's interpretation—a context that shows how discussions of Gen 3:16a and the pain of childbirth existed before the discovery of anesthesia and persisted long after anesthesia was accepted in obstetrical circles.

By 1860, many of the objections to chemical anesthesia had subsided. In spite of this, questions concerning Gen 3:16a's prescriptive nature did not vanish. In the mid-twentieth century another obstetrical breakthrough, the fear/tension/pain syndrome theory and the painless childbirth movement, became the subject of debate. One of the questions raised addressed the morality of the breathing techniques used to relieve parturition pains. Did they go against scriptural teaching?

Perhaps the most noted voice of the painless childbirth movement was that of British obstetrician Grantly Dick Read. Read's book, *Childbirth without Fear* (1944), went through multiple printings, was translated into several languages, had at least five editions, and was tremendously popular in the United States.

Read argued that "for the perfect labor anaesthesia is unnecessary because there is no pain" (Caton 1999, 185). Instead, childbirth pains were frequently the result of fears and anxieties raised by superstitions or cultural expectations of women. While Read admitted that *some* fears and anxieties concerning labor were justifiable, he insisted that more cultured societies historically viewed the very act of childbirth as essentially painful and dangerous. Such attitudes, Read argued, evoked fear and the anticipation of pain that, in turn, produced muscular tension in women's minds and bodies. Thus natural tension (fear) influenced women's muscles, which prevented childbirth from functioning naturally (that is, painlessly). Read therefore saw fear, tension, and pain as the three evils that opposed the natural design of childbirth. To relieve tension, Read argued, one must overcome women's fears. Only then could the pain of childbirth be relieved (Read 1984, 196–97).

For Read, one source of fear lay in the Bible:

> The most important of all historical writings, and the most likely to be read, is the Bible. It is still the world's best-selling book. Many women read and study their Bibles—and many have been influenced to believe that childbirth is a grievous and painful experience because of passages in the King James Version like Genesis 3:16, which quotes the Lord as having said to Eve: "I will greatly multiply thy sorrow and the conception; in sorrow thou shalt bring forth children." This passage has been known as the "curse of Eve," with its assumption that misery, pain, and sorrow automatically accompany every birth. Thus many still are of the opinion today that the teaching of natural childbirth is contrary to the Bible. (Read 1984, 164)

Thus Read, like Simpson before him, entered the exegetical arena to defend his medical theory. For Read, the problem with Gen 3:16a was one of translation:

> For those who believe the translators and others who compiled the various editions of the Bible were under Divine guidance no argument will be of any avail, but if this word had Divine inspiration it is likely that the writers of the original manuscripts were inspired, and not the translators of the various editions in different languages. . . . Being interested in this subject myself for many years, I have acquired in my library a considerable collection of Bibles and find that some of the translations differ from those of the great King James Version. (Read 1984, 164–65)

Through his own comparative analysis of English versions, Read concluded that translations of Gen 3:16a often reflected the medical assumptions of the translators. Since many were writing before the technology to relieve pain had been discovered, their translations were not informed by later scientific advances. To support his own exegesis, Read quoted from his correspondence with a Rev. B. D. Glass, whom Read identified as a Hebrew scholar. Glass admitted that biblical passages referring to childbirth as dangerous and painful had always been perplexing. Read's book had prompted Glass to exegete Gen 3:16a and passages like it. After a lengthy discussion of *'eṣeb* (which would have done credit to any commentary), Glass concluded the term had many meanings (i.e., toil, labor, etc.) but did not mean "pain" (Read 1984, 165–66).

Read also indicted the church in perpetuating the fear of childbirth. As proof, he cited the Anglican prayer book's service for "The Churching of Women." Basically intended to be a thanksgiving after childbirth, it instructed new mothers as follows: "Oh, Almighty God, we give Thee humble thanks for that Thou hast vouchsafed to deliver this woman, Thy servant, from the great pain and peril of childbirth" (Read 1984, 167). Read argued that such sentiments reinforced the idea that childbirth had to be painful and communicated fear to potential mothers in the congregation. His own paraphrase reveals how he saw such words functioning as they were heard by mothers and mothers-to-be: "Thank you very much for having allowed ME to come through all that frightfulness unscathed; it is nice to be alive in spite of having performed the greatest of all natural functions for which You especially built me, although you did make it dangerous and painful for me" (168). Read called such understandings of childbirth (and God) a "travesty of truth" (169).

The painless childbirth movement drew ecclesial attention and comment. On January 8, 1956, Pope Pius XII addressed a group of Catholic gynecologists and obstetricians. After giving an overview of the theory and practice of painless childbirth in Britain and Russia, Pius XII commented on its moral and spiritual aspects. Morally, Pius concluded that "In itself it contains nothing that can be criticized" (Read 1984, 167) and commended Read's work, preferring its philosophical and metaphysical postulates over those of the Russian researchers (165).

Pius XII's response concerning the scriptural dimension of painless childbirth focused on Gen 3:16a:

> In order to understand this saying correctly, it is necessary to consider the condemnation declared by God in the whole of its context. In inflicting this punishment on our first parents and their descendants, God did not wish to forbid and did not forbid men to seek and make use of all the riches of creation, to make progress step by step in culture, to make life in this world more bearable and more beautiful.... Similarly, in punishing Eve, God did not wish to forbid and did not forbid mothers to make use of means that would render childbirth easier and less painful. (Pius XII 1978, 169)

Pius concluded his remarks with a reminder that, although women can accept the new technique of pain relief without any scruple of conscience, they are not obliged to do so. Suffering, Pius reminded his listeners, "can be a source of good, if it is borne with God and in obedience to His will" (171). Editions of Read's *Childbirth without Fear* published after Pius XII's remarks capitalized on what was seen as a papal endorsement of Read's approach.

Read's reading of Gen 3:16a curiously echoed Cotton Mather's in one important respect. Like Mather, Read made a connection between the pain of childbirth and a woman's piety. Whereas Mather saw the process as driving the expectant mother to her knees to seek forgiveness, Read saw women's piety helping them to achieve a painless delivery. For Read, the few women he knew who had no fears of childbirth were those "women who faithfully believed in the rightness of their God and the sanctity of their bodies" (Read 1984, 171). Childbirth, as Read perceived it, was "fundamentally a spiritual as well as a physical achievement" (171). It was monument of joy, not an experience of terror. At the moment of her child's birth, Read argued, a woman was inexplicably "transfigured." Read identified what he called "four pillars of parturition": Elation, Relaxation, Inattentiveness, and Exaltation (209).

Read embraced a "mystical faith in motherhood" (Caton 1999, 173). It was, in his opinion, woman's goal and purpose in life. For Read, "Woman fails when she ceases to desire the children for which she was primarily made. Her true emancipation lies in freedom to fulfill her biological purpose" (185).

With the shift of emphasis from pain to pleasure in childbirth, Read reversed, for many, the image of painful childbirth found in seventeenth- and eighteenth-century medical tracts. Read retained, however, the association of childbirth and women's piety. Whereas Mather associated pregnancy with a chance to increase women's piety (when they feared the possibility of their own death), Read saw pregnancy/painless childbirth as evidence of piety. Thus, for those women who could not deliver painlessly, or worse, those who could not or chose not to have children at all, Read's philosophy suggested that they had somehow failed to do that for which they were created. Ironically, for these women, Read's comments would, in the end, be just as oppressive as Mather's had been centuries before.

Works Cited

Anonymous. 1848. Professor Simpson and the Fanatics. *Lancet* 1:111.

Arms, Suzanne. 1975. *Immaculate Deception: A New Look at Women and Childbirth in America.* Boston: Houghton Mifflin.

Bealle Otho T., Jr. 1963. *Aristotle's Master Piece* in America: A Landmark in the Folklore of Medicine. *William & Mary Quarterly* 20:207–22.

Caton, Donald. 1999. *What a Blessing She Had Chloroform: The Medical and Social Response to the Pain of Childbirth from 1800 to the Present.* New Haven: Yale University Press.

Channing, Walter. 1848. *A Treatise on Etherization in Childbirth: Illustrated by Five Hundred and Eighty-One Cases.* Boston: Ticknor.

Duffy, John. 1964. Anglo-American Reaction to Obstetrical Anesthesia. *Bulletin of the History of Medicine* 38:32–44.

Duns, J. 1873. *Memoir of Sir James Y. Simpson.* Edinburgh: Edmonston & Douglas.

Farr, A. D. 1983. Religious Opposition to Obstetric Anaesthesia: A Myth? *Annals of Science* 40:159–77.

Gordon, Henry L. 1898. *Sir James Young Simpson and Chloroform (1811–1870)*. New York: Longmans, Green & Co.

Graham, Harvey. 1951. *Eternal Eve: The History of Gynaecology and Obstetrics*. Garden City, N.Y.: Doubleday.

Keys, Thomas E. 1945. *The History of Surgical Anesthesia*. Park Ridge, Ill.: Wood Library, Museum of Anesthesiology.

Mather, Cotton. 1972. Elizabeth in Her Holy Retirement. Pages 235–48 in *The Angel of Bethesda*. Edited by Gordon W. Jones. Barre, Mass.: American Antiquarian Society & Barre.

Miller, Peter. 1804. *An Essay on the Means of Lessening the Pains of Parturition*. Philadelphia: Hugh Maxwell.

Pope Pius XII. 1978. Address of Pope Pius XII to a Group of Catholic Obstetricians and Gynecologists: January 8, 1956. Pages 160–72 in *Love and Sexuality*. Edited by Odile M. Liebard. Wilmington, N.C.: McGrath.

Read, Grantly Dick. 1984. *Childbirth without Fear: The Original Approach to Natural Childbirth*, 5th ed. New York: Harper & Row.

Rush, Benjamin. 1803. Article V. On the Means of Lessening the Pains and Danger of Child-Bearing, and of Preventing Its Consequent Diseases; in a Letter to Dr. Edward Miller. *Medical Repository* 6:26–31.

Simpson, James Y. 1849. *Anaesthesia or the Employment of Chloroform and Ether in Surgery, Midwifery, etc.* Philadelphia: Lindsay & Blakiston.

———. 1872. Same Subject Continued, in a Letter to Dr. Protheroe Smith, of London: Edinburgh, July 1848. Pages 56–64 in *Anaesthesia, Hospitalism, Hermaphroditism, and a Proposal to Stamp Out Small-Pox and Other Contagious Diseases*. Edited by W. G. Simpson. New York: Appleton.

Smith, Hilda. 1976. Gynecology and Ideology in Seventeenth-Century England. Pages 97–114 in *Liberating Women's History: Theoretical and Critical Essays*. Edited by Berenice A. Carroll. Urbana: University of Illinois Press.

Smith, Protheroe. 1848. *Scriptural Authority for the Mitigation of the Pains of Labour, by Chloroform and Other Anaesthetic Agents*. London: Highley.

Thatcher, Virginia. 1984. *History of Anesthesia: With Emphasis on the Nurse Specialist*. New York: Garland.

Thulesius, Olav. 1994. Nicholas Culpeper, Father of English Midwifery. *Journal of the Royal Society of Medicine* 87:552–56.

Wertz, Richard W., and Dorothy C. Wertz. 1979. *Lying-In: A History of Childbirth in America*. New York: Schocken.

7

Rethinking the "Virtuous" Woman (Proverbs 31)

A MOTHER IN NEED OF HOLIDAY

Cheryl A. Kirk-Duggan

Some mothers love their sons and raise their daughters. That is, by doting on their sons, who, in the mothers' eyes, are incapable of wrongdoing, these mothers emotionally cripple the sons.[1] These sons often develop into self-centered, emotionally crippled arrogant men who believe that everyone must cater to them. These mothers train daughters to be self-sufficient and competent around the home and often overachievers at work. Such mothers usually try to be everything to everyone—a Mother Goose, Mother Jones, and Mommie Dearest[2]—folded into "Mother

---

1. Consider Tennessee Williams and Gore Vidal's screenplay for the 1959 movie *Suddenly Last Summer*: in New Orleans in 1937, a rich widow, Mrs. Venable (Katherine Hepburn), plans to fund a hospital building for a state asylum, if Dr. Cukrowicz will perform a lobotomy on her niece Catherine (Elizabeth Taylor). Mrs. Venable is distraught over the death of her son Sebastian. Sebastian and his mother used to travel abroad together every summer, except the previous summer, when he took his cousin Catherine instead. Catherine appeared to go mad the day that Sebastian died under mysterious (cannibalistic and homosexual) circumstances.

2. *Mommie Dearest* (1981) is an account of the life and times of one of our greatest actresses as seen through the eyes of an adopted darling daughter. The huge burden of following in the footsteps of Joan Crawford (Faye Dunaway) by a daughter Christina (Diana Scarwid) desiring to please her mother brings an almost insurmountable load of pressure to bear on her. The film was based on the book about Joan Crawford, one of the great Hollywood actresses of our time, written by her adopted daughter Christina Crawford. Joan decides to adopt children of her own to fill a void in her life. Yet her problems with alcohol, men, and the pressures of show business get in the way of her personal life, turning her into a mentally abusive wreck seen through the eyes of Christina and her brother Christopher, who unwillingly bore the burden of life that was unseen behind the closed doors of "The Most Beautiful House in Brentwood."

Courage."[3] Such mothers tell fascinating stories, are organizers, teachers, seamstresses, and may be abusive parents or self-effacing. This Mother Goose, Mother Jones, and Mommie Dearest combination may very well be the so-called "Mother Courage" of Prov 31.

Is the wife-mother in Prov 31 an admirable, persuasive role model? My essay profiles the mother-wife in Prov 31 from a womanist, psychosocial, spiritual perspective. Following an overview of my methodology, I construct from Prov 31: (1) a prototype of the mother focusing on the expectations of her husband, society, and children; (2) an analysis of the role of patriarchy in establishing this picture of mother-wife; (3) an overview of the many pathologies codified in this biblical mother; and (4) a prescriptive rereading of this wisdom mother toward a balanced experience as mother and woman.

Perspective for Reading Proverbs 31

Renita Weems posits that womanist biblical hermeneutics underscores multiple identities, intelligences, scholarship, and activism toward recognizing the ways such scholars find themselves immersed between postcolonial, diasporic, woman-centered conversations with two-thirds world global women and the dialogue with privileged, hegemonic theories of Western feminism. Such discourse knows the marginalization of black women readers and the privilege of Western Eurocentric feminist interpreters. This paradoxical intellectual legacy, socioeconomic cosmology, and politically disruptive baggage shapes how one hears, reads, and interprets. Womanist biblical hermeneutics begins with the often-ignored experiences of African and African diasporan women as they survive and flourish amid systemic oppressions that prove continuously threatening. That threat includes the ways biblical texts and their interpretations have legitimated slavery and disregarded and dehumanized African peoples. Womanist biblical hermeneutics work to liberate: (1) to change people's consciousness, transform reality, and help people problematize an inspirational text toward radical readings for justice; and (2) to read these texts and use these stories to share, change, and understand human identities. With liberative womanist biblical hermeneutics, one reads texts in an analytical manner, often against accepted parlance toward liberation, empowerment, and shared power (Weems 2003, 20–32).

---

3. Mother Courage (German *Mutter Courage*) is a character from a Grimmelshausen novel *Lebensbeschreibung der Ertzbetrügerin und Landstörtzerin Courasche* (*The Runagate Courage*) dating from around 1670. The character had played a cameo role in *Der abentheuerliche Simplicissimus Teutsch* (1668). The Bertolt Brecht play (1939) *Mutter Courage und ihre Kinder* (*Mother Courage and Her Children*), gave her currency in the twentieth century. Brecht casts Mother Courage as a walking contradiction. She is torn between protecting her children from the war and profiting out of the war. See http://en.wikipedia.org/wiki/Mother_Courage.

A liberative womanist biblical hermeneutics challenges the queen mother of ancient Israel as paradigmatic for twenty-first-century women. Many pastors and parents teach contemporary women that the mother in Prov 31 is *the* quintessential woman, wife, and mother. Usually, contemporary women of faith's forays into this text miss the patriarchal framing and systemic ecclesial oppression, shaping their accepted social mores. Some even hear a critique of the superwoman, without rejecting patriarchy and seeing the overwhelming power of capitalism and individualism that shape gender roles and family life.[4] I read this text with suspicion, or tempered cynicism, to grasp the helpful/harmful continuum, given complex societies and individuals, and how contemporary women experience identity as a self, family member, and member of society. With courage and creativity, I question customary interpretations particularly in areas of sexuality and expectations of mothers. Commitment to justice-seeking and discovery with candor exposes pathological oppressions masking control and manipulation. Curiosity and a need to discredit the sanctity of misinterpretations that imprison women of faith and a sense of the comedic undergird my reading, keeping me simultaneously sane and challenged (Kirk-Duggan 2003, 40). With spirited vigor, as iconoclast and instigator, I turn to explore the woman of Prov 31 as wife, then as mother.

Prototype: The Queen Mother/Warrior Woman of Proverbs 31

Scholars debate whether this woman is symbolic as personified woman wisdom or an actual wife who embodies wisdom. Most late twentieth-century scholars posit that she is historical and incarnates wisdom ideals. For them, Prov 31:10–31 constructs the woman as a capable homemaker and conceptualizes woman-wisdom as composite teacher, prophet, and mediatrix. Noting that these characterizations are lopsided, Waltke says that to get to the truth one must combine all proverbs into a logical montage—proverbs self-correct themselves. Viewing her as a premier wise-woman role model for all time is problematic and erroneous. Readers are to think through an appropriate life application of various proverbs (Waltke 2005, 517). Too often people read Prov 31 and make universal assumptions about womanhood, unaware of ancient Israel's socioreligious ethos.

In ancient Israel's patrilineal, patrilocal, patriarchal society,[5] men handled crops, livestock, and property and dominated public space. Women produced pottery, baskets, food, textiles; bore and raised children; helped with harvesting; managed household worship; sought oracles; and dis-

---

4. Conversation with my colleague, scholar-activist, Mikeal Broadway, Associate Professor of Theology and Ethics, Shaw University Divinity School, Raleigh, May 2007.

5. In such a male-dominated society, land inheritance passed to the oldest male, and women lived in their husbands' homes.

seminated information. Under the Davidic monarchy, women and men were equals in daily life and highly respected the law. Gender-based roles and place and a prescribed cosmic order with sexual boundaries were strictly upheld under threat of harsh punishment. As *'ēšet ḥayil*, the queen mother as a superb household manager and her male counterpart as *geber* set the tone for Hebrew Bible theology and Western civilization sacred texts.[6] Blumenthal argues that the Hebrew root *'hb*, love as affection, is not in this text because for the *'ēšet ḥayil* love is solid household management and orderly family living amid divine blessing and order. She is the ideal Jewish woman (Blumenthal 2005, 17–26). Various biblical versions translate *ḥayil* as "capable," "trustworthy," "valiant," "worthy," or "good." Within the wider semantic range, *ḥayil* is a warrior-hearted woman who encompasses her socioeconomic, personal, military, and sexual power, notes Wilda Gafney (2000, 25–27).[7] In sum, the Queen/Warrior-Hearted Mother of Prov 31 (hence Queen/Mother-Warrior) deemed faithful mother and virtuous wife is *larger* than life: a wealthy housewife who helps her husband advance his business (Keil and Delitzsch 1978, 325).

Yet for all of her gifts and accomplishments, this Queen/Mother-Warrior is not independent: her husband owns her; she is a possession and commodity. While her capacity for industry honors good stewardship, what are her thoughts about her life and world? Her compulsive work ethic exacts what cost? Given that many verbs and language about this woman are masculine and military as she girds her loins, is her sexual identity in question (verse 17)? Does intense masculine language press the question for a transgendered identity? Does she have an obsessive-compulsive personality disorder? Her costly attire and having maids signal class status and privilege; ergo, her life does not parallel the lives of most women then or now. Can her husband really respect her when he owns her? Is she a workaholic because she is an object? Does that same woman today smother herself with work to run away from life and from herself? As manager, does she ever delegate work? Responses to these questions frame the prescriptive reading of this Queen/Mother-Warrior in the concluding section of this essay.

From a literary perspective, the so-called ideal, life-giving woman of Prov 31 is juxtaposed with the alleged strange, bad, death-inducing woman of Prov 1–9. Szlos posits that these women are complex; the ideal woman, a doer, has some power in a system that also limits her power. Second, Prov 31 describes the ideal woman with five words of power—physical and socio-economic strength and capacity, unusual as these terms usually describe YHWH, men, and military contexts. Third, body parts in the text

---

6. The three monotheistic religions and secular Western civilization owe their beginnings to ancient Israel's patriarchal-rural life.

7. Wilda Gafney connects the sexual power of Queen/Mother-Warrior with Ruth's seduction of Boaz (2000).

either actually or metaphorically indicate she works or has power.[8] Intriguingly, nowhere else does the Hebrew Bible use the term "loins" to describe a woman. An additional military term, her having booty or spoils of war, engenders male-power. Fourth, marketing and commerce language focuses on her prosperity and industrious capacities. Fifth, the use of third feminine possessive pronominal suffixes—from her value, her food, to her sons and her husband—presses her audience to pay attention to and remember her regarding household management (Szlos 2000, 97–103).

A strong ethic of solidarity rooted in the interdependence of household members is central to households in ancient Israel: relations of blood, marriage, workers, servants, secondary wives, and slaves. Religiously speaking, the household holds two important values: the election or chosenness of the ancestors, foundational to the nation of Israel; and a God who creates and sustains the cosmos, the family, and each individual, where the monarchy had ceased to exist. Proverbs 31, an economic text about consumption and production, includes household activities of nurture, reproduction, education, and judicial dynamics (Perdue 2000, 276–77).

Most scholars view Prov 31 as two poems: "The Noble King" (vv. 2–9); and an acrostic poem "The Valiant Wife" (vv. 10–31). The superscription of verse 1 accords authorship of the entire oracle to Lemuel's mother. Viewing the received chapter as one text, we see the mother speak to her son, and her character unfolds in silence. Interestingly, the wife's husband sits in the gate, not the throne. His son is king. Waltke suggests that the sage uses metonymy, a figure of speech where an idea or thing or symbol is represented by another idea or thing or symbol that has some connection with it: strength signals virility, and might symbolizes sexual vigor. First, she tells him to avoid compromising sexual relationships, especially with women from the harem placed there for deception or conspiracy.[9] Obsession with sexual gratification can distort the king's power, distract him, undermine his leadership, and expose him to trickery and subversion.[10] Second, she encourages him to avoid excessive drinking, which hinders one's capacity to promote justice and have compassion for the poor, widows, and orphans. Third, the Queen/Mother-Warrior contends that Lemuel can find others who ought to have alcohol: alcohol will allow them to forget their dire conditions. However, no one is to become inebriated,[11] even with the sarcastic command to let the impoverished drink. Rather, the king is to rescue the suffering from their poverty and misery.

---

8. Body parts indicating power include hands, palm, arms, and loins.
9. Consider the biblical story of Solomon and his wives and concubines.
10. Consider the biblical saga of King David.
11. Consider the biblical story of Lot and his daughters. There would not be total prohibition against drink given the implication that the king has wine cellars.

Fourth, she tells Lemuel to speak on behalf of the speechless, as a noble, responsible king (Crenshaw 1998, 9–10, 14–18). Ultimately, the king must be present for people, especially the poor; otherwise, they will have no voice (Waltke 2005, 501–9). This new king, the "son of my womb," "son of my vows," implying a mother's promise to respond actively to God for divine gift or protection, is to live with integrity and justice by defending human rights (Perdue 2000, 272–74).

Two Biblical proverbs (Prov 1:8; 6:20) mention the mother and the father's teaching (*tôrāh*). While fathers are usually heard in parental instruction, these texts signal that both parents instructed their sons in ethical principles. In Prov 31:26, mother invokes wisdom and integrity amid compassionate responsibility in sharing her wisdom and teachings. This unnamed non-Israelite Queen/Mother-Warrior from Massa in the Transjordan, with much rhetorical fanfare, spiritually and physically cares for her special son, Lemuel, like Hannah did for Samuel before his birth. Queen/Mother-Warrior admonishes her son four times about various issues.

In Jungian analysis, a positive mother complex provides children with value, an unquestionable right to exist, space to develop healthy ego activity, and life in a world that supplies their needs. The child experiences love, safety, and emotional intimacy. With strong ego strength, children can separate from parents to know freedom. Parents must guard against projecting expectations onto their children, while parents also free themselves from their own parents (the children's grandparents). With a good mother complex, mother nurtures, protects, and gives the child a sense of well-being. At the right time, mother pushes the child away in a freeing gesture. Otherwise, the child is smothered (Kast 1997, 2–5, 14–15, 42). Is the Queen/Mother-Warrior in Proverbs a good mother, or a dysfunctional one?

Patriarchy Takes Center Stage

Many ideologies about mothering exist. A patriarchal-mothering ideology prescribes personal identity and selfhood that requires women to participate in biological reproduction as natural. As such, patriarchy has almost turned mothering into an isolating, estranged labor. Such reductionist strictures on motherhood potentially trap women where they stop valuing their own lives and cannot work for communal freedom. "Mothers are romanticized as life giving, self-sacrificing, and forgiving [or] demonized as smothering, overly involved, and destructive" (Glenn 1994, 11). Either extreme robs mothers of their personhood and agency. Mothering ideologies tend to disavow the labor of mothering and the import of caring. Bifurcations organic to Western philosophy subordinate and construct mothering amid oppositions: nature/culture, reason/emotion, mind/body, public/private, and labor/love (9–15).

Some mothers hold shameful secrets about how their feelings or behavior damage their children. An ideological, patriarchal, sentimental portrait of mothers can overshadow real mothers with guilt. Historically, a perfect, ideal mother and formulas, absolutes, or easy answers about mothering do not exist. Exposing useless, perfect mothers' paradigms can be liberating for real mothers. Romantic notions of mothers who can always love their children unconditionally and whose children always flourish and behave are unrealistic. Notions of mothering and child-rearing evolve. When mother and child bond, the child loves and needs the mother in profound, exclusive ways. Similarly, socializing with children is not always gratifying and will seem endless and thankless. Hiding conflicts about mothering exacerbates such problems. Styles of mothering are not universal; they are culturally derived, shaped by community mores, familial traditions, and individual tastes.

Twenty-first-century standards of good mothering in the United States are contradictory, intangible, daunting, and self-denying. While infants need lots of affection and touch, mothers must let go of children as they age. If there is an imbalance in a mother's love or disregard for the child, the child may experience permanent harm. Images of the Virgin Mary, fairy godmothers, and embracing patriarchal cultural norms have bolstered the ideal, perfect mother. Literature, film, and music reflect visions of "maternally induced psychic paralysis" (Thurer 1994, xvii). Amid apparent maternal power, these mothers often lose themselves. Their needs become lost, and desires shift or vanish or get sublimated to their children's needs. Recently, the role of mother became more complicated: her responsibilities increased to include tending to everyone's needs. She often receives criticism when she works outside the home, although throughout history most mothers have had duties beyond child care and have delegated some tasks to others. In Western literary tradition, mothers often do not get to speak and are idealized, trivialized, or disparaged, particularly regarding sexuality. For public sentiment, maternity and sexuality mix like oil and water.[12] While much psychological literature blames the mother[13] for many children's problems,[14] these theories do not consider how war, classism, racism, heterosexism, and sexism can thwart any mother's best endeavors to be loving and supportive. With the nurture versus nature quagmire, today many in the public blame nurture for any problems with children. Not only are our ideals about mothers tied to culture, history-specific

12. For example, Hamlet believes his mother marries too soon after his father's murder. In stories such as *Madame Bovary*, *The Scarlet Letter*, *Anna Karenina*, *The Graduate*, and *The Good Mother*, sensual mothers get punished, which is often self-inflicted.

13. It is only recently that science learned that autism in children is caused by physical brain damage rather than neglect by unemotional mothers who failed to bond with their offspring.

14. The mother is often intrusive and overprotective or cold and narcissistic.

epochs, fashion, population pressures, technology, biology, and specula-
tions about women's nature, as men claim their part in procreation and
intensify patriarchy, but mothers have been dehumanized and idealized
or degraded and reduced to that of brood mare (Thurer 1994, xi–xxvi).
Mothers are often defined by their roles and functions as child breeders,
often to their own detriment. Many mothers have not learned to say no
to fathers, husbands, children, and grandchildren and have not learned to
set boundaries.[15]

Boundaries, important psychological tools for safeguarding personal
rights and integrity, protect us from violations of our bodies, self-esteem,
sexuality, privacy, and possessions. When one's boundaries are broached
or compromised, one's core self gets lost. Unaware of personal choice,
some persons become victims of familial physical, psychological, or sexual
abuse. One can choose to overcome dysfunctional, familial dynamics of
denial and repression toward self-affirmation, self-expression, and self-
defense. Boundaries help people sustain balanced, healthy relationships:
they protect and preserve individual rights and temper the impact of patriarchy. Clear boundaries support lucid, open communication. Experiences
of mistrust, resentment, sadness, anger, and shame are frequent where
familial addiction, abuse, and codependency reside. Codependency happens when one depends on a loved one for direction and stability, as well
as for solving problems and handling responsibilities. In families with active addictions, much energy gets wasted trying to control the addicted
person's behavior. Amid feelings of inadequacy or ambivalence, one can
set boundaries and confront challenges. When a woman has a healthy
family of origin, she may still have to confront societal bias due to gender, class, race, and ability. Some embrace a life philosophy where one
lives in the present, protects boundaries in personal and professional life,
and embraces one's creativity, vision, and completion. In life, one must
learn to negotiate family systems, moving from dependency to balance,
independence, and discipline. Women often trained to be nurturing—as
self-sacrificing, submissive, and tolerant—need to temper these traits with
healthy self-respect and not to become victims or martyrs trapped in emotional and mental illness or addictive, dysfunctional behaviors (Wallace
1997, xii–23; 188–93). Is Queen/Mother-Warrior a potential victim or a balanced, fulfilled leader? What do we learn about this mother based upon
her relationship with her royal son?

The words of Queen/Mother-Warrior to her son raise questions of
boundaries. The mother forbids her son—son of her womb, of her vows
(v. 2)—negating any intimacy or connectedness to her husband or to his father regarding the son's birth or current relationships, to give his strength
to women. Is she fantasizing about her relationship with her son? Is her

---

15. "Mending Wall" (Robert Frost, 1914): "Good fences make good neighbors."

husband so dysfunctional that she places all of her efforts in grooming her son to be the "husband" she wished she had? While she is correct in cautioning her son to live a life with integrity, she does not mention how he should relate solely to men in the community per se, unless one focuses on her caution to him that he should not give his ways to those who destroy kings. When imagining this mother-son relationship, such overtones of control and undertones of sexual tension where the Queen Mother warns the son to not give his strength to women (v. 3) reminds one of Sophocles's Oedipus saga. An oracle warns Laius, king of Thebes, that his son will kill him. When Laius's wife, Jocasta, gives birth to a son, Laius takes the infant and leaves him exposed on a mountainside, but a shepherd saves the infant Oedipus, and the king of Corinth adopts him. As a young man, Oedipus travels toward Thebes and meets Laius, who provokes a quarrel; they fight, and Oedipus unknowingly kills his father. Next Oedipus answers the Sphinx's riddle and rids Thebes of her destructive presence. As a reward for this heroic deed, he is given the throne of Thebes and the hand of the widowed queen—his mother—and they have four children. When they finally learn the truth about their identities, Jocasta commits suicide, and Oedipus blinds himself and goes into exile. While the text does not implicate the Queen Mother and her son, given legend and daily occurrences of global incest, it is not too far-fetched that the queen at the least fantasized about being sexually intimate with her son (see Sophocles 1877). The Queen Mother/Warrior's final words to her son regarding taking care of the unfortunate is a marvelous gesture (v. 9), yet in and of itself does not expose patriarchy, is not incompatible with them having an incestuous relationship or her fantasizing about her son and him about her.

Many men in United States culture have unresolved issues regarding their relationships with their mothers because growing up the two developed a strong psychological connection: mother nurtured son, and son emotionally nurtured mother in a way that an absent husband (working, divorced, or removed from the setting) did not. Loving their sons, some mothers fail to raise them toward helping them deal with their maleness and their psychological, spiritual, emotional selves. Whether from maternal or paternal neglect, abuse, abandonment, or absence, these problems color how mothers nurture their sons. Gurian notes that confusion arises for mother and son when there is conflict between loving each other, while not creating a so-called "momma's boy": not being too close or too distant. A patriarchal, heterosexist, sexist culture oppresses and stereotypes women and mothers. Sons are often conflicted, confused, and wounded. Though wounds also abound in father-son relationships, Prov 31 begins with complex mother-son relationships, often fueled with delusions, hidden hostilities, and the pain of sons from larger society and mother's cosmology. Overmothered and underfathered, many sons enter adulthood lacking the capacity for intimacy, discerning meaning, or em-

bracing personal empowerment. These sons feel overwhelmed by their
mother's affection and neglected by limited intimacy with their fathers. In
response to the isolation and codependency on mother that often thwarts
healthy connections with older men, these sons try to become accepted as
men through a series of rituals connecting them to male spirituality and
responsibility. Without these initiations, these sons never really mature,
understand power, know fulfillment, or have healthy relationships with
women. Gurian posits that even where there is little to no dysfunctional-
ity, mothers tend to rescue their boys emotionally; fathers tend to require
their boys to earn their dad's respect. When either parent goes overboard,
mothers tend to smother; fathers may become authoritarian. Ultimately,
sons must separate from parents and mentors toward intimacy, altru-
ism, empowerment, and selfhood (Gurian 1994, 4–9, 17–28). Mothering is
complex.

Controversy rises and falls over women's place as mothers in society—
from questions of family and maternity leave, reproductive rights, and
ordination, to being on the "mommie track"—and what mothering and
motherhood means. Universal and essentialist meaning collapse around
how people socially construct mothering. Mothering, not a biological in-
scription, varies, though some forms are denigrated and ignored via race
and class. Glenn notes that United States' society has often commodified
Asian American, African American, and Latina women to see them only
as laborers—not full-time, stay-at-home mothers or integral parts of family units. In many communities, the household shares and cooperates in
mothering and doing chores. Many African American families are multi-
generational, where nurturing kin involves children, elders, and female
and male adults. Glenn finds that white mothers tend to deal with isolation
and gender oppression amid idealized motherhood and patriarchy; mothers of color often have to deal with the physical survival of community
and children. These two different scenarios juxtapose powerlessness and
power in the mother's lived reality, thus calling into question the import of
self-definition amid building collective and individual racial identity. Most
working women have to take the brunt of taxing, physical work that is not
experienced by women of privilege. Those working mothers often have to
neglect their children to care for other privileged women's children and/or
elderly parents, due to limited options, training, legal status, or language
problems (Glenn 1994, 1–8). Recently, some young-adult middle-class
women have stopped working full time to raise their children—an option
that is feasible only if a partner or husband has substantial income or the
woman has independent means.

There are many traits of Queen/Mother Warrior that most women
ought not to aspire to if they are to have healthy, balanced lives. The litany
of her attributes begins with a rhetorical question using a figure of speech
that implies the negative: Who can find a valiant woman? The implied
answer is no one (see Ps 90:11; Hos 14:9; Isa. 53:1). Such a wife with value

beyond measure can come only from God; the standards are almost impossible. Reading her positively, the demands on this woman intensifies as her husband trusts her, a trust usually only relegated to God; that trust involves the husband's well-being (Prov 31:11). Apparently wife and husband have a strong spiritual relationship, for he lacks for nothing since his wife wins for him the basics. She intentionally does the good, that which is beneficial physically and economically. Whatever she does, she is *always* successful. This wife has great value to all in her family and her community. She helps the impoverished, the poor, and her husband to boost the region's leadership. An entrepreneur, she provides economic resources for her household, exemplifying industriousness and intellect. Her trade affords her funds to purchase food from distant lands: she is a visionary, skilled trader, and aware of haute cuisine. Though named a preying lioness, a queen would not hunt for food at night like the lioness. She strategizes her every move and so multitasks that she helps clear the field and plants the best vines. Her wealth and privilege do not prohibit her from doing menial work. Psychologically and spiritually, she does strenuous, physical work. Her work yields enduring wealth, which is good. Waltke suggests that the phrase that her lamp does not go out signals the woman's enduring affluence and success. Her spoken wisdom shapes her actions and the work she does with her hands. She empowers her husband to embrace justice and righteousness, and she helps the distressed, disabled, or destitute (Waltke 2005, 520–25). This woman is unbelievable and unbalanced.

Pathologies Codified

The virtuous woman's attributes taken together overwhelm, seem neurotic, pathological, and impossible to achieve—then and now. Many commentators conclude that these attributes involve a compilation of a virtuous woman's qualities and do not depict one *actual* woman. In United States' society, the prototype of the virtuous, ideal woman continues to change, particularly for Euro-American women, whose ideal shifted from a domestic, demure, well-dressed, well-coifed stay-at-home mom who often had an African American maid, to today's woman with low-rider jeans, who is often a soccer mom driving an SUV. Most white girls received mixed messages from "assert yourself" to "avoid being pushy." In pursuit of being an ideal, virtuous woman, women often torture themselves about their body images, focusing on the external and forgetting the internal.[16] The more some obsess, the more stressed and addictive they become. As people-pleasers, ultimately they please no one, including themselves. Some women gauge their worth based on their possessions and achievements. They fail to know the worthiness of being made in God's image. Much

---

16. In pursuit of the ideal body image, some women pursue plastic surgery, anorexia, and bulimia.

has changed regarding being efficient and the required daily work for the Queen/Mother Warrior of ancient Israel and today. That both women do so much for others is intriguing and ironic, for what happens if she is depressed and in need? In this text, no one regards her needs (Courtney 2004, 4–5, 7, 28, 33–47, 50–55, 81). This woman has no room to be or make mistakes like mothers who are ill and may physically, psychologically, and spiritually harm their children.

People tend to ignore, deny, and discredit female sexual abuse of children because they find it too difficult to acknowledge. Disbelief, secrecy, ideology, and fear of ignoring male sexual abuse must impede studying female sexual abuse. Often adults, even clinicians, disbelieve reports of female sexual abuse of minors and males and accuse victims of fantasizing.[17] Many believe anyone without a penis cannot commit sexual abuse. Female and male victims of female sexual assault can have tortured lives of addictions, attempted suicide, emotional trauma, chronic depression as well as gender and personal identity problems, traumatic relationships, fear of touching their own children. They sometimes become sexual abusers themselves (Eliot 1993, v–vii; 8–10). Given the discussion earlier about the echoes of Oedipus-Jocasta and the son—Queen-Mother Warrior woman, it would not be impossible that this son later becomes an abuser. Because the texts never inform us about the mother's feelings, previous life, or worldview other than that of industry and work, it is conceivable that such a woman would abuse in the guise of love because of her own pain, the implied rejection or at least distance of her husband from her, and the need to get some type of intimacy with her son.

Sexual abuse or misconduct occurs when someone forces, manipulates, or coerces a person, particularly a child, to do or have sexual acts done to her or his body by an authority figure—a person in care of, control of, or power over that child. These acts cause great harm.[18] Longdon notes that the damage increases exponentially when others disavow the possibility of female sexual assault. Often female family members, who resist believing the abused child, are hurtful and vindictive. Some are so resistant because historically society has believed that children were safe with women. Female sexual abuse evokes feelings of distrust and insecurity, shattering healthy notions of family values. Female abusers range from mothers and nuns to babysitters and school teachers. Neither age, gender, race, nor socioeconomics protect children from sexual abuse. Types of abuse range from fondling to aggressive, brutal acts, including vaginal and anal penetration with objects, severe humiliation and degradation,

---

17. Freud believes that the daughters of his friends were fantasizing and not telling the truth when reporting paternal incest.

18. Acts of sexual assault can include one being forced to participate in or watching others engage in sexual acts, talk, movies, pictures, etc. beyond that child's psychological and sexual development.

oral sex, sadomasochism, bestiality, and masturbation, sometimes in concert with emotional and physical abuse. Some abuse is long-term. When victims do come forward, it is important to listen to them and to get them to a safe, reputable therapist so they can express the repressed pent-up emotions they have carried for years and move toward being able to take charge of their own lives (Longdon 1993, 48–56). While the text sings only praises for Queen/Mother Warrior, even she is not above wrongdoing. Such tireless, relentless care of everyone else can cause her to scapegoat and resent her children when she finally gets so exhausted that the payoff of everyone singing her praises minus loving her without having to do anything finally wears thin. For example, does she rely on her children to provide a kind of nurture that she is lacking from their father? Is such a demand fair of her to require of her children?

While her biblical record, problematically, is too perfect, there are some intriguing hermeneutic twists regarding the mother of Prov 31. What do we know about her spouse? Waltke argues that Proverbs uses the term *ba'al*, which means lord or owner, for husband, particularly as it relates to *'ēšet ḥayil*, although *'îš* (man) is usually used for husband outside of Proverbs (Waltke 2005, 510). However, the concept of lord or owner speaks more to the reality of her domestic situation: she is property, without rights. Her lord/husband/owner trusts her, and she brings him home spoils of war. The text does not inform us as to whether she can trust him.

This wise, competent woman does so much that she is too good to be true. Bailey sees her as a Type A personality in an oppressive situation, valued mostly for her economic activities. She hustles all day while her lord/husband/owner pontificates at the gate, where he receives respect. What about her? This paradigm is an unhealthy, socially dangerous model for twenty-first-century socialization, marriage, and family (Bailey 1992, 26–27). She seems to be obsessive compulsive. How much does she delegate? Does she help her children learn how to participate in the household? Could the husband be a domestic-violence perpetrator who, when frustrated that she was not delivering quickly enough and with the proper duty, would react against her with physical, psychological, or intellectual abuse? In his 2003 novel, *Living Water*, a midrash on the "woman at the well" (John 4), Obery Hendricks creates a story of a woman who experiences love amidst violence through a rough coming-of-age, as she struggles to hold back her passion for life in a sociocultural milieu committed to breaking her spirit. No one wanted a *gibbôrâ*-minded girl running around. *Gibbôr* men are men of strength, boldness, and bravery. This is good. To be a *gibbôrâ* woman was blasphemy (Hendricks 2003, 4–5). How might the Queen/Warrior woman dampen the spirit of her *gibbôrâ*-minded girls, given her own experience? Further, masculine, military-type language regarding this woman intensifies in verse 17, where she "girds her loins" with strength, reiterating that *the best woman is a man* (Hendricks 2003, 27) and questioning whether this is really a woman with strong so-called masculine/aggressive traits. Is she a lesbian or perhaps a trans-gendered person? Verbs that describe her actions move her beyond the everyday woman of ancient Israel.

That she has maids situates her within the elite. She wears clothing with colors symbolizing prosperity and wealth, reflecting character as a woman of strength, dignity, splendor, and majesty amid her laughter, indicating some balance. Her sons (Waltke 2003, 513) or her children, depending on the translator, call her blessed, and her lord/husband/owner praises her.[19] Proverbs 31 reflects a woman who is too flawless, too ideal and perfect, with children and a lord/husband/owner who are under her complete control. Does this scenario seem credible anywhere, at any time?

This poem ends by calling for this Queen/Mother-Warrior's commemoration (see Ps 145:10). Works praise her at the city gates, the center of the community's activity. The poet parallels praise for the warrior-woman with the cosmic praise afforded YHWH in Psalms (Van Leeuwen 1997, 263). This unnamed mother shares traits in common with Jochebed, Moses' mother. When Jochebed sees her son, Moses, she pronounces him good, *kî ṭôb*, just as Elohim spoke of creation in the Priestly narrative of Gen 1. Further, Jochebed parallels Noah's actions when she builds an ark, a *tēbâ*, to protect her child. The narrator compares Jochebed, the *'ēšet ḥayil* of Exodus, with the *'ēšet ḥayil* of Prov 31. In sum, biblical writers signal that the best woman is not just a woman, wife, or mother of excellence, but actually she is a god or, better yet, a better man (Bailey 1995, 32–34).

Prescriptive Rereading of the Valiant Queen/Mother Warrior

The flurry of activity in the text of this Queen/Mother Warrior is exhausting, impossible for any one person to perform, and it begs the question of weighting industry versus intimacy toward realized identity. This mother/wife is a workaholic, is overly industrious. She creates, builds, and produces. Intimacy is nonexistent. She receives words of praise and thanksgiving for her work, which ultimately cannot define who she is. Her emotional and spiritual well-being remains a mystery. Such long-term behavior in the twenty-first century could be deadly, at the least not healthy. She has the best organizational strategies of a Mother Jones, the creativity of a Mother Goose, and, ultimately, if pressed, she could end up being a consummate Mommie Dearest, the day she explodes, rife with rage and resentment for being used and taken for granted.

A liberative womanist biblical interpretation of the Queen/Mother Warrior in Prov 31 exposes patriarchal framing and systemic oppression

---

19. Waltke suggests that her sons praise her in verse 28 in parallel with her daughters in verse 29, not her children. Her many daughters produce and do much, but not as much as she does. Some commentators state that many women, not daughters, produce much, hinting at competition and judgment.

codified by the church and Western social mores, with the intent of encouraging a healthy communal response to patriarchal, socioeconomic pressures devouring our families and us. Suspicion, or tempered cynicism shows that this text creates an impossible, harmful paradigm. She advises her son, yet has no voice regarding herself. Courage and creativity unmask tensions regarding her compulsive industriousness, where she is an automaton, possibly crippling her children, with a leech for a husband. Commitment to justice-seeking and discovery reflect her charitable works amid elitism and privilege, coupled with her objectification and implied self-identity via being industrious, tells her to run from Queen/Mother Warrior as model. Besides, Queen/Mother Warrior is a composite, not an individual ideal. Curiosity unveils potential for sexual misconduct and manipulation by Queen/Mother Warrior. Masculine language describing her skews her sexual identity, ultimately replacing her with a god or man, a notion lost when one is unaware of Hebrew. The comedic finds the last laugh on us, for the text tells us from the very beginning that such a woman does not exist!

Works Cited

Bailey, Randall C. 1992. Doing the Wrong Thing: Male-Female Relationships in the Hebrew Canon. Pages 18–29 in *We Belong Together: The Churches in Solidarity with Women*. Edited by Sarah Cunningham. New York: Friendship.

———. 1995. Is That Any Name for a Nice Hebrew Boy?": Exodus 2:1–10: The De-Africanization of an Israelite Hero. Pages 25–36 in *The Recovery of Black Presence: An Interdisciplinary Exploration*. Edited by Randall C. Bailey and Jacqueline Grant. Nashville: Abingdon.

Blumenthal, David R. 2005. The Images of Women in the Hebrew Bible. Pages 15–60 in *Marriage, Sex, and Family in Judaism*. Edited by Michael J. Broyde and Michael Ausubel. Lanham, Md.: Rowman & Littlefield.

Courtney, Vicki. 2004. *The Virtuous Woman: Shattering the Superwoman Myth*. Nashville: Broadman & Holman.

Crenshaw, James L. 1998. A Mother's Instruction to Her Son (Proverbs 31:1–9). Pages 9–22 in *Perspectives on the Hebrew Bible: Essays in Honor of Walter J. Harrelson*. Edited by James L. Crenshaw. Macon, Ga.: Mercer University Press.

Elliot, Michele, ed. 1993. *Female Sexual Abuse of Children*. New York: Guildford.

Gafney, Wilda. 2000. Who Can Find a Militant Feminist. *A.M.E. Zion Quarterly Review* 112.2:25–31.

Glenn, Evelyn Nakano. 1994. Social Constructions of Mothering: A Thematic Overview. Pages 1–32 in *Mothering: Ideology, Experience, and Agency*. Edited by Evelyn Nakano Glenn, Grace Chang, and Linda Rennie Forcey. New York: Routledge.

Gurian, Michael. 1994. *Mothers, Sons and Lovers: How a Man's Relationship with his Mother Affects the Rest of His Life*. Boston: Shambhala.

Hendricks, Obery. 2003. *Living Water: A Novel*. New York: HarperSanFrancisco.

Kast, Verena. 1997. *Father-Daughter, Mother-Son: Freeing Ourselves from the Complexes That Bind Us*. Shaftesbury, Dorset: Element Books.

Keil, Carl F., and Franz Delitzsch. 1978. *Proverbs, Ecclesiastes, Song of Solomon*. Vol. 6 of *Commentary on the Old Testament in Ten Volumes*. Grand Rapids: Eerdmans.

Kirk-Duggan, Cheryl. 2003. Slingshots, Ships, and Personal Psychosis: Murder, Sexual Intrigue, and Power in the Lives of David and Othello. Pages 37–70 in *Pregnant Passion: Gender, Sex, and Violence in the Bible*. Edited by Cheryl A. Kirk-Duggan. SemeiaSt 44. Atlanta: Society of Biblical Literature.

Longdon, Cianne. 1993. A Survivor and Therapist's Viewpoint. Pages 47–56 in *Female Sexual Abuse of Children*. Edited by Michele Elliot. New York: Guildford.

Perdue, Leo G. 2000. *Proverbs*. IBC. Louisville: John Knox.

Sophocles. 1977. *The Oedipus Cycle: Oedipus Rex, Oedipus at Colonus, Antigone*. Translated by by Dudley Fitts and Robert Fitzgerald. Orlando: Harcourt.

Szlos, M. Beth. 2000. A Portrait of Power: A Literary-Critical Study of the Depiction of the Woman in Proverbs 31:10–31. *USQR* 54:97–103.

Thurer, Shari. 1994. *The Myths of Motherhood: How Culture Reinvents the Good Mother*. New York: Penguin.

Van Leeuwen, Raymond C. 1997. The Book of Proverbs. *NIB* 5:19–264.

Wallace, Ann Cope. 1997. *Setting Psychological Boundaries: A Handbook for Women*. Westport, Conn.: Bergin & Garvey.

Waltke, Bruce K. 2005. *The Book of Proverbs: Chapters 15–31*. Grand Rapids: Eerdmans.

Weems, Renita. 2003. Re-reading for Liberation: African American Women and the Bible. Pages 19–32 in *Feminist Interpretation of the Bible and the Hermeneutics of Liberation*. Edited by Silvia Schroer and Sophia Bietenhard. JSOTSup 374. London: Sheffield Academic Press.

8

Reading the Religious Romance
SEXUALITY, SPIRITUALITY, AND MOTHERHOOD IN THE BIBLE AND TODAY

Mark Roncace and Deborah Whitehead

Feminist theologian Sarah Coakley writes about the "profound, but messy, entanglement of our human sexual desires and our desire for God," a theme she traces back to the early trinitarian Christian tradition (1). A recent episode of *South Park* makes the connection explicit when the character Cartman decides to start a Christian rock band. When his friends wonder where they will get their material, Cartman suggests they simply graft religious language onto existing popular songs: "All we have to do is cross out words like 'baby' and 'darling' and replace them with 'Jesus.'" Hilarity ensues as the sexual subtexts in the band's performances go from implied to overt, to the great discomfort of their Christian audiences. This essay explores this "messy entanglement" of sexual desire and desire for God as it intersects with the role of motherhood in biblical texts and in popular culture today. Specifically, we offer a linguistic and literary examination of germane Hebrew Bible texts, a brief analysis of how the messy entanglements are manifested in Christian tradition, and, finally, a cultural critique of contemporary evangelical women's literature.

Dubious Conceptions

Throughout the Bible, God is typically present in the act of procreation. The deity and motherhood are closely associated. While scholars have noted this phenomenon, they have not seemed to appreciate its ubiquity and thus significance. In nearly every story of conception in the Hebrew Bible, God either opens wombs, gives seed, or perhaps even fathers the child. The New Testament features two prominent stories of conception—that of John the Baptist and Jesus—neither of which will be discussed in detail here. That God is intimately involved in the conception of Jesus hardly needs comment. In Luke's version, Mary is literally impregnated by divine action (Luke 1:35). John's birth story is subject to the same analysis as the annunciation type-scene found in the Hebrew Bible, which we discuss in some detail below. But let us begin at the beginning.

In Gen 4:1 Eve claims, "I have created/acquired a man with the Lord" (קניתי איש את־יהוה). The Hebrew of this verse is notoriously difficult and has evoked a wide variety of interpretations and translations.[1] Certainly one way to understand Eve's statement is that she and the Lord together produce a man. He is the father; she is the mother. To be sure, Gen 4:1 clearly states that "Adam knew his wife Eve." Eve, however, credits the deity, not her husband, as the creative partner. When Cain subsequently kills his brother Abel, it is the Lord who confronts Cain, punishes him, and protects him from death (Gen 4:6–15). The Lord, not Adam, acts as Cain's father. The Lord's role as the father is highlighted further by the fact that the relationship between the father (the Lord) and his sons—blatant paternal favoritism of the younger son, which results in fraternal conflict—foreshadows the later interaction between Abraham and his sons (Ishmael and Isaac), Isaac and his sons (Jacob and Esau), and Jacob and his sons (the ten elder ones and Joseph). That is, the unifying literary themes present in the book of Genesis invite one to read the Lord as the father of Cain and Abel. Adam is conspicuously absent.

Later, when Eve bears Seth, her naming speech again connects her conception to divine action: "God has placed for me another seed [אחר שת לי אלהים זרע] instead of Abel" (Gen 4:25). Again, the translations and interpretations of this verse vary significantly. The verb שית has a wide semantic range, but the most common meaning is to "put," place," or "set." Similarly, זרע can be rendered a variety of ways, but the most basic meaning is "seed." Many translations conceal the scandalous ambiguity by rendering, for example, God has "appointed for me another child" (NRSV) or "provided with me another offspring" (NJPS), but a more literal reading of Eve's speech is that God put his seed in Eve. How striking that in Eve's two naming speeches—the first such maternal pronouncements in the Bible—God is so closely associated with conception: the mother's own words suggest that the deity is the father.

When we move out of the primeval history and to the stories of the mothers of Israel, we encounter the well-known "barren woman" motif. In these stories, both barrenness and fertility are traced directly to God. For example, Isaac appeals to God concerning the infertility of his wife, Rebekah (Gen 25:21). Jacob says to the exasperated Rachel: "Am I in the place of God, who has withheld from you the fruit of the womb" (Gen 30:2–3; see also Gen 33:5). God "opens the womb" of both Leah (29:31) and Rachel (30:22), and both mothers give their children theophoric names, which further strengthens the connection between the deity and motherhood (Gen 29:32–33, 35; 30:23–24).

---

1. For a discussion of the various possibilities, see Pardes 1992, 43–47.

Closely associated with the barren woman motif is what Robert Alter has identified as the annunciation type-scene, which consists of the following elements: (1) the woman is barren; (2) a messenger from God appears to the woman; (3) the messenger promises a son; (4) the announcement is confirmed despite human doubt; and (5) conception occurs, the son is born, and he becomes a significant person in the story. This pattern is seen most clearly in the stories of Sarah, Samson's mother, and Hannah. Since this story-form and these texts have received close scrutiny by others, our analysis focuses strictly on the idea that in all of these stories the paternity of the child—whether it is God or the human husband—is ambiguous.

In her first speech, Sarai claims, "The LORD has prevented me from bearing children" (Gen 16:2). If the Lord produced children with Eve, now he denies Sarai the pleasure of his partnership and the resulting conception. The Lord promises to Abraham concerning Sarai: "I will bless her, and moreover I will give you a son by her" (Gen 17:16). The phrase "by her" (ממנה) recalls that Sarah had previously told Abraham to take Hagar so that "I shall obtain children by her [ממנה]" (Gen 16:2). When Abraham fathered a child with Hagar, the offspring was considered Sarah's even though she had nothing to do with the conception or birth. Thus, when God declares that God will provide a son "by her," it suggests that the Lord and Sarah have relations, but the child is Abraham's even though he has nothing to do with the conception. Other elements in the text leave open this possibility. Nowhere does the narrative report that Abraham had sexual intercourse with Sarah; contrast the situation with Abraham and Hagar (Gen 16:4). Instead, when the Lord visits Abraham and Sarah, the "three men" are clearly more interested in Sarah. They ask Abraham where she is (Gen 18:9) and then announce: "I will surely return to you in due season, and your wife Sarah will have a son" (Gen 18:10). The narrative subsequently reports that "The LORD visited [פקד] Sarah as he said [אמר], and the LORD did [עשה] to/for Sarah as he spoke [דבר]. And Sarah conceived and bore a son for Abraham" (21:1–2). The verb פקד has a broad semantic range, but it can, in fact, signal sexual desire (see Judg 15:1). The verb עשה may not have explicitly sexual connotations, but it is difficult to dismiss that possibility given the context. The very fact that the deity—rather than Abraham—is the subject who is "doing" is significant. God's actions render a barren woman pregnant. Furthermore, אמר and דבר recall the creative power of divine speech in Gen 1, suggesting that perhaps here God's word has again created life—this time in Sarah's womb. The syntax here is also suggestive. The *waw* consecutive—ותהר ("and she conceived")—implies that the conception is a result of divine action (see also Bal 1988, 266; Klein 1990, 111).

Samson's paternity is also clouded in ambiguity. An "angel of the LORD" appeared to the barren and unnamed wife of Manoah and announced the birth of a son (Judg 13:3). Although Manoah requests that the messenger return "to us" so that "we" will know what to do, the angel appears a second time only to the woman (Judg 13:9). The clandestine encounter, as others have observed, has a sexual aspect (see also Bal 1988, 74; Reinhartz 1994, 166–68; Klein 1990, 114). Further, the phrase "came to the woman" is the same phrase used in Ruth 4:13 (see below), where it is typically understood as a euphemism for intercourse and is rendered "they came together." As with Abraham and Sarah, the text never reports that Manoah and his wife had sexual intercourse. Instead, after the angel departs, the narrative laconically states, "The woman bore a son and named him Samson. The boy grew, and the LORD blessed him. The spirit of the LORD began to stir him" (Judg 13:24–25). Not only is Manoah absent, but the Lord is mentioned twice immediately after the birth of Samson, which contributes to the suspicion of divine paternity. The numerous superhuman feats of Samson only serve to support this notion.

The story of Hannah parallels that of Rebekah and Rachel in many ways. Her womb is closed by the Lord (1 Sam 1:5–6), so Hannah appeals to God, not her husband, for a son. The priest Eli serves as the messenger from God who announces the birth of a son (1:17), to whom Hannah gives a theophoric name (1:20). The narrator reports that "Elkanah knew his wife Hannah, and the LORD remembered her, and in due time Hannah conceived and bore a son." Unlike other cases (see Gen 4:1, 17), where the text states "X knew his wife and she conceived and bore," here the Lord intervenes textually—and, symbolically, sexually—between Elkanah's actions and Hannah's conception. The human husband does his part, but without the Lord there is no conception. Hannah, of course, gives the son back to the Lord (1 Sam 1:27–28); the transaction is between Hannah and the deity. Elkanah can do nothing but assent to Hannah's plan (1:23). Further, the narrative concludes Hannah's story by reporting that, "The LORD visited [פקד] Hannah, and she conceived and bore three sons and two daughters" (1 Sam 2:21). As was the case with the Lord and Sarah, פקד may not have an explicit sexual meaning, but those connotations echo in the background.[2]

Another instance of dubious paternity is the story of the great woman of Shunem and Elisha (2 Kgs 4:8–37). As others have noted, this episode subverts the annunciation type-scene (Shields 1993, 63). The woman is not barren. There is no messenger from God to announce the birth of a son. The promised son is not given a name and he has no significance in Israelite history. In its "proper" form, the annunciation scene hints that the deity is the father, but by substituting Elisha for God this story further subverts the "proper" type-scene. Several elements in the text point to Elisha as the father (see Van Dijk-Hemmes 1994, 225–27). As with Sarah and Samson's mother, the text does not indicate sexual relations between the woman and her husband. Instead, Elisha announces, "At this season, in due time, you

---

2. Klein (1994, 77–92) demonstrates the special relationship between the Lord and Hannah in contrast to Hannah's marginalization by her human husband.

will embrace a son" (1 Kgs 4:16); the narrative then reports the fulfillment of the word: "The woman conceived and bore a son" (2 Kgs 4:17). The juxtaposition of announcement and its fulfillment leaves no room for the husband to act. Furthermore, the husband is largely absent throughout the story. In his lone appearance, he takes no responsibility for or interest in the child but instead instructs his servants to take the sick boy to "his mother" (2 Kgs 4:19). Accordingly, when the woman discovers her son's illness, she immediately contacts Elisha. In short, this text's subversion of the annunciation type-scene supports the notion that the "proper" question is whether the father is God or the human husband.

One other text needs to be mentioned briefly—Ruth. Like the great woman of Shunem, Ruth is not barren. Yet even though no miracle is needed, the deity is closely involved in the conception: "When he [Boaz] came to her, the LORD gave to her conception, and she bore a son" (Ruth 4:13). The phrase "to give conception" appears nowhere else in the Hebrew Bible. Its significance is further underscored by the fact that it is only the second time in the book of Ruth where God is the subject of the verb (see 1:6). Appropriately, the women acknowledge the deity's life-giving power (4:14). Boaz's role is strikingly minimized.

While the human father's role is minimized, omitted, or left ambiguous in these biblical texts, the mother and her relationship with God are elevated in importance. Leila Leah Bronner argues that biblical mothers enjoy a much higher level of status and power than do other biblical women: a form of "unassigned power," or "unofficial influence and persuasion," unconventional forms of power within a patriarchal system (ix). But if the textual ambiguities surrounding conception and motherhood leave more room for biblical women to maneuver, they also call into question representations of masculinity and fatherhood in the texts. Howard Eilberg-Schwartz contends that "divine representations can also be sources of competition and rivalry," for "if it is the divine father who is responsible for opening a woman's womb, it is not clear at all what role the human father plays" (17). This theme of competition between God and human fathers resurfaces in slightly altered form in the contemporary evangelical Christian texts discussed below, where competition for love and affection replaces competition over reproduction.

When one surveys, albeit briefly, these Hebrew Bible stories, one senses that the ambiguity surrounding the Lord's sexual activity has been routinely overlooked in the history of interpretation—subconsciously perhaps—because of its scandalous nature. It is curious that Christian tradition affirms the virgin birth, though it has not given serious consideration to the "pregnant" gaps in the Hebrew narratives. Indeed, many people have noted the connection between the barren wife stories—particularly the account of Hannah—and the New Testament's stories of Mary (and Elizabeth). Susan Ackerman, for example, observes: "Both these types of empty wombs [barren and virginal], moreover, can only be filled through God's miraculous intervention. . . . The Mary narrative—despite its stress on virginity—[is] an illustration of the 'barren' woman tale" (201). However, in the case of early Christian texts, despite similarities to the Hebrew Bible annunciation scenes, any ambiguity surrounding the conception of Jesus in the earliest sources gives way to a heavy-handed stress on divine paternity and Mary's virgin motherhood as a means of emphasizing the uniqueness and purity of the Christ.[3] In short, the literary connections between miraculous birth stories in the Hebrew Bible and New Testament invite consideration of the deity's role in all the texts. The preceding comments have proposed that the divine role in narratives of special conception in the Hebrew Bible is rather ambiguous, leaving sufficient room to read God as the father.

Erotic Desire and Desire for God

The link between God and sexuality appears in various later strands of the Christian tradition, where it is often associated with the allegorical interpretation of Song of Songs and the "bride of Christ" imagery. Coakley identifies in patristic texts a careful wrestling with the nexus of erotic desire and desire for God, along with a provocative, though cautious, metaphorical rendering of contemplation and mystical ascent with the language of erotic desire. The richness of this imagery of desire exceeds our modern understanding of desire as sublimation and invites us to rediscover the ancient tradition anew: "Instead of thinking of God-language as really being about sex (Freud's reductive ploy)," she writes, we moderns need to take a clue from the ancients and "understand sex as really about God, and about the deep desire that we feel for God—the clue that is woven into our existence about the final and ultimate union that we seek" (4).

Beginning in the twelfth century, women mystics frequently employed erotic, sexual, and marital language and imagery to convey the experience of union between the soul and Christ, a development that occurred along with the greater use of feminized and affective language, more positive valuations of marriage and motherhood, and an emphasis on the humanity and physicality of Christ.[4] Becoming one with Christ meant uniting

---

3. See Schaberg 1987 for a discussion of the tradition and interpretation of the illegitimacy of Jesus. By the second century C.E., apocryphal texts such as *Protoevangelium of James* took great pains to eliminate all ambiguity regarding the divine manner of Jesus's conception (see Schaberg 1998).

4. See, e.g., Bynum 1982; Jantzen 1995; and Hollywood 1995. It is important to note that such bodily metaphors were not restricted to female mystics only, although they often differ quite strikingly from the writings of male mystics, and certainly were conditioned by the tendency to associate women more closely with the body, women's lack of access to theological training and clerical office (accounting for less spiritualized and more literal renderings of bride of Christ imagery), and also by women's very real experiences of physical suffering in this period.

with him in his bodily, suffering form. Sexual and erotic imagery, often borrowed from the courtly love tradition, became one way to describe this experience of "dependence and union" among certain writers of this period, both male and female.[5]

From a modern perspective, such an experience is easily read (reductively) as sublimated desire.[6] Yet Bynum and other interpreters of female mysticism caution against such readings, reminding us that "in the Eucharist and in ecstasy, a male Christ was handled and loved; sexual feelings were not so much translated into another medium as simply set free" (Bynum 1987, 248). Far from being intellectualized or allegorized, women mystics participated in what Jantzen calls a "direct, highly charged, passionate encounter between Christ and the writer" (133). The Christ worshiped and loved by medieval women was not the Christ of the theologians and clergy but the physical, fleshly Jesus of the Gospels: "Christ the baby, Christ the bridegroom, Christ the tortured body on the cross." Imagining themselves as mothers, medieval women physically constituted a kind of anti-establishment *imitatio* in which clerical authority was circumvented, implicitly critiqued, or appropriated (Bynum 1992, 130; 135).

Jumping ahead several centuries, we encounter another nexus of gender, affective metaphors, and religious devotion in the sentimentalized theology and spirituality of nineteenth-century American Victorian culture. The Victorian cult of true womanhood associated women with spirituality, motherhood, and higher virtue, while a more affective theology of feminine and maternal imagery replaced traditional Calvinist theology. A growing preference for a humanized, "liberal" Jesus as opposed to a removed, judging God marked a shift to models of the divine as tender parent and friend, "newly sensitized and feminized in image, defined as a lover of all the world's 'little ones'" (Douglas 1998, 125, 130). At the same time, women were celebrated and sentimentalized—but also circumscribed—in their roles as wives and mothers, nurturers and passive exemplars of piety and virtue. Sunday was a "weekly Mother's Day," since it provided the opportunity for men and children to experience a full course of gentle "womanly persuasion" on their day of rest in the home (111). Women were understood to be closer to God because of their supposedly more affective nature and ability to mediate religiosity to men, while Jesus came to resemble a romanticized portrait of Victorian masculinity.

Traces of both the medieval mystical and Victorian sentimental traditions linger in the present, along with a post-Freudian understanding of

---

5. Bynum 1982, 161. Another way was through the use of maternal imagery. As Bynum notes, maternal imagery had the advantage over sexual imagery in that it avoided the problem of requiring monks to express union with God by identifying themselves as female in relation to a male deity.

6. See, e.g., Jacques Lacan's interpretation of Teresa of Avila in his lectures on *Feminine Sexuality* (147).

sexuality, a popular preference for "spirituality" over "religion" (the former understood as "true" religious commitment, the latter as mere exercise), and ongoing cultural and religious struggles over traditional gender roles. This context shapes both the writing and reception of the contemporary evangelical Christian literature to which we now turn, a literature that is marketed to and written for (and in many cases by) evangelical Christian mothers. If biblical mothers enjoy a special—or, as we have seen, even sexual—relationship with the deity, and if the link between sexuality, spirituality, and motherhood persists in Christian history and culture, mothers in today's evangelical tradition are portrayed as seeking the same intimate relationship with God. Just as the biblical narrative highlights the connection between God and the women, not between the women and their husbands or children, yet has implications for how those relationships and roles are conceptualized, so too the "religious romance" found in evangelical Christian women's literature reflects continuing contestation of gender identities and roles.

"God the Ageless Romancer": Jesus/God as Lover in Contemporary Evangelical Women's Literature

In chronicling her experiences with the religious right, Donna Minkowitz was struck by the ways in which sexuality and spirituality converge in Pentecostal and charismatic evangelical Christian worship services. It is as if, she writes, "all the sexuality in the world had been compressed into the relationship between God and believer" (148). Minkowitz observes the following scene at a service led by a charismatic women's group:

> On the stage, Alicia, a twenty-two-year-old with long hair and a voice like Debbie Gibson, starts singing about Jesus as though he were a perfect boyfriend: "'Tis so sweet to trust in Jesus, / Just to take him at his word. / Just to rest upon his promise" . . . she cheeps endless variations on this happy theme: song after song about how he's going to come and make her whole again, fulfill all her yearnings, free her from everything that isn't beautiful. By the fifth ballad, women are looking up at God with private smiles. "Jesus, Jesus, how I trust him," Alicia warbles, "How I trust him night and day." Women start to jump and holler, as though they had just remembered a steamy date. "Oh, she really gets me *on fire!*" Gina says when she takes over from the singer. Gina, who's a professional cosmetologist with a ravenous air, gets the atmosphere even hotter. "He is so madly in love with you," she croons. (169)

Later, the worship leaders invite all the mothers in the audience onstage, where they begin to pray together, chant, speak in tongues, and become "slain in the Spirit," falling backward ecstatically into each other's arms. More women come forward as the atmosphere becomes more and more emotionally charged: "Women pitch and totter as Gina invites Jesus to enter them ('In Jesus' name! In Jesus' name! Oh God, fill her, fill her, fill her, *in Jesus' name!'*), invokes S/M [sadomasochistic] imagery ('Oh, I pray you bring the harnesses upon her, Lord!'), and makes teasing noises like a coquette ('*Ohhh* God! *Ohhh* Holy Spirit!')." Finally, the eroticism culminates in audience call and response chants of "*Ain't nobody do me like Jesus!*" (169).

The use of erotic language to describe closeness to the divine persists in charismatic worship services like those Minkowitz describes as well as in the broader evangelical Christian movement's publications.[7] The bestseller *The Sacred Romance*, which has sold over 400,000 copies to date, invites readers to see the biblical text as a "great Love Story" in which the hero is God, the "Ageless Romancer," and human beings the Beloved. God is a "wild," "passionate," "fiery" lover who has "loved us before the beginning of time, has come for us, and now calls us to journey toward him, with him, for the consummation of our love," the authors assert (97). In a sequel to the book written for women, we read that "every woman in her heart of hearts longs for three things: to be romanced, to play an irreplaceable role in a great adventure, and to unveil beauty," much like in a fairy tale or epic romance.[8] Woman "at her core was made for romance," and should look to Eve as her model, "glorious, powerful, and captivating," the crown of all creation and the pinnacle of both God's and Adam's desire (19). The book concludes by rapturously exhorting women to respond to Jesus' "invitation," declaring, "You are sought after, pursued, romanced, the passionate desire of your Fiancé, Jesus" (217). While *The Sacred Romance* and its sequels may be the most popular examples, they repeat themes common to evangelical women's literature in which desire for union with the deity is often expressed in sexualized language.

The back cover of Cynthia Held's book *Becoming a Woman of Prayer* promises to help readers "respond to God's invitation to deeper intimacy with Him." The first chapter, entitled "An Invitation to Intimacy," begins by declaring: "The eternal, majestic God of the universe wants to be intimate with us! He longs to love, to refresh, to encourage us." She explains how "Scriptures portray God's desire for our intimacy with Him." Elizabeth George's book, *A Woman after God's Own Heart*, boasts 600,000 copies in print and several editions. George writes: "To be God's woman, to love Him fervently with a whole heart, is our sole desire" (14). She encourages readers to "start fresh with God by giving him all that you are, all that you have. . . . Give God 'your life' and 'your body' and 'place them in God's

---

7. In his study of Pentecostal spirituality, Cox notes that, while sensitive to sexual subtext or, as he puts it, charges of "sexual hanky panky under cover of prayer," the image of God as lover, "wooing" and "courting" human beings and being "heartbroken" when they reject "his gentle advances," remains primary in the tradition (Cox 2001, 200–201).

8. Indeed, *Captivating* (Eldredge and Eldredge 2005, 8) quotes the stories of Cinderella and Anna and the King, as well as such films as *Pretty Woman*, *Titanic*, and *Lord of the Rings*, almost as often as it quotes scripture to support its assertions.

loving hands to do with them what He will' " (19). She instructs readers to "develop the habit of drawing near to God"; she then considers where one might do that: "Right now my bed is my place" (31). Later she writes, "I know that, like me, you want to walk so closely with Him that his fragrance permeates all of your life" (44). Kay Arthur's book, winner of the Gold Medallion, is suggestively entitled *His Imprint, My Expression: Changed Forever by the Master's Touch.* The back cover indicates that the book "Identifies the soul's deep longing to be shaped by the Master's own hand." Equally suggestive in its title is *Fingerprints of God: Recognizing God's Touch on Your Life*, by Jennifer Rothschild, which reveals that "God's touch is not skin to skin, but it's just as real. No human touch can be so intimate, so true." Catherine Martin dedicates her book *A Heart That Dances: Satisfy Your Desire for Intimacy with God* to her "intimate friends," the first of whom is "Jesus Christ, the lover of my soul / Who was the first One to call me friend / Who has been faithful to the uttermost / Who has moved and romanced me / From the very beginning." Her husband follows next, after Jesus.

Other books employ "romance theology" even more explicitly and consistently. In *Sex and the Soul of a Woman: The Reality of Love and Romance in an Age of Casual Sex*, Paula Rinehart advises women who need time to heal from a relationship or who have made poor choices in their relationships:

> Immerse yourself in a relationship with a very different man, one who will never let you down—the Son of Man, Jesus. He is more real than anyone you or I will ever share a meal or a bed with. I can promise that you will be safe in his company as have women throughout the ages. You will be valued, protected, and enjoyed. . . . Innumerable women echo just that: "No one ever loved me like Jesus." (134–35).

Rinehart explains that "there is something incredibly attractive about Jesus as a man. There has to be, because throughout the ages women who feel like cast-off rejects, who fear they've screwed up their lives beyond recognition, have found the shelter of a huge rock in Jesus Christ." Rinehart encourages readers to "get to know him" and that "getting to know him is mostly about letting him in—letting ourselves be loved by him. . . . He is jealous of your love. His purifying gaze will heal even as it penetrates your soul." When human sex fails, Rinehart encourages readers to look to God for a fulfilling, meaningful relationship. As she recounts the stories of various women she has counseled, Rinehart's book is peppered with phrases such as "For six months, God and I dated exclusively" (152).

A book that shows up on the recommended reading list on a number of websites for Christian women is *Do You Think I'm Beautiful? The Question Every Woman Asks*, by Angela Thomas. The book comes with companion *Bible Study and Journal: A Guide to Answering the Question Every Woman Asks*. Thomas invites readers "to awaken your passion and glimpse your deepest desires. To voice your longing to be loved with an ultimate love. And to fall into the embrace of the One who asks you to dance." Thomas prefers passionate love with the divine because human men fall short: "A good man can be wonderful, but he can never be enough, and he can never make you whole. You and I were made for even more. We were made for God." Similarly, "He is swept away by your beauty. He has given you other lovers as gifts, but He is the only Lover who can fill your soul. He is the only One who will ever be enough" (57). In a prayer to God, Thomas writes:

> Are You the One who longs for me—the One who can fill this desire to be known? . . . What will You do with me if I show You everything? Every desire? Every longing? . . . If I am exposed before You, will You still love me? . . . Will You hold me and care for me in the dark? Oh, God, hold me, please hold me and tell me that You love me. Tell me that I am desirable. Tell me that You'll fight for me. Tell me that I am beautiful. (12)

She then says that she heard God "speak into my heart": "Yes, Angela, I think you are beautiful. . . . Are you tired of hoping that someone else could fill the place that was meant for Me? I see you, all of you, and you do not have to hide anymore. . . . I am crazy about you. I am the answer for your longing" (12–13). The book is replete with similar prayers and responses from the deity. One more example: "Take all of me, please, take everything. Turn on Your floodlight in my soul and do not leave anything in the shadows. Lay me open. . . . I'm ready to show You everything. . . . Whatever it's going to take, let's do it now. Break me if that is what it takes. Don't hold back. Don't string me along. Bring it on" (186).

As a final example, we consider one book directed specifically to mothers: *The Contemplative Mom: Restoring Rich Relationship with God in the Midst of Motherhood*, by Ann Kroeker, a tome rife with sexualized language. The first chapter, entitled "Our Richest Relationship," and begins this way:

> Imagine the early days of a romance. Late-night phone calls, long walks hand-in-hand. Whispered secrets. Emotional electricity. Legs that turn to butter when you make eye contact across a crowded room. Remember the racing heartbeat, those adoring eyes . . . sweaty palms? . . . Recall the sensations, pleasure, and delight, the inexpressible joy of being with your beloved. . . . Now consider this: God wants this with you. . . . He longs for the inexpressible joy with you . . . the fresh thrill of enthusiastic love, the passion for His presence. . . . He wants us to know Him in a way we might equate with a healthy marriage. (1)

She continues, "As the Holy Spirit, He penetrates and inhabits us, knowing us more intimately than our husbands do" (2). Kroeker asserts that, since it takes more time to develop intimacy with the Lord than it does with one's husband, mothers are to schedule "Time Alone with the Beloved," the title of the second chapter. She writes: "When we do find a place and time to bare our souls to the Lord, . . . we experience Him at a level we might never have thought possible—especially if we've been satisfying ourselves with nothing more than a quick devotional thought before sprinting out the door" (20). For Kroeker, "quickies" with God are good, but finding quality time to experience real intimacy is much better. God, indeed, is the ultimate and ideal lover: "We wish for exclusive time with our Prince, our King, our Bridegroom. . . . He stands by our side, defending us, like a supernatural knight in shining armor. He embodies relational ideals and surpasses them all. Oh, how we crave a depth of relationship with God beyond our wildest imagination!" (3).

Of course, being a mother makes pursuing intimacy with God more difficult, as she notes in detail: "There is this big glitch. It's the whole 'mom' thing. Doggone it. If we were strictly 'contemplatives,' as we might picture a nun, let's say, then maybe we could easily foster this kind of intimacy with God" (3). She then wistfully describes at length the life of a nun. She writes, "There would be so many advantages we don't have now: We'd slip on a symbolic ring to represent a marriage of sorts to the Lord Jesus Christ."[9] For Kroeker, the ideal life is one of marriage to God; her life as a mother pales in comparison and creates "restrictions" and "challenges" to developing intimacy with God. As one of the blurbs on the back cover appropriately explains, the book "gives busy, loving, kid-centered mothers permission to rest, like a tired child, in God's strong arms."

All of the above books, or most of them, are recommended reading on websites for Christian mothers. In looking at this material, the language of relationship and union with God expressed in sexualized and romanticized terms is apparent. The writers emphasize the care, concern, and tenderness of the divine, but equally if not more important is the *maleness* of Jesus and God because it becomes a central feature by which women can enter into close relationship with the deity. This is in contrast to the complexity of biblical and medieval imagery, which often link care, gentleness, and tenderness with maternal aspects of God. Elisabeth Schüssler Fiorenza has noted that today's preoccupation with the maleness of Jesus occurs in tandem with wider political and cultural issues. In the context of the religious right, "the combination of Protestant revival methods with the cultural romance narrative—Jesus loves me so!—seeks to secure the loyalty of Christian wo/men. Jesus becomes commodified and commercialized in terms of heterosexuality and wo/men's desire for the perfect man, the knight in shining armor who will rescue and truly love them" (145).

In her classic study *Reading the Romance*, Janice Radway analyzes the popularity of romance novels among middle-class white women in the United States. She argues that these texts have special appeal for women

---

9. It is interesting to note that Kroeker, as well as the authors in the Sacred Romance series, reference and romanticize the contemplative and mystical traditions as examples of the kind of relationship with God that they advocate. Indeed, *The Sacred Romance* and *Captivating* cite medieval women mystics repeatedly. This has occasioned no small amount of approbation from Christian critics that their theology is heretical for both its views of God as a desiring being and women as the object of that desire.

who are wives and mothers, as it allows a form of escape from the burden of traditional caregiving roles. As readers and writers of romance novels, Radway argues,

> these women are participating in a collectively elaborated female fantasy that unfailingly ends at the precise moment when the heroine is gathered into the arms of the hero who declares his intention to protect her forever because of his desperate love and need for her. These women are telling themselves a story whose central vision is one of total surrender where all danger has been expunged, thus permitting the heroine to relinquish self-control. Passivity *is* at the heart of the romance experience in the sense that the final goal of each narrative is the creation of that perfect union where the ideal male, who is masculine and strong yet nurturant too, finally recognizes the intrinsic worth of the heroine. Thereafter, she is required to do nothing more than *exist* as the center of this paragon's attention. Romantic escape is, therefore, a temporary but literal denial of the demands women recognize as an integral part of their roles as nurturing wives and mothers. It is also a figurative journey to a utopian state of total receptiveness where the reader, as a result of her identification with the heroine, feels herself the *object* of someone else's attention and solicitude. Ultimately, the romance permits its reader the experience of feeling cared for and the sense of having been reconstituted affectively, even if both are lived only vicariously. (97)

In that sense, Radway claims, romance novels are "compensatory literature," providing women with an "emotional release" from the confines of traditional caregiving roles. Similarly, the evangelical Christian women's texts discussed above can be said to construct another kind of female fantasy, one of "total surrender" to perfect union with the ideal male par excellence, Jesus/God, who is seen to embody that ideal romance-hero combination of masculinity, strength, and care.[10] Passively constituted by the all-encompassing, overwhelming love and devotion of the divine, her intrinsic worth recognized and her salvation assured, the female subject is free to "relinquish self-control" and, if only temporarily, escape from her demanding roles as wife and mother, surrendering herself to perfect union with a divine lover in whose arms she can rest.

The romance motif functions also to construct an alternative, ideal family in contrast to the inevitable disappointments of the real one. Marie Griffith suggests that imagery of Jesus as lover indicates an implicit critique of the status quo: "In place of uncommunicative and generally inadequate husbands, God or Jesus may act as the romantic lover-husband, ever

---

10. Indeed, an analysis of popular artistic representations of Jesus indicates a move from more "feminized" portrayals of Christ to more "masculine" ones during the course of the twentieth century, the latter portrayals bearing sometimes striking resemblances to the stylized male heroes on the covers of romance novels. See McDannell 1995, 186–93.

faithful and solicitous of his beloved's needs" (178). Through the power of prayer, evangelical women are encouraged to feel totally accepted and loved by Jesus/God even as they also accept their imperfect husbands and restrictive, often unsatisfying caregiving roles. Yet prayer also becomes the powerful medium by which these roles may be transformed. That is, imagining Jesus as one's husband or conversely one's husband as Jesus and acting accordingly may produce real and lasting effects in one's relationships, based on the "conviction that God can transform men into tender creatures more closely resembling the gentle Jesus whom they adore" (207).

Conclusion

The preceding analysis indicates that when evangelical women today represent God and Jesus as lover and husband, they are tapping into a long tradition in which sexuality and spirituality are associated. From the ambiguous stories of conception in the Hebrew Bible, to anxiety in the earliest Christian texts regarding the manner of Mary's conception of Jesus, to the rich use of the language of erotic desire in the patristic and medieval mystical traditions, to the ideology of romance and the fantasy of the "perfect man" that we see today, sexuality and spirituality persist in a "messy entanglement." Some of the richness and ambiguity of the past has been lost in the present discourse, however, as much of the contemporary rhetoric of God/Jesus as lover/husband depends on pop-culture stereotypes about what women need: a strong, masculine, yet nurturing lover-hero who actively pursues and protects, convinced of "his" woman's intrinsic self-worth. Above all, the rhetoric presumes an adherence to traditionally circumscribed social roles of wife and mother, even while it recognizes the burdens of those roles and the need for vicarious escape from them. As literature written for evangelical Christian women who are mothers, the rhetoric of "religious romance" acquires part of its appeal by invoking cultural romance fantasies while simultaneously tapping into the erotic imagery in the biblical and Christian traditions. In so doing, the potentially subversive elements of the Hebrew Bible and Christian mysticism are tempered by a heavy-handed stress on gender essentialism and a naturalized theology of gender roles.

The messy entanglement of sexual desire and desire for God thus intersects with motherhood in such a way as to allow mothers temporary and vicarious escape from their divinely ordained roles as caregivers. They are lovers but also daughters of God, claiming to find "the true path to liberation and this-worldly fulfillment in a committed relationship with a Jesus who is at once father figure and lover" (207). The relationship with their own husbands, sons, and daughters, then, becomes of secondary importance as they commune with the divine. This is a thread that seemingly runs all the way back to the biblical tradition, where the relationship between the mothers—Eve, Sarah, Samson's mother, Hannah, Ruth, and Mary—and their sons is barely developed at all in the narrative. Yet while there may be implicit critique or explicit escape, the underlying theological and cultural framework in which such experiences are interpreted today functions to preserve the status quo by romanticizing and naturalizing it. In this way, the biblical and contemporary mothers analyzed here may be closest to the Mother Goose archetype, with its elements of fairy tale and fantasy.

Works Cited

Ackerman, Susan. 1998. *Warrior, Dancer, Seductress, Queen: Women in Judges and Biblical Israel.* New York: Doubleday.

Alter, Robert. 1983. How Convention Helps Us Read: The Case of the Bible's Annunciation Type-Scene. *Prooftexts* 3:115–30.

Arthur, Kay. 1996. *His Imprint, My Expression: Changed Forever by the Master's Touch.* Eugene, Ore.: Harvest House.

Bal, Mieke. 1988. *Death and Dissymmetry: The Politics of Coherence in the Book of Judges.* Chicago: University of Chicago Press.

Bronner, Leila Leah. 2004. *Stories of Biblical Mothers: Maternal Power in the Hebrew Bible.* Lanham, Md.: University Press of America.

Bynum, Caroline Walker. 1982. *Jesus as Mother: Studies in the Spirituality of the High Middle Ages.* Berkeley and Los Angeles: University of California Press.

———. 1987. *Holy Feast and Holy Fast: The Religious Significance of Food to Medieval Women.* Berkeley and Los Angeles: University of California Press.

———. 1992. *Fragmentation and Redemption: Essays on Gender and the Human Body in Medieval Religion.* New York: Zone Books.

Coakley, Sarah. 1999. The Trinity, Prayer, and Sexuality: A Neglected Nexus in the Fathers and Beyond. Unpublished paper presented as the Wattson/White Memorial Lecture, Centro Pro Unione, 16 December 1999.

Cox, Harvey. 2001. *Fire from Heaven: The Rise of Pentecostal Spirituality and the Reshaping of Religion in the Twenty-First Century.* Cambridge: Da Capo.

Curtis, Brent, and John Eldredge. 1997. *The Sacred Romance: Drawing Closer to the Heart of God.* Nashville: Nelson.

Douglas, Ann. 1998. *The Feminization of American Culture.* New York: Noonday Press.

Eilberg-Schwartz, Howard. 1994. *God's Phallus and Other Problems for Men and Monotheism.* Boston: Beacon.

Eldredge, John, and Stasi Eldredge. 2005. *Captivating: Unveiling the Mystery of a Woman's Soul.* Nashville: Nelson.

George, Elizabeth. 1997. *A Woman after God's Own Heart.* Eugene, Ore.: Harvest House.

Griffith, R. Marie. 1997. *God's Daughters: Evangelical Women and the Power of Submission.* Berkeley and Los Angeles: University of California Press.

Held, Cynthia. 2005. *Becoming a Woman of Prayer.* Colorado Springs: NavPress.

Hollywood, Amy. 1995. *The Soul as Virgin Wife: Mechthild of Magdeburg, Marguerite Porete, and Meister Eckhart.* Notre Dame, Ind.: University of Notre Dame Press.

Jantzen, Grace. 1995. *Power, Gender, and Christian Mysticism.* Cambridge Studies in Ideology and Religion 8. Cambridge: Cambridge University Press.

Klein, Lillian. 1990. *The Triumph of Irony in the Book of Judges*. Sheffield: Sheffield Academic Press.

———. 1994. Hannah: Marginalized Victim and Social Redeemer. Pages 77–92 in *A Feminist Companion to Samuel and Kings*. Edited by Athalya Brenner. Sheffield: Sheffield Academic Press.

Kroeker, Ann. 2000. *The Contemplative Mom: Restoring Rich Relationship with God in the Midst of Motherhood*. Colorado Springs: Shaw.

Lacan, Jacques. 1985. *Feminine Sexuality*. Edited by Juliet Mitchell and Jacqueline Rose. New York: W. W. Norton.

Martin, Catherine. 2003. *A Heart That Dances: Satisfy Your Desire for Intimacy with God*. Colorado Springs: NavPress.

McDannell, Colleen. 1995. *Material Christianity: Religion and Popular Culture in America*. New Haven: Yale University Press.

Miller, Julie. 1999. Eroticized Violence in Medieval Women's Mystical Literature: A Call for a Feminist Critique. *JFSR* 15:25–49.

Minkowitz, Donna. 1998. *Ferocious Romance: What My Encounters with the Right Taught Me about Sex, God, and Fury*. New York: Free Press.

Pardes, Ilana. 1992. *Countertraditions in the Bible: A Feminist Approach*. Cambridge: Harvard University Press.

Radway, Janice. 1984. *Reading the Romance: Women, Patriarchy, and Popular Culture*. Chapel Hill: University of North Carolina Press.

Reinhartz, Adele. 1994. Samson's Mother: An Unnamed Protagonist. Pages 157–70 in *A Feminist Companion to Judges*. Edited by Athalya Brenner. Sheffield: Sheffield Academic Press.

Rinehart, Paula. 2004. *Sex and the Soul of a Woman: The Reality of Love and Romance in an Age of Casual Sex*. Grand Rapids: Zondervan.

Rothschild, Jennifer. 2005. *Fingerprints of God: Recognizing God's Touch on Your Life*. Sisters, Ore.: Multnomah.

Schaberg, Jane. 1987. *The Illegitimacy of Jesus: A Feminist Theological Interpretation of the Infancy Narratives*. San Francisco: Harper and Row.

———. 1998. The Infancy of Mary of Nazareth. Pages 708–27 in *A Feminist Commentary*. Vol. 2 of *Searching the Scriptures*. Edited by Elisabeth Schüssler Fiorenza. New York: Crossroad.

Schüssler Fiorenza, Elisabeth. 2000. *Jesus and the Politics of Interpretation*. New York: Continuum, 2000.

Shields, Mary. 1993. Subverting a Man of God, Elevating a Woman: Role and Power Reversals in 2 Kings 4. *JSOT* 58:59–69.

Thomas, Angela. 2003. *Do You Think I'm Beautiful? The Question Every Woman Asks*. Nashville: Nelson.

Van Dijk-Hemmes, Fokkelien. 1994. The Great Woman of Shunem and the Man of God: A Dual Interpretation of 2 Kings 4:8–37. Pages 218–30 in *A Feminist Companion to Samuel and Kings*. Edited by Athalya Brenner. Sheffield: Sheffield Academic Press.

9

Jesus and His Mother

AN ANALYSIS OF THEIR PUBLIC RELATIONSHIP AS A PARADIGM FOR AFRICAN WOMEN (WIDOWS) WHO MUST CIRCUMVENT TRADITIONAL AUTHORITY IN ORDER TO THRIVE IN SOCIETY

Andrew M. Mbuvi

> *But if [African] women appropriate both our Christian and African heritages, we can be social commentators on behalf of justice and true religion as well as cultic functionaries. We can be prophets in our churches, like Anna, who saw in the baby Jesus the vision of a New World (Luke 2:36–38), as well as prophets like the Ahemaa and the Iyalode who stood for social justice and women's participation in political decisions.*
>
> —M. A. Oduyoye (2002, 174)

Introduction

The typical African church's characterization of Mary as "mama Maria" (a Mother Goose caricature) seems to subjugate her image to the norms of society's expectation of women (timid, submissive, voiceless, etc.), instead of challenging them. The resultant perpetuation of the traditional patriarchal African marginalization of women (widows) must be confronted by a different understanding of Mary based upon an analysis of the public relationship between Mary (a widow?) and her son Jesus. The scourge of HIV/AIDS, by exponentially expanding the population of widows in the continent, has made the plight of the widow in Africa a desperate concern that demands immediate attention" (Bongmba 2007, 110–15).

To get a glimpse of the African widow's plight, listen to the following account:

Imagine being an African woman with 8 children, trying to make ends meet by living on the average Kenyan wage of $1 a day. Up by 4:00 am building a fire to make tea for the kids. While the fire is gaining some momentum, she rushes to a neighbor's house to buy some fresh milk. By 5:30 am she pulls the kids out of bed, bathes them, gives them a cup of tea (no bread because she can't afford it) then by 6:30 [am] she sends them off to school. They have to leave so early because of the two mile walk and if they are there a minute past 8:00 [am], they will be beaten and sent back home. After the kids leave for school, the African woman washes some clothes (by hand) then sets out walking from garden to garden looking for work, weeding, digging, anything that will bring that $1 so she can buy a meager amount of corn maize and vegetables so the kids don't have to go to bed hungry like they did last night. After a long days work digging, she gets a few shillings, enough to give the kids something for dinner. She arrives home at 7:00 pm to find a small pile of wood the children collected on their way home from school. She builds the fire and cooks the food. By 9:00 pm serves the children dinner. After the meal is finished, she washed the dishes and by 11:30 pm, climbs into bed, exhausted, discouraged, hopeless. The only thing keeping her going is knowing that her children can't survive without her. As she drifts to sleep, she dreams of the days when her husband was alive, when she didn't worry about the 8 mouth's [sic] to feed, when she enjoyed cooking for her family, when life wasn't such a burden. The story of the African widow is all to [sic] common. Everywhere I look, everywhere I go, I see her, struggling for her life and for the lives of her children. (Lipparelli 2007)

Traditionally, the extended family played a significant role in taking care of widows in African communities, with even some, like the Luo of Kenya, providing a sibling to marry the widow (levirate marriage) in order to keep her provided for by the husband's family. But with rapid migration, urbanization, and transformation of African economies by colonialism and postcolonialism, the strain on the family unit has virtually shredded the extended family. Compounding this, HIV/AIDS has reduced the age of the average widow from middle-aged and above to between the mid-twenties and fifty. The widow and the orphan, the most vulnerable in society, have lost the support they used to have.

In the case of the Luos, for example, it has forced a change of the levirate marriage system as siblings refuse to marry a widow, especially if her husband died of HIV/AIDS (Bongmba 2007, 51–117). The result is a two-fold stigma—the family rejects her and then no one else wants her, especially if she is herself potentially infected with the disease. As a result, such widows, often with their children, are essentially kicked out of their deceased husband's families and denied any inheritance, ending up with no one to provide for them (Bongmba 2007, 113).

Putting it in rather stark terms, the United Nations' secretary general's special envoy on HIV/AIDS for African states, Stephen Lewis, states, "For the African continent it means economic and social survival. For the women and girls of Africa, it's a matter of life or death (Bongmba 2007, 35). Given the African church's crucial role in the ministry to many widows, it has an indispensible responsibility in calling to task the aspects of the patriarchal social structure that have inhibited the empowerment of widows, resulting in the devastation of the HIV/AIDS pandemic (Bongmba 2007, 114).

This paper reconstitutes an image of Mary that can inspire the African widow by arguing for an understanding of Mary as widow who manages to overcome serious odds raised by the cultural structures of her community, a Mother Jones image. An examination of the public relationship of Mary and Jesus is an important window through which we will see how Mary negotiates these cultural norms. Hopefully, that image would become an inspiration to the African widow (woman) as a catalyst of subversive tendencies that would challenge the negative impact of patriarchal African cultural norms, which, in effect, have only served as a vehicle in spreading HIV/AIDS.

Reconstituting the Image of Mary for Africa

In a recent book titled *Mary for Evangelicals*, Tim Perry identifies two ways in which Mary is depicted in the New Testament: as "a symbol" and as "a person" (Perry 2006, 263).[1] It is the latter image of Mary the person that needs to be recovered in order for the ordinary folk like the poor African widow to be able to identify with her. As Gaventa and Rigby rightly assert, "[t]o elevate Mary to a status beyond ordinary personhood is to abdicate the very hope of the incarnation" (Gaventa and Rigby 2002, 3). The church, especially the Roman Catholic Church, by projecting a medieval image of Mary that highlights her basically as "mother of God," completely loses the image of a vulnerable, bold, and courageous young widow who confronts society's structural norms. Part of recovering of the image of Mary the person is to see how the New Testament texts portray Mary, who in the midst of her very human struggles, manages to navigate subversively through cultural norms that sought to confine her. This is the image of Mary that the African church should strive to recover (Bongmba 2007, 110–12).

Establishing Mary's Widowhood

Recovery of Mary the person must include clarification of her status as a widow. While it is not possible to be absolutely conclusive on the matter, I believe there is sufficient ground on which to view Mary as a widow by the time of Jesus' public ministry. Several factors support this conclusion. First, none of the public encounters of Jesus and his family includes his father (Mark 3:31–35; Matt 12:46–50; Luke 8:19–21; John 2:1–12). The only exception of Joseph in a public interaction with Jesus is in the Lukan nar-

---

1. While Tim Perry proceeds to talk of the significance of the *Theotokos* in this endeavor, our interest in this paper does not take us in that direction.

rative of Jesus, as a twelve-year-old, being left behind in Jerusalem (Luke 2:40–52).

Second, when the Gospel of Mark, which does not have Jesus' infancy narratives, lists Jesus' family members, there is no connection to Joseph and, strangely, identifies Jesus with his mother instead (Mark 3:31–35; 6.3; 15:40; see also Matt 13:55). Even when put in the mouths of his village mates who took offense at his words, the identification of Jesus with Mary instead of Joseph is most peculiar (Mark 6:1–3).[2] In comparison, while James and John abandon their families to follow Jesus (Mark 1:16–20), they are always referred to as the sons of Zebedee, their father (Mark 3:17; 10:35; see also "James son of Alpheus" in Mark 3:18 and "Judas son of James" in Luke 6:16).

One could argue that it may simply be a way in which the community was denigrating Jesus' ministry, but that would not make complete sense. If the people were trying to shame Jesus, why omit reference to the father figure who is the public face of the family? But if Joseph is dead and Jesus has failed to take his role as the oldest male representative of the family, then Mary may have been forced to assume the public face of her family, thereby subverting some aspects of the community's norms (see Matt 7:29; Mark 1:21–22; Luke 4:32). This in and of itself would make Jesus' family something of a laughing stock in the community and partly explain the community's reluctance to embrace Jesus and his claims (Mark 6:3).

Third, the Fourth Gospel has Mary somewhat forcing Jesus' hand when she makes him respond to the potentially embarrassing lack of a sufficient amount of wine at a wedding in Cana by miraculously turning water into wine (John 2:1–12). Again, there is no indication that Joseph is present. In fact, at the end of the Fourth Gospel, Jesus hands over his mother to "adoption" by the beloved disciple, who takes her into his own home (John 19:25–27). If Joseph were still alive, there is absolutely no way this would happen. How can a young friend of Mary's son adopt her, if Mary has a husband to take care of her?

Fourth, the Luke-Acts list of people gathering with the disciples at the upper room after Jesus' resurrection (Acts 1:14) includes "Mary the mother of Jesus and his brothers."[3] Once again, there is no mention of Joseph.

Cumulatively, these texts strongly suggest a total absence of Joseph in the family during Jesus' public ministry, which can best be explained by death. If Joseph were still alive at this point, this consistent avoidance of identifying him would be virtually unlikely, given the fact that in patriar-

---

2. Even if one was to argue that later redactors with the intention of establishing a higher Christology eliminated any human fatherhood for Jesus in these references, the move is still quite unprecedented.

3. Even when Luke 8:19–21 copies this list from Mark 3:31–35, he omits the reference to "sisters."

chal societies the father is one with whom the family is publically identified (Elliot 1993, 129).

Jesus and His Mother: An Evaluation of Their Public Encounters

The reports of Jesus as a young person (Matt 1–2; Luke 1–3) indicate the presence of a father.[4] As we have seen, however, subsequent listings of Jesus' family strangely omit any reference to Joseph, allowing for postulation as to his demise before Jesus' public ministry (Mark 3:31–35; see also 6:3; Matt 12:46–50; John 2:3–10; 19:25–27). The death of the father would allow for a less precarious widow situation if they had a son: "When the father dies he will not seem to be dead, for he has left behind him one like himself, whom in his life he looked upon with joy and at death, without grief" (Sir 30:4–6). However, Jesus may have failed to follow through on this family responsibility of family leadership when he began his public ministry, leading to the tension-filled public encounters with his mother.

As Stegemann and Stegemann have pointed out, "Gender-specific behavior was generally embedded in the fundamental values of Mediterranean societies and was oriented toward the concepts of honor, shame, and disgrace" (1999, 367). For this reason, John H. Elliott explains, "the honor and shame of the family are symbolized by the male family head (paterfamilias) and his sons and by his wife and daughters, respectively" (Elliott 1993, 129). In fact, in a list in 1 Macc 5:23, the men seem to be distinct from the rest of their families, which are grouped together with property: "Simon brought the Jews of Galilee and Arbatta, along with their families and their possessions, to Judea. When they arrived, everyone was shouting and celebrating."

The expectation for the son is not only to continue the legacy of his family, but also to assume some of the *paterfamilias* roles that used to be played by the father, defending both the honor and interests of the family (Balla 2005, 86–105). For example, the son becomes the rightful heir of the family property and, if old enough, assumes role of the breadwinner for the family (Stegemann and Stegemann 1999, 367–69; Elliott 1993, 129). In this regard, the son that is old enough (thirteen years and above?) has the mandate to take the reins of the household at the demise of the father, overshadowing the mother. He becomes the public face (the male domain) of the family (Balla 2005, 87).

Thus it is no surprise, then, that whenever we encounter Jesus and his

---

4. Luke includes a caveat in his genealogy when he includes an aside that indicated Joseph was really not the biological father of Jesus even though people thought it to be so (Luke 3:23). Even in the Lukan narrative of Jesus as a twelve-year-old mistakenly left behind in Jerusalem, it is Mary who assumes the role of the parent-spokesperson by reprimanding Jesus, while Joseph silently stands by (Luke 2:40–52).

mother's public interactions in the Gospels, they usually appear to be ill at ease, somewhat strained, and even, to say the least, conflict ridden. The conversations seem to revolve around what the mother perceives Jesus should be doing and how he should be dealing with the given situations, be it a private wedding (John 2:1–12) or public preaching ministry (Mark 3:31–35).

While the Gospels do not address the absence of Joseph prior to the listings, it is rather peculiar that it is the mother with whom Jesus' family is identified (Mark 3:31; 6:3). If Joseph is indeed dead, as we have maintained, then one might have expected that the more appropriate social listing for the Gospel writers to maintain would be identifying the brothers of Jesus (male progeny) first, and then the mother, and then sisters (Elliott 1993, 129). As such, perhaps the Gospel writers might be intent on highlighting Christianity's peculiar cultural transformation or a downplaying of gender roles (see Gal 3:28) by shifting around the order of names. This might be the Gospel writers' way of surreptitiously and subtly handing the traditional role of the *paterfamilias* to the widow, the matriarch of the family (*materfamilias?*).

Jesus, being the firstborn, would have naturally assumed this mantle in his family. However, the itinerancy of his public ministry seems to suggest that Jesus might have sidestepped these social duties, causing some consternation in the family (see Mark 6:3–5). At some point, Jesus' mother, together with his siblings, comes to the conclusion that her son has become a public disgrace to the family and is probably not in his right mind (Mark 3:31–35; Matt 12:46–50; Luke 8:19–21). Because of this recognition, she sets out on a mission to ensure that Jesus leaves the public sphere and returns to the family fold, where he would exercise his socially mandated role. According to Bruce Malina, it was normal for families to seek out and try to conceal a member whose behavior was perceived as potentially shameful for the family (Malina 1993, 80).

Such a move by the mother of Jesus has to be perceived as a fairly bold one, since first-century Mediterranean societies maintained a strict dichotomy between public domain (male centered) and private domain (female centered) (Malina 1993, 129). Jesus' mother, in the tradition of Jewish heroines (Judith, Deborah, mother of the seven sons in 4 Macc 14–17), challenges a cultural mandate of male leadership by assuming the role of her now-deceased husband as family head and giving voice to her needs and concerns. Negotiating, and perhaps even stretching these boundaries by Mary, is what provides for the awkward public encounters of Jesus and his mother.

The image of Mary that emerges is not that of a docile and reclusive widow but one not afraid to bend or break rules and challenge customs, one who is determined not to be smothered by the cultural norms that seek to subjugate her. In the midst of what I consider a tenuous argument about the illegitimacy of Jesus, Jane Schaberg rightly maintains that:

> Mary *is a woman who has access to the sacred outside the patriarchal family and its control.* The illegitimate turns out to be a grace not a disgrace, order within disorder. On the basis of belief in the Holy Spirit who empowers the conception of Jesus and his resurrection, and who creates and elects all, a community is believed possible. (Schaberg 1990, 199, emphasis added)

I think Schaberg's point of Mary's "access" unbridled by society's cultural norms needs to be pushed a little further and point to its transformation of the emerging Christian society. Ultimately, these liberation and egalitarian tendencies embodied in Mary can provide a premise or template on which to ground a biblical emancipation of the widow in the African community, to which we now turn.

African Patriarchy, HIV/AIDS, and African Widows

The Roman Catholic Church's characterization of Mary as the "Mother of God" seems to preclude any balanced analysis of the relationship between Jesus and Mary in its basic human terms (Gaventa and Rigby 2002, 3). The Protestant church's reaction of virtually ignoring the significance of Mary in the relationship with her son Jesus is no less misplaced (ix–xii). Beyond the Christmas story, Mary does not seem to play any significant role in the daily spiritual life of most in the Protestant church.

Tim Perry uses the categories of "Mary the symbol" and "Mary the person" to distinguish between the ecclesial and biblical construction of Mary, respectively. Perry correctly points out that "Mary the symbol" has so overwhelmed "Mary the person" in the history of the Western church that the latter has almost virtually disappeared (Perry 2006, 263). Accordingly, the need to focus on "Mary the person" must be maintained to balance things and recover a more relevant image of Mary. The more pertinent element, however, is how Perry describes the latter Mary as "one who hovers on the margins of her society and on the fringes of the biblical text" (263). This same statement, *mutatis mutandis*, would aptly characterize the African widow who, in various ways, is marginalized and on the fringes of society.

Needless to say, then, the recovery of "Mary the person" would inevitably be inextricably bound in the recovery of the plight of the African widow. As Nwachuku explains, "the African widow is a neglected and deserted lonely woman" (Nwachuku 1992, 61). Nwachuku thus insists on the need to treat the African woman as a "whole person" worthy of dignity (71). The worth and value of the woman cannot simply remain within the African traditional parameters of assessment: marriage and procreation (Nasimiyu-Wasike 1992, 106). A different denominator must emerge.

The picture thus painted needs to be compared to the African widow and the scourge of the HIV/AIDS pandemic in Africa that has left many women as widows and heads of households. With the pandemic of HIV/

AIDS in Africa, it is the mother who seems to be suffering the loss of husband and sons (Bongmba 2007, 2–10). This does not mean that women and children are not dying or being affected; rather, the ones already suffering on the margins of society are now even worse off. The characterization of Mary in Africa mainly as "mama Maria" tends more or less to subsume her within the African tradition, which while respecting her as "mother," still confines her to the domestic sphere (Nasimiyu-Wasike 1997, 175). Maria is the picture of a humble, obedient, and uncontroversial figure. However, as it has been maintained so far, this docile image of Mary, especially when read in relation to her public relationship to her son Jesus, cannot be upheld and is not healthy or helpful.

The medieval church's portrayal of Mary as simply the image of virtue and piety, which was transferred "hook, line, and sinker" into the Africa community by European missionaries with little regard to its biblical context or relevance for the people of Africa has to be replaced (see Nasimiyu-Wasike 1997, 175; Oduyoye 2002, 185–87; Okure 1995, 196–210; Maseno 2004, 125–35). This image of Mary does little to identify with and challenge the poverty and suffering of women in Africa. She is a sanitized Mary who is far removed from the image of Mary found in the biblical texts, who in her own humble estate and widowhood would identify with that of the African widow. Her courage in challenging the social structures of first-century Jewish Palestine would provide the model for the African widow to be resourceful and challenge the African church to support her, forcing the society to rethink its not-so-useful traditions (Bongmba 2007, 111).

Traditionally, the place of the mother in the African culture is one of supreme importance and recognition. A mother is honored and respected. One of the worst-case scenarios is for a child to bring shame or dishonor to his or her mother by disregard or affront. Insulting one's mother amounts to committing sacrilege, and society frowns at it. Yet, with no right to inheritance in most of these African communities, the widow (and the orphan) has borne the brunt of the worst impact of HIV/AIDS on African communities. Not surprisingly, then, the widows—the face of vulnerability, suffering, and neglect—have become the growing concern of the African -church (Bongmba 2007, 1–4). The African church itself continues to falter partly by uncritically perpetuating within its own structure the same African patriarchal system that gives very little voice to women.

The African widow must be encouraged by the church, in its reconstruction of Mary the person, to seek proactive means that would subversively empower her and alleviate her from her plight as victim of society and of the ills of HIV/AIDS. Finding ways to challenge the system to action on her behalf is a significant motivation given by the mother of Jesus and is the challenge given to the African church. The patriarchal structure and its subjugation of women (widows), even within the church, have to be challenged by a biblical reconstruction of Mary the person. The African widow must become a catalyst of subversive tendencies, especially in the church, that would challenge the negative impact of the cultural norms of patriarchal African society, which, in effect, have only served as a vehicle in spreading the HIV/AIDS disease in the continent.

Writing on the plight of widows in Africa, Daisy Nwachuku decries the situation: "There is today a great deal of ambivalence or dualism among many African Christians when issues touch on life threatening traditional beliefs or superstitions: this explains the continued ritualistic treatment of the widow even when she is a Christian" (Nwachuku 1992, 61). By essentially perpetuating the patriarchal structures within the church, leaving the predominantly male leadership with a false sense of cultural and "biblical" entitlement has only sustained the maltreatment and neglect of widows. As Mercy Oduyoye maintains, concerning the use of biblical characters as premises for inspiration to African Christian women's struggles, "It is essential that we Christian women celebrate such collaboration as we struggle for liberation from patriarchal structures, political, ecclesiological, and economic. Without these foresisters, . . . we have no history" (Oduyoye and Kanyaro 1992, 182).

While acknowledging complicity of African women in their treatment in society, Oduyoye emphasizes the need for African women to take matters in their own hands, so to speak. Without their involved and engaged participation in the issues that pertain to the society's structure, the status quo will prevail and the suffering of the women (widows) persist: "We must also demand the opportunity to live as independent persons capable of participating in all areas of life, and to develop this model of woman's being in home, church, and country" (Oduyoye and Kanyaro 1992, 184). This is not simply some naïve pontification on the part of Oduyoye. She is fully aware of the challenges that lie ahead: "The most difficult part of re-imaging ourselves and affirming our experience is to articulate our oppression. Our inhibitions are valid because we have been brought up to smile—even when suffering. Any collective hurts we identify are immediately personalized and particularized. We must, therefore, find ways of acting not just as individuals but collectively" (184).

As I have maintained, the recovery of "Mary the person" may perhaps best be determined from her personal public relationship with her son Jesus. In this complex parent-child relationship Mary confronts the traditional strictures of systemic societal binaries of *private* (female) versus *public* (male) spheres (true to both African and first-century Mediterranean cultures). This Mary's actions evoke a Mother Jones–type figure who is willing to challenge those boundaries drawn by society.

Conclusion

Oduyoye is resolutely emphatic and could not be more persuasive when she encourages the African women "to engage in a continuing synthesis of

... past experiences and present possibilities instead of simply accepting the dogmas and lifestyles imposed upon [them] ... by religion or culture" (Oduyoye 2002, 173–74). To this end, she admonishes a reading of the Bible with an openness to possibilities of revitalized understandings that would transform the way we may have thought about things in the past. I have maintained in this paper that the subversive role of Mary in her relationship to Jesus models a way forward for African women (widows). With the help of the Christian community, African widows can circumvent the societal and cultural constrictions, making way for a more liberative experience of their own relationship with Christ and the community. Empowering African women, and widows in particular, would especially be crucial in winning the battle against the HIV/AIDS pandemic in Africa, and a rereading and recasting of the biblical public relationship of Mary and Jesus is an essential starting point.

Works Cited

Balla, Peter. 2005. *Child-Parent Relationship in the New Testament and Its Environment.* Tubingen: Mohr Siebeck, 2003. Repr., Peabody, Mass.: Hendrickson.

Bongmba, Elias Kifon. 2007. *Facing a Pandemic: The African Church and the Crisis of HIV/AIDS.* Waco, Tex.: Baylor University Press.

Elliott, John H. 1993. *What Is Social-Scientific Criticism?* Minneapolis: Fortress.

Gaventa, Beverly, and Cynthia Rigby, eds. 2002. *Blessed One: Protestant Perspectives on Mary.* Louisville: Westminster John Knox.

Katongole, Emmanuel, ed. 2002. *African Theology Today.* Scranton, Pa.: University of Scranton Press.

Kinoti, Hannah W., and John M. Waliggo, eds. 1997. *The Bible in African Christianity: Essays in Biblical Theology.* Nairobi: Acton.

Lipparelli, Daniel. 2007. The African Widow. Online: http://transformedinternational.org/updates.php.

Malina, Bruce. 1993. *Windows on the Time of Jesus: Time Travel in Ancient Judea.* Louisville, Ky.: Westminster John Knox.

Maseno, Loreen. 2004. Feminist Theology in West and East Africa: Convergences and Divergences. *Norsk kvinnelig teologforening* 3–4:125–35.

Meyers, Carol L., Toni Craven, and Ross Shepard Kraemer, eds. 2000. *Women in Scripture: A Dictionary of Named and Unnamed Women in the Hebrew Bible, the Apocryphal/ Deuterocanonical Books, and New Testament.* Grand Rapids: Eerdmans.

Nasimiyu-Wasike, Anne. 1997. Mary the Pilgrim of Faith for African Women. Pages 165–78 in *The Bible in African Christianity: Essays in Biblical Theology.* Edited by Hannah W. Kinoti and John M. Waliggo. Nairobi: Acton.

Nwachuku, Daisy N. 1992. The Christian Widow in African Culture. Pages 54–73 in *The Will to Arise: Women, Tradition, and the Church in Africa.* Edited by Mercy Oduyoye and Musimbi Kanyoro. Maryknoll, N.Y.: Orbis

Oduyoye, M. A. 2002. Acting as Women. Pages 171–88 in *African Theology Today,* vol. 1. Edited by Emmanuel Katongole. Scranton, Pa.: University of Scranton Press.

Oduyoye, Mercy, and Musimbi Kanyoro, eds. 1992. *The Will to Arise: Women, Tradition, and the Church in Africa.* Maryknoll, N.Y.: Orbis.

Okure, Teresa. 1995. The Mother of Jesus in the New Testament: Implications for Women in Mission. *Journal of Inculturation Theology* 3/2:196–210.

Perry, Tim. 2006. *Mary for Evangelicals: Toward an Understanding of the Mother of Our Lord*. Downers Grove, Ill.: InterVarsity Press.

Schaberg, Jane. 1990. *The Illegitimacy of Jesus: A Feminist Theological Interpretation of the Infancy Narratives*. New York: Crossroads.

Stegemann, Ekkehard W., and Wolfgang Stegemann. 1999. *The Jesus Movement: A Social History of Its First Century*. Translated by O. C. Dean. Minneapolis: Fortress.

10

Jesus as Fantasy Mother

Tina Pippin

Jerusalem, Jerusalem, the city that kills the prophets and stones those who are sent to it! How often have I desired to gather your children together as a hen gathers her brood under her wings, and you were not willing! See, your house is left to you, desolate. For I tell you, you will not see me again until you say, "Blessed is the one who comes in the name of the Lord."

— Matthew 23:37–39 [par. Luke 13:33–35]

In fantasy and fairy-tale literature, mothers take on many forms, and in most cases they are absent (*Cinderella* and *Beauty and the Beast*, among others). The interpretive emphasis on both the Matthean and Lukan stories of Jesus' lament over Jerusalem has been on the metaphor of a motherly Jesus, a hen caringly protecting her brood from harm. But what follows in this passage is an apocalyptic judge/ment; unruly (and murderous) children bring about the disappearance of Jesus from their city. I want to examine the Jesus in this passage as an abusive mother who is mirrored in his abusive children, at least as far as the metaphor can extend. The promise of comfort is held out and withdrawn. Fantasy and fairy-tale literature mothers and birds have significant roles—and share themes of flight. I also explore the image of the city as accused murderer, on the verge of a response to the eschatological offer of Jesus.

I want to thank George Aichele for his wonderful insights on an earlier draft of this article.

141

Mother Goose Comes Home to Roost

Mother Goose comes home to roost
Her brood won't follow after.
The Mother calls
The whole world falls
When Mother Goose comes home to roost.

— from *The Apocalyptic Mother Goose*[1]

Mother Goose has been the archetypal grandmotherly teller of children's rhyme. The vision of her in downy white feathers, bonnet, and spectacles brings forth feelings of comfort. She makes finger plays and sings silly songs and lullabies. Even when she sings about bad things happening to misbehaving children, grown-ups, and animals, there is light-hearted rhyme behind the mischief and violence. The eclectic collection of children's poetry creates a fantasyland that mirrors this world over the centuries since the purported first book in around 1765, John Newberry's *Mother Goose's Melody, or Sonnets for the Cradle* (Warner 1998, 195). The multiple authors of the Mother Goose collection have given some universal rhymes and silly stories of humans and animals to us. As John Goldthwaite discovered, "It is not surprising that nursery rhymes should be our most common cultural currency after the Bible. It is Mother Goose who first introduces us to who we are in the world, and it is she who brings us our first make-believe" (Goldthwaite 1996, 15). The nonsense helps children make sense of the world.[2] The fantasy or "make-believe" (Goldthwaite's term) of the Bible also helps to order the chaos of life, and there are many stories directed to children,[3] but Mother Goose has other, less silly, and more sobering tales to tell—of punishment, sickness, and death.

The image of this often-airborne mother on a goose, or as a "quaint old bird" (Goldthwaite 1996, 27)—for all the surface maternal symbols—plays with the gendered image, since the mother is a plurality of anonymous storytellers. Marina Warner notes: "The problem of Mother Goose's dou-

---

1. *The Apocalyptic Mother Goose* is, like all Mother Goose, a made-up book as well as a collection out of my imagination. And like many Mother Goose rhymes, this book includes themes of punishment and judgment. I encourage others to write for this pretend volume.

2. Rather than accept the binary sense-nonsense, Goldthwaite proposes a definition that leads to harmony: "Nonsense might be defined more accurately as a flirtation with disorder, a turning upside down of the world for the pleasure of seeing it come right side up again" (Goldthwaite 1996, 15). In this way apocalyptic literature is nonsensical, but with a more dangerous undertone that leads to destruction, not harmony.

3. Goldthwaite notes that the collection in the book of Proverbs is "the world's oldest surviving children's book" (1996, 4). He acknowledges that there are even older separate stories, like David and Goliath that would have been directed at youth (1996, 361, n. 2).

ble tongue remains: is she truly a female storyteller, only now and then in drag, or does the drag constitute a claim on credence, advanced by men invoking something more authentic in themselves?" (1994, 187). As Mother Goose is a mixed image, so is the Gospel's mother hen. Jesus in drag provokes both male and female interpreters to draw near, to want to be part of her brood, to believe in the authenticity of her stories.

I have always felt an apocalyptic chill when I read some of Mother Goose's rhymes. For example, in "Sing a Song of Sixpence," the blackbird pie baked for the king and queen turns into a Hitchcockian nightmare. The pie is opened, the "four and twenty blackbirds" sing "Wasn't that a dainty dish to set before the king?" then attack the maid: "The maid was in the garden, hanging out the clothes, / When down came a blackbird and snapped off her nose" (DePaola 1985, 13; Addams 1995). In Tomie dePaola's illustration, the birds sit innocently on the castle; one sits on the clothesline near the maid. But in Charles Addams more wicked interpretation, the birds fly around the tower; two are dangerously close to the king and queen, and one nose-dives toward the long nose of the maid. The baker looks on in horror as birds emerge from his pie, while a guard with a crossbow aims at a bird. Similarly, the drawings for "There was an old woman / Lived under a hill, / And if she isn't gone, / She lives there still" vary greatly. DePaola shows the old woman looking out her front door from the green hillside (DePaola 1985, 56). Addams shows a blind woman, with her knitting, her cat, and a warm stove safely ensconced in a brown hill. Outside the landscape is a charred ruins, the burned remains of a nuclear attack.[4]

Both traditional and feminist readings of the Matthean and Lukan versions of Jesus' lament over Jerusalem see a compassionate, maternal Mother Goose figure. Here the mother (Jesus) becomes the bird—a great, protective, winged creature. Consider Joseph Fitzmyer's reading in his commentary on Luke:

> In comparing himself to a mother bird, Jesus uses a readily understood figure for his own love and concern for his contemporaries, manifesting thereby in a new way the salvific interest of God himself, which he was sent to proclaim (Luke 4:43). But Jerusalem will not seek the security of

---

4. On the back cover of the Addams collection, cartoonist Roz Chast adds, "Charles Addams doesn't *have* to alter the original Mother Goose because his drawings take us directly into these little rhymes' creepy, dark heart—the heart we always knew was there from the first time we heard about the four-and twenty blackbirds baked in a pie." I continue to find it curious that, like most children's editions of Mother Goose, biblical scholars alter the apocalyptic biblical texts to make them more palatable. In the *Left Behind* books, LaHaye and Jenkins at least acknowledge the horror of the apocalypse, although in their warped and perverse way they also buy into the violence and anti-Semitism. Neither interpretation rejects the madness of biblical apocalypse(s).

> the protective wings of "heaven-sent wisdom." So it will be left a helpless
> fledgling, its "house" will be left abandoned. (Fitzmeyer 1981–85, 2:1035)

Fitzmeyer interprets this passage as the compassionate bird mother protecting her brood and announcing the coming kingdom. In the midst of
potential anti-Jewish sentiments, Jesus is offering an inclusive protection
package, safe shelter to all who come under his or her wings. A.-J. Levine
comments: "The patriarchal associations of the city are ironically contrasted to Jesus' feminine language: rather than divide individuals into
elites and marginals, he would have gathered the children of Jerusalem
together" (Levine 1988, 53). So Jesus' intentions were good. Levine opts for
an inclusive reading of this passage; Jesus as a mother is a unity figure, and
all who live in the city are her brood. Jesus longs to shelter all of them from
the destruction, but they refuse her. The onus is on them, not Jesus.

The comforting mother-hen image is on the surface a calming image
of maternal competence. Despite all her best efforts and chick-raising techniques, her brood turns against her. Her children are a murderous bunch.
Mother hen laments the loss. R. S. Sugitharajah cites the hermeneutics of
a nineteenth-century Anglican missionary, James Long, who took the side
of oppressed indigo workers in Bangladesh (Sugitharajah 2005, 98). Long
used many metaphors to describe Jesus, but his interpretation of Jesus
as mother hen is interesting. Sugitharajah explains: "As a mother hen, he
nourished them by his great 'drop of blood.' The image of hen had its
limitations, as Long explained, since the hen forgets the young when they
are grown up" (130). In the Gospel versions, the mother hen continues
to desire to shelter the brood, forgetting them only when they refuse her
protection. This mother hen refuses to forget her chicks; she gets revenge:
"See, your house is left to you, desolate" (Matt 23:38). Mother Goose turns
into Mommie Dearest, serving as the very cause of her lament, wrecking
havoc in their lives and prophesying that one day, after great suffering
and desolation, the children will show their gratitude.

But who exactly are these children? The text refers to Jerusalem's
children, so is Jesus a surrogate mother? Are there two mothers in this passage—Mother Jerusalem and the mother hen Jesus? Is Mother Jerusalem
protecting her kids against an angry, apocalyptic deity?

The Early Bird Gets . . . Post-Traumatic Stress Syndrome

In the apocalyptic story of the flood, birds figure prominently. Some repre-
sentatives are taken on the boat, while the rest are destroyed in the flood.
The birds Noah sends out to check the progress of the flood vary in their
surveying ability. The raven makes the first attempt, not returning to the
ark. In the Epic of Gilgamesh flood story, the last bird sent out, the raven,
also does not come back to the ship. Then the more obedient dove flies
out and back but comes back when there is no dry land. On the third try,
the dove returns with an olive leaf. After a week Noah sends the dove out

again, and it does not return (Gen 8:6–12). What have the raven and dove seen on their journeys from the ark? What is floating on the water? What is in the mud and muck? At the end of the flood, where has the genocide been washed—the destroyed temples, homes, animals, and piles of bodies—cholera in the ruins?

Norman Cohn refers to the role of the raven in the rabbinical midrash Genesis Rabbah. In that retelling, "The raven caused Noah much embarrassment," arguing with Noah and refusing to fly away because he suspected that Noah "had designs on his mate, the female raven" (Cohn 1996, 35–6; Gen. Rab. 33.5). Ravens have a bad reputation throughout folktale tradition, pronouncing and partaking in destruction, such as feeding on corpses.[5] According to Leonard Lutwack, corpses play a prominent role in much of the bird imagery (Lutwack 1994, 120). Doves have a better image and represent the gentler traits of peace and love. In Christianity, doves get the honor of representing the Holy Spirit. Overall, birds have a mixed history in the Bible and in literature. Lutwack notes, "Birds were seen as an ambivalent symbol standing at the close as well as at the beginning of life on earth, at the destruction as well as the creation of the world" (1994, 239). The image of Jesus as a bird is not so far-fetched, since God's birdlike creation over the waters of chaos, winged members of the heavenly court, and birdlike goddesses appear in the ancient world. But Jesus as a bird is a mixed image, much more than soft, downy, feathery, encompassing compassion—hardly an ancestor of Big Bird.

Mary Ann Beavis sides with the majority in finding the positive in this feminine imagery for Jesus: "The range of the avian images—from homely domestic fowl to powerful wild predator—points to a divine that is both nurturing and awe-full, motherly and destructive, familiar and other" (Beavis 2003, 127). Beavis points to the Septuagint version of Prov 16:16 and Sir 1:15a, in which Sophia Wisdom is a mother bird with a brood and nest (122 n. 13). The link between Jesus and Sophia has been made by several feminist scholars; Jesus embodies the feminine spirit who breathes life into believers. Elizabeth Johnson quotes Anselm of Canterbury, who sees the chicks as an analogy for the sinner's soul: "And you, my soul, dead in yourself, / run under the wings of Jesus your mother / and lament your griefs under his feathers" (Johnson 1994, 150, quoting Anselm 1973, 153–56). Jesus will offer believers cover against the evil world.

The mother-goddess-bird is a dynamic image in the ancient world, and both Judaism and Christianity used it. Silvia Schroer suggests:

> A strong connection was made in the Ancient Near East between the
> Mother-Goddess and the vulture, to which rich notions of protection

---

5. In his book on the flood, Cohn includes a drawing from the Basel Speculum of 1476 of the raven of the ark devouring a beast's corpse as Noah and family look on and as the dove approaches the boat with the olive branch (Cohn 1996, 36).

and regeneration were attributed. Whenever there is mention of the protective wings of YHWH, the motherliness of YHWH is not particularly emphasized. Nevertheless, it is definitely present [Deut 22:6]. In this respect, YHWH is the successor to the Goddess. (Schroer 1998, 280)

Wings symbolize more than protection and shelter. There is also the connection of wings to genitals, especially when mentioned with "feet" (e.g., Ruth 3:9; Isa 6:2). In any event, eroticism is in the air, although most scholars avoid the topic and avoid linking angels to bird imagery. The protection of the wings is more the normative topic. Schroer points out that "The Near East thought much more dynamically of 'being born anew,' and about the new strength that results from protection and shelter" (281). There is healing in the bird's wings, although ironically these birds are unclean (Lev 11:13; Deut 14:12; see Schroer 1998, 269). Where Schroer sees healing in the shadow of the wings, I also see shadows—a foreboding of judgment and destruction. However, she sees the eagle as more of a goose-vulture. Schroer links the shadows with the vulture-goddess Mut, whose letters, *mwt*, relate to both womb and coffin. Schroer continues

At the same time, the goose-vulture stands also for *nrt* or *nrw*, terror—a persuasive illustration of the ambivalence of the *tremendum et fascinosum* of the holy. It is very likely the terror of death that is symbolically associated with the vulture, of which we read in Isa 31:5: "Like birds . . . hovering so YHWH Sabaoth will encircle Jerusalem, encircle and rob, flit around and embowel it." (Schroer 1998, 271 n. 13)

The ancient rabbis were onto something in their interpretation of the flood birds; the raven circles the boat, keeping a watchful eye on a bestial Noah. Although in Matthew and Luke Jesus is not a vulture but a hen, I think the connection with protection of a brood still holds. The image of mother hen is multifaceted: protective mother-goddess, but also abandonment, ominous apocalypse. There must be another raven in this passage, circling Jerusalem, watching the great hen (who, like Noah, cannot fly) and who has promised the city's destruction.

The goddess imagery is problematic and has a mixed history in the Bible. The winged goddess-bird of creation in Gen 1 flies over the waters of chaos to tame them. The winged serpent appears in artwork of Gen 2–3, a female head on a snake body, only to be grounded by God. Then God makes periodic appearances as a bird (e.g., Exod 19:4; Deut 32:10–11). By the New Testament birds appear at baptism, in parables, as messengers (angels or eagles), and as feeders on road kill. In the role of mother hen, Jesus takes over for mother-goddess, like some male actor in a Shakespearean play in the sixteenth century. Jesus puts on a chicken costume. Is Mother Goose a counterpart to Lilith?

The creation-destruction loop is my focus here. For Catherine Keller, the winged creation dragon of Babylon, Tiamat, becomes thoroughly demonized by Rev 12, in which the new "Eve" faces the demonized serpent-beast who threatens to eat her newly born, messianic son. Keller notes, "Thus the text promotes the snake back up from garden-variety creep to cosmic Evil worthy to oppose the Good. Apocalypse does not casually *reverse* Genesis. The 'fall' of the first creation narrative is *replayed*, taken into the spiral, in order to solve it—to end it" (Keller 1996, 69; see also 203 n. 23). Serpent and bird imagery becomes mixed into strange interspecies versions. The appearance of the winged serpent beast brings forth the earth goddess and the archangel Michael, who protect the woman clothed with the sun. The woman also protects herself: "But the woman was given the two wings of the great eagle, so that she could fly from the serpent into the wilderness to her place where she is nourished for a time, and times, and half a time" (Rev 12:13).[6] The Apocalypse is full of wings: of serpents; of angels; of an eagle who cries prophecies; of the Sun Woman; and of the carnivorous birds of midheaven. Wings are symbols of power, of destruction, and of supernatural realms intersecting, once again, with the human. These wings stir up trouble. What is behind and inside these wings? If one enters the cover of the wings, are they a portal that provides safe passage—to renewal, to a new world? Or are the wings a temporary holding cell and one awakes to the devastation of a postapocalyptic world, to rebuild among the heaps of bodies and carnage, like Noah? Is there a happy ending to this lament?

Isaiah 34:14–15 comments on the judgment and chaos that will befall the enemy nations: "Wildcats shall meet with hyenas, goat-demons shall call to each other; there too Lilith shall repose, and find a place to rest. There shall the owl nest and lay and hatch and brood in its shadow; there too the buzzards shall gather, each one with its mate." The apocalyptic birds of Ezek 39 bring destruction upon Gog and Magog and their nation friends. God instructs Ezekiel:

> Speak to the birds of every kind and to all the wild animals: Assemble and come, gather from all around the sacrificial feast that I am preparing for you, a great sacrificial feast on the mountains of Israel, and you shall eat flesh and drink blood. You shall eat the flesh of the mighty, and drink the blood of the princes of the earth. (Ezek 39:17–18)

These vampiric birds gorge themselves on the damned. An equally gory scene occurs in the Apocalypse of John, when the birds of midheaven feast on those who feasted on the whore of Babylon. The visionary John tells us, "Then I saw an angel standing in the sun, and with a loud voice he called to all the birds that fly in midheaven, 'Come, gather for the great supper of God, to eat the flesh of kings, the flesh of captains, the flesh of the mighty, the flesh of horses and their riders—flesh of all, both free and slave, both small and great'" (Rev 19:17–19). Then the beast and false prophet are

---

6. Scientists debate whether or not dinosaurs were the precursors to birds; those who argue for evolution argue similarities in tailbones, toes, etc.

thrown into the fiery lake. "And the rest were killed by the sword of the rider on the horse, the sword that came from his mouth; and all the birds were gorged with their flesh" (Rev 19:21). There is an emphasis in Ezekiel and the Apocalypse on how overfull—and drunk in Ezekiel—the birds become. "You shall eat fat until you are filled and drink blood until you are drunk, at the sacrificial feast that I am preparing for you" (Ezek 39:19). Following these visions comes restoration—of Israel (Ezekiel) and Jerusalem (Apocalypse). The sacrificial meal provides the necessary ritual for purifying the sacred land. I wonder what the mother hen eats?

Birds Gone Wild

I hardly think a few birds are going to bring about the end of the world.
— Mrs. Bundy in *The Birds*

Most of the birds I have encountered are in recovery. They sit nicely on their branches and sing, and unless you try to bother a nest, they will leave you alone. But apocalyptic birds are on a mission; they invert the norm; they create fantasy space. The apocalyptic birds made their major film appearance in Alfred Hitchcock's famous psycho thriller, *The Birds* (1963). The story is of a socialite from San Francisco, Melanie Daniels, following a lawyer, Mitch Brenner, whom she met in a pet store in the northern California seaside hamlet where his mother and sister live. While there she meets Mitch's overprotective mother, who does not want to share her son with any woman. The birds gradually begin attacking, the townspeople are terrified, and by the end of the film an ominous group of birds watches the survivors leave the farm. These are the birds of midheaven, gathered for the feast on fears.

The tension builds slowly. One of the townspeople, Mrs. Bundy, reassures, "Birds are not aggressive creatures. They bring beauty into the world. It is mankind, rather, who insists upon making it difficult for life to exist upon this planet." Later she rethinks her initial observation on the birds: "Doesn't it seem odd that they'd wait all that time [140 million years] to start a war against humanity?" There is no explanation of why the birds attack, and unlike the biblical apocalyptic birds, no clear direct order comes from the deity.

The Birds indulges the viewer in a potential end time, or at least in apocalyptic horrors that, if left unchecked, could bring about the end of humanity. Alfred Hitchcock called his characters in the film, "victims of Judgment Day" (Spoto 1983, 479). The birds are normal birds: seagulls, crows, and such. They are not mutant beasts or alien species, and they do not have supernatural powers. This image of regular birds heightens the apocalyptic fear. Žižek observes that "in what is surely Hitchcock's final irony—the 'unnatural' element that disturbs everyday life is the birds, i.e., *nature itself*" (1991, 178 n. 3). The invaders are creatures we see every day.

The reason the birds attack is uncertain. There is no real ending to the film, only a mention of other bird attacks in the region. There is a hint of the subversion of the normal hierarchy of living beings, a hint that the disaster is spreading.

Žižek explores the film's focal points: "The birds' subjective view of the town creates a menacing effect, even though our view—the camera's view—is that of the birds and not that of their prey, because we are inscribed in the scene as inhabitants of the town; that is, we identify with the menaced inhabitants" (Žižek 1991, 178 n. 9). For Žižek, "birds function as the embodiment of a cruel and obscene superegoic agency" (1991, 18). For one reading Lacan while watching Hitchcock, *The Birds* becomes a film about the "maternal superego." As in several Hitchcock films, there is an absent father and an overbearing, controlling mother. Žižek notes the build-up through the films of birds, or "the figure of a threat in the shape of birds": the airplane that attacks Cary Grant in *North by Northwest*, the stuffed birds in Norman Bates's room in *Psycho*, and, finally, the hoards of birds in *The Birds* (Žižek 1991, 99). He continues:

> the terrifying figure of the birds is actually the embodiment in the real of a discord, an unresolved tension in intersubjective relations. In the film, the birds are like the plague in Oedipus's Thebes: they are the incarnation of a fundamental disorder in family relationships—the father is absent, the paternal function (the function of pacifying law, the Name-of-the-Father) is suspended and that vacuum is filled by the "irrational" maternal superego, arbitrary, wicked, blocking "normal" sexual relationship (only possible under the sign of the paternal metaphor). (Žižek 1991, 99)

The birds serve as a cover for the messed-up family relationships, and the overbearing mother is the one responsible for the mess. From a feminist perspective, this reading is of course problematic, even if the mother in this film is guilty. Žižek's explanation is that the birds attack because there is no father to pacify the maternal superego, so that ego takes over all the relationships in the family, including and especially any women who attempt to usurp the mother's position of dominance with her son. Žižek calls this derailment of the normal caused by the mother a "pathological narcissism," a phrase he borrows from Christopher Lasch, who believes these mothers cannot meet the needs of their child: "in the child's fantasies the mother appears as a devouring bird" (Žižek 1991, 99, quoting Lasch 1991, 176).

The whole Lacanian notion (from Freud) of the maternal superego has its points and ambiguities; the part of our unconscious that is shaped by maternal and paternal moral cues and the effects of bad parenting on human moral development. But in the story of Hitchcock's *The Birds* and in the biblical story of Jesus as Big (Devouring) Bird, I find some useful points. In lamenting his inevitable destruction of Jerusalem, Jesus chastises the city's children (1) for killing the prophets and stoning others sent by God; and (2) for not being willing to gather and seek protection in his or her wings. In Matthew, Jesus' temple speech is near the end of a section of "woes" on the religious authorities. Jesus holds them responsible for *all* the murders of the Hebrew heroes and prophets, from Abel to Zechariah (Matt 23:35). When the authorities claim that the blame is on their ancestors, Jesus replies: "Fill up, then, the measure of your ancestors. You snakes, you brood of vipers! How can you escape being sentenced to hell?" (Matt 23:32–33). The lament is a catch-22: the city's children cannot possibly go to Jesus because he has already rejected them and damned them to eternal damnation. The correct answer is that they will not escape; they will be made desolate, covered with "all the righteous blood shed on earth" (Matt 23:35), and their "house" (city, temple) utterly destroyed. It is difficult, if not impossible, to by-pass the anti-Jewish tone of this apocalyptic muttering or of biblical apocalypse in general.

For Hitchcock, who needs the supernatural when the natural will do just fine? The Gospel writers use a common farm image, a hen with her chicks, and bump it up to the supernatural. The domestic image is striking in the midst of a proclamation of supernatural judgment. But the hen is deceptive. Unzip the costume, and out pops Jesus. The chicks had better run for their lives or, as Mike Davis would suggest, organize to resist the insanity. At various points throughout the Bible, God puts on a bird costume; God is king or queen of the birds. In grand Marduk-like fashion (or the wolf in "Little Red Riding Hood"), God disembowels the hovering bird and uses the disguise to lure the unsuspected. Are we as readers being lulled by this image so that we miss the apocalypse that God promises? Not all birds in the Bible are possessed by the deity's apocalyptic spirit, but here we encounter the "vision of a cruel, arbitrary, and impenetrable God who can bring down catastrophe at any moment" (Žižek 1991, 97). The threat, the uncertainty of timing, is psychologically abusive. The victims of such apocalyptic, revenge-filled rage are required to respond at the new millennium, "Blessed is the one who comes in the name of the Lord" (Matt 23:39). The apocalyptic torture chamber will bring a forced confession and submission to Jesus' authority. The lament is a threat—of total destruction—of what God desires to do to humanity but holds back until some predetermined but seemingly arbitrary time. No wonder the children of Jerusalem refuse this promise of protection. It is an empty promise, made too late, after the end-time prophecy has been pronounced. Jesus sounds rather disingenuous, as a male cross-dressing as a mother acting out his own issues of childhood. "I really wanted to be able to protect you, you naughty children, but you had to go and kill the prophets, and now I'm going to have to punish you with blood and total annihilation." That is the way divine apocalypse works: a vengeful deity offers safety under the guise of compassion and at a cost. Even civilian noncombatants are targeted. There is not a "hidden cruelty" in this image of Jesus; the rage is powerful.

This mother hen is "the Monster at our door," as Mike Davis (2006) calls the avian flu epidemic. Whereas bird flu is a natural phenomenon (albeit caused by bad poultry practices), an apocalyptic god is a Plague of plagues. A Janus-faced Christ (one side man, one side chicken?) pronounces: "Listen! I am standing at the door, knocking; if you hear my voice and open the door, I will come in to you and eat with you and you with me" (Rev 3:20). Davis sees a "pandemic clock ominously approaching midnight." He stresses, "Now, with a real Monster at our door—as terrible as any in science fiction—will we wake up in time?" (2006, 176–77). One current prophecy preacher, ironically with the last name Hitchcock, believes: "If the Rapture were to happen soon, a virus such as the bird flu could be one of the apocalyptic plagues God uses to bring judgment on the Earth. It's just a matter of time" (Hitchcock 2005). The mother hen in (Matthew) or approaching (Luke) Jerusalem brings a pandemic of his or her own. Davis calls on humans to unite to resist the deadly disease by putting the survival of the poor above the profits of the pharmaceutical industry (Davis 2006, 176). The civilian noncombatants of Jerusalem are doomed. Restorative justice is not part of the equation.

The monster mother stands knocking at the door in Matthew and Luke, too. Keller traces the revealing of this monster mother by feminist theologians; they are engaged in a reclaiming of the *tehom* (Keller 2003, 34–36).[7] However, in Matt 23 and Luke 13 something different is happening than in Genesis: here is God in drag again, neutralizing the monster mother into a seemingly harmless chicken, a storytelling Mother Goose. The creative spirit becomes utterly destructive. There is a perverse inversing of the creative mother. She has been killed off (or put in exile, like the woman clothed with the sun in Rev 12?).

The ability to fly is not limited to birds in the Apocalypse. In apocalyptic text and art there are wings everywhere—angels, beasts, dragons, birds, a flying woman—it is difficult to tell which winged creatures are dangerous, and I would argue that all of them are. One, "the fourth living creature like a flying eagle" (Rev 4:7), guards the throne of God with three other beastly creatures (lion, ox, human face). All the throne guards wear "six wings, are full of eyes all around and inside" (Rev 4:8). They also sing a choir of praise for the one on the throne. Warner notes that, with only a few exceptions, "Research shows that birdsong correlates with high levels of testosterone" (1998, 229).

The angels are the largest flying figures in Western apocalyptic art. There are no cute little winged babies here. Angels arrive as oversized eagles to guide the seer, to pronounce the prophecies, and to defeat the enemy beasts. They lead the charge as an army for God, and they com-

---

7. Keller relates that Tiamat appears in the text: "Indeed the Babylonian myth was otherwise long dead, returned to dust and sand, but for its captivity in the second verse of the Bible" (Keller 2003, 249 n. 23).

mand their fellow winged fellows, the largest collection of birds in the
Bible and a subunit of God's army, the birds of midheaven (Rev 19:17–
21). The phrase "to take someone under one's wing" refers here to a bit
of apocalyptic mentoring. *The Angel Standing in the Sun* from Beatus of
Liébana's *Commentary on the Apocalypse* (ca. 950) is surrounded by color-
ful birds that he has called together for "the great supper of God" in Rev
19:17 (Grubb 1997, 34). *Babylon Invaded by Demons* from *The Apocalypse of
Angers* (ca. 1373–81) shows the birds of midheaven attacking the beasts in
the city as the people flee. The Berry Apocalypse (ca. 1400) shows three
angry birds—one with an elongated beak—diving toward their supper,
three people, and two horses.[8] An angel looks on, smiles, and points the
way. One folio of the Spanish Apocalypse of St-Sever (ca. 1076) features a
bird-god prominently. The bird is a beautiful green, red, blue, and yellow
creature; its face is kindly. If you block off the serpent part, the bird radi-
ates a kind of innocence, as if it still dwells in Eden. Frederick van der Meer
comments on the art that accompanies Beatus's commentary (ca. 785):
"'Bird and Serpent' is an allegory of Redemption: the Bird, divine Wisdom,
hid his bright feathers under the mud of Man's earthly nature at the Incarnation, and thus he was able to approach and kill the Old Serpent, which
did not recognize him. In the miniature, the Bird grips the reptile with its
claws, a cloud of dirt hanging over its head" (van der Meer 1978, 113). The
death grip of the bird's mighty talons causes blood to trickle down the
serpent, and its beak holds the snake at eye level. Van der Meer continues:
"Bird and Serpent: [is] a symbol of Satan beguiled and overcome by God's
'disguise' in the Incarnation of the Logos" (van der Meer 1978, 119). I wonder if the incarnation of Jesus as mother hen is not also a clever disguise to
capture victims for the Last Judgment. If this story were a fairy tale, Jesus
might be a good fairy in disguise.[9]

I think I am beginning to suffer from a bout of ornithophobia. Imagine
all the biblical birds gathering together; imagine them outside your house
right now. Would you go outside? Would you seek the protective wings?
Look to the sky; they are gathering now.

---

8. Lutwack (1994, 120) notes that corpses are present in much bird imagery
in literature.

9. There is also a tradition of fairy godmothers in fairy tales (*Cinderella*, among
others). Jesus is certainly no fairy godmother here; he dispenses plague not pleasure. Warner (1994, 215) discusses the role of the good fairy, usually configured
in less than beautiful disguise. According to Warner, "If the storyteller is an old
woman . . . she may be offering herself as a surrogate to the vanished mother in the
story. . . . Mother Goose enters the story to work wonders on behalf of her brood"
(1994, 215). Does Jesus' appearance as mother hen point to an absent mother in
the text? Why is Mother Jerusalem silenced? What kind of motherhood is Jesus
modeling?

A Fowl Apocalypse, or Jesus' Coop d'Etat

The good news is that the Jesus of the New Testament also teaches love and nonviolence, especially toward children. In fact, he never advocates punishing children (Greven 1990, 219). I would be overgeneralizing to say that Jesus never advocates violence or, on the other hand, that he advocates violence. I have no real idea what Jesus advocated; all I have are the mixed and too often problematic accounts of the Gospel writers. As an activist committed to peacemaking, I learn from the radical justice of Jesus' messages of peace and transformative justice. I want to believe, with Walter Wink, who firmly believes that Jesus teaches a "Third Way" of non-violence, that "We know that nonviolence is the New Testament pattern" (Wink 2003, 103). But the apocalyptic messages woven throughout the New Testament—into its very fibers—cannot be extricated or ignored or easily explained away or relegated to Mark 13 and parallels plus the Apocalypse of John. The apocalypse is the winged shadow hovering over the canon, and Jesus is an apocalyptic attack bird in this lament over Jerusalem.

Mother-church imagery in medieval art has an interesting connection to the bird imagery. Mother church guards believers in her winglike robes. Christopher Hitchens reminds us of what happened in Rwanda in the 1994 genocide when Tutsi (and some Hutu) took refuge in churches. Priests were Hutu collaborators, and thousands of people were executed in these spaces (Hitchens 2007, 191). The wings or arms of the mother did not offer protection.

In his typical cranky style, Hitchens comments about apocalyptic *Schadenfreude*, "guilty joy," of a scene of millions of birds in the *Left Behind* series: first, one's own death is cancelled—or perhaps repaid or compensated—by the obliteration of all others; second, it can always be egotistically hoped that one will be personally spared, gathered contentedly to the bosom of the mass exterminator, and from a safe place observe the suffering of those less fortunate (Hitchens 2007, 57). In Jesus' statement, Jerusalem's children (all of them?) will be massacred (or at least left to die after their world is destroyed), so does this leave room for the believing reader to step into mother hen's wings? Is the reader being lured into such guilty joy of the sort Tim LaHaye and Jerry Jenkins promote endlessly in their endless series? In these books, Jesus flies down in the rapture to gather up his brood of believers and again at the end of the tribulation to defeat the antichrist-Satan. The very cross of Jesus seems to fly; the crossbeam transforms into wings, with Jesus offering his outstretched arms to take us with him. I hear only the planes of 9/11, the cries of the desolate in a senseless war. Our relation to Jesus as mother hen is even more problematic when viewed in the shadow of these wings. Anyone wanting to recover this image as one of compassion must look deeper into the feathers. Mother Jerusalem is right to keep her children—even her bad children—away from such protection. In this fairy tale the mother is still absent, replaced by a ferocious male deity disguised as a loving mother hen. In fairy tales there is often an absent mother; the good mother dies and "is supplanted by a monster," the evil stepmother (Warner 1994, 201). This image of the "wicked stepmother" has, of course, been damaging to women, but in this case the archetype holds, further embedding the sexist image.

I went searching for a sign, something to convince me this image of mother hen has any salvageable ethical meaning. I live in a state full of chickens, so I thought to look locally for a sign. Then I thought of egg imagery, since every mother hen has eggs. Eggs are a sign of fertility, of spring, of resurrection at Easter. The cosmic egg that is the focus of Hildegard of Bingen holds all creation. Keller relates, "the etymological connotation of brooding has always emitted the mythical associations of the mother bird laying the world-egg" (Keller 2003, 233). The spirit must brood over the chaos or Tehom, for there to be life: "Apart from the spirit 'brooding o'er the chaos,' Tehom remains a sterile possibility and 'God' remains mere Word, fleshless abstraction, and power code" (Keller 2003, 233) The cosmic egg is the very stuff of the universe, down to its smallest particle. "If the wing served to make the bird miraculously free of earth, the egg bound the bird to earth, and the brooding hen became a symbol of the miracle of life" (Lutwack 1994, 81–82).

I find this reading of Gen 1 and the history of the cosmic egg very hopeful and like to dwell here instead of the apocalyptic New Testament. But I return to the sections of destroyed cities and peoples in Jesus' speech. The apocalyptic egg in our times is the nuclear bomb, the egg dropped on Hiroshima and Nagasaki. My home state of Georgia broods over such nuclear eggs: Trident submarines, and "white trains," and other trains and trucks carrying nuclear waste pass through and are held by these "wings." There is a picture that members of Nuclear Watch South (formerly Georgians against Nuclear Energy) took in the early 1990s about a mile from my house. In the photo, members of the group dressed from head to toe in white antiradiation suits, stand within twelve feet of a train container full of high-level nuclear waste that passed through and stopped in a heavily populated urban area. The container is an "egg" that must never crack open.

I continued my search for something more comforting and wound up in Marietta, Georgia, at the "Big Chicken," a famous (around here, at least) and huge red and white chicken with moving beak and eyes. Mother hen sits atop a Kentucky Fried Chicken restaurant and beckons the hungry to come inside her protective wings. I had found "comfort food," as we call it in the South. This supersized hen promises nourishment. She even offers her body for food! She beckons, "Eat my flesh and. . . ." But she brings obesity and heart disease to all who abide in her wings too long. My search continues.

Will it take a Mother Jones to stand up to this apocalyptic Mother Goose? Who will call Jesus out of his or her apocalyptic disguise? Who will stand in solidarity beneath the coming shadows of bird wings?

In the midst of the hopeful feminist reconstruction of the divine feminine and reclaiming of Jesus as mother bird, I appear as a negative doomsayer and unwelcome party crasher. "Who invited *her*?" they say as I walk into the party, smiling sweetly, holding a great big bucket of southern fried chicken.

Works Cited

Addams, Charles. 1995. *Mother Goose*. New York: Simon & Schuster

Anselm. 1973. Prayer to St. Paul. Pages 153–56 in *The Prayers and Meditations of St. Anselm*. Translated by S. Benedicta Ward. New York: Penguin.

Beavis, Mary Ann. 2003. "I Like the Bird": Luke 13:34, Avian Metaphors and Feminist Theology. *Feminist Theology* 12:119–28.

Cohn, Norman. 1996. *Noah's Flood: The Genesis Story in Western Thought*. New Haven: Yale University Press.

Davis. Mike. 2006. *The Monster at Our Door: The Global Threat of Avian Flu*. New York: Henry Holt.

DePaola, Tomie. 1985. *Tomie DePaola's Mother Goose*. New York: Putnam.

Fitzmyer, Joseph A. 1981–85. *The Gospel according to Luke: Introduction, Translation, and Notes*. 2 vols. AB 28–28A. Garden City, N.Y.: Doubleday.

Goldthwaite, John. 1996. *The Natural History of Make-Believe*. New York: Oxford University Press.

Greven, Philip. 1990. *Spare the Child: The Religious Roots of Punishment and the Psychological Impact of Physical Abuse*. New York: Vintage.

Grubb, Nancy. 1997. *Revelations: Art of the Apocalypse*. New York: Abbeville.

Hitchcock, Mark. 2005. Bird Flu and the Apocalypse. Online: http://www.leftbehind.com.

Hitchens, Christopher. 2007. *God Is Not Great: How Religion Poisons Everything*. New York: Twelve.

Johnson, Elizabeth A. 1994. *She Who Is: The Mystery of God in Feminist Theological Discourse*. New York: Crossroad.

Keller, Catherine. 2003. *Face of the Deep: A Theology of Becoming*. London: Routledge.

Landes, Richard. 1996. On Owls, Roosters, and Apocalyptic Time: A Historical Method for Reading a Refractory Documentation. *USQR* 49:165–85.

Lasch, Christopher. 1991. *The Culture of Narcissisms in American Life in an Age of Diminishing Expectations*. New York: Norton.

Levine, Amy-Jill. 1988. *The Social and Ethnic Dimensions of Matthean Salvation History*. Lewiston, N.Y.: Mellen.

Lutwack, Leonard. 1994. *Birds in Literature*. Gainesville: University of Florida Press.

Meer, Frederick van der. 1978. *Apocalypse: Visions from the Book of Revelation in Western Art*. New York: Alspine Fine Arts Collection.

Miller, Alice. 1983. *For Your Own Good: Hidden Cruelty in Child-Rearing and the Roots of Violence*. New York: Farrar, Straus & Giroux.

Schroer, Silvia. 1998. "Under the Shadow of Your Wings": The Metaphor of God's Wings in the Psalms, Exodus 19.4, Deuteronomy 32.11 and Malachi 3.20, as Seen Through the Perspectives of Feminism and the History of Religion. Pages 264–82 in *Wisdom and Psalms*. Edited by Athalya Brenner and Carole R. Fontaine. FCB 2/2. Sheffield: Sheffield Academic Press.

Spoto, Donald. 1983. *The Dark Side of Genius: The Life of Alfred Hitchcock*. Boston: Little, Brown.

Sugitharajah, R. S. 2005. *The Bible and Empire: Postcolonial Explorations*. Cambridge: Cambridge University Press.

Warner, Marina. 1994. *From the Beast to the Blonde: On Fairy Tales and Their Tellers*. New York: Farrar, Straus & Giroux.

———. 1999. *No Go the Boogeyman: Scaring, Lulling and Making Mock*. New York: Farrar, Straus & Giroux.

Wallace, Mark I. 1993. The Wild Bird Who Heals: Recovering the Spirit in Nature. *ThTo* 50:13–28.

Wink, Walter. 2003. *Jesus and Nonviolence: A Third Way*. Minneapolis: Fortress.

Žižek, Slavoj. 1991. *Looking Awry: An Introduction to Jacques Lacan through Popular Culture*. Cambridge: MIT Press.

11

BMW

BIBLICAL MOTHER WORKING/WRECKING, BLACK MOTHER WORKING/WRECKING

Stephanie Buckhanon Crowder

Introduction

Julia. Florida Evans. Mrs. Thomas. Louise Jefferson, or "Weezie." Claire Huxtable. Nikki Parker. These are television images of mothers—black mothers—who worked to support their families. They are women who worked, sometimes with husbands or partners, sometimes without, to put a roof over their children's heads and food on the table. There are other images: Hattie McDaniel's "Mammy," Ethel Waters in *Pinkie*, Beah Richards as the "Mother Preacher" in *Beloved*. Time will not forget the plethora of nameless so-called mammies and matriarchs who during slavery and the Reconstruction nursed not only their children but massah's children as well. These were hard-working, burden-bearing, heavy-load-carrying foremothers who from sunup to sundown worked in the fields only to go home and provide for their own sons and daughters.

The African American community cannot forget unwed mothers, "other" mothers, or "neighborhood" mothers who took responsibility for any and every child in the community long before daycare became a business. Our community must tell the story of hot mommas and hoochie mommas alongside side our narrating the contributions of church mothers. These are all historical and yet vibrant images of black women, black mothers. These sisters represent the reality of black mothers who have a history of working and have a foundation of hard work. Some need to work in order to survive. For others it is a matter of choice and personal fulfillment. Yet common to all is the belief that our identity, my identity as a black woman, a black mother, and a black working mother is interrelated and in many cases one in the same.

This essay, an exegetical exercise based on Matthew's portrayal of the

Canaanite woman pleading for Jesus to intervene on behalf of her demon-possessed daughter (Matt 15:21–28 // Mark 7:24–30), explores the dynamics of black mothering and work as that of advocacy as well as commitment to family. I chose Matthew's version because of the negative "Canaanite" descriptive the author applies to the mother and the way in which the disciples reject her by urging Jesus to send her away. I also found intriguing the concept of faith as evident in Matthew and lacking in Mark. For Matthew, the Canaanite woman's faith is expressed through her mediating on behalf of another—in this case, her daughter. Thus work is rooted in and the fruit of one's faith.

I engage a womanist maternal theological framework. According to Stephanie Mitchem, womanism starts with an analysis of roles assigned to black (my addition) or African diasporan women by their families and the dominant culture, the persistent stereotypes about black women, the combination of race with gender and class (my addition), and the recognition of diversity among women (Mitchem 2002, 23). Delores Williams asserts that a womanist theology challenges all oppressive forces impeding black women's struggle for survival and for the development of a positive, productive quality of life conducive to the women's and the family's freedom and well-being. As a means of differentiating itself from other approaches to feminist hermeneutics, womanist theology branches off in its own direction, introducing new issues and constructing new analytical categories needed to interpret simultaneously black women's and the black community's experience in the context of theology or God-talk (my addition; Williams 1993, xiv).

Bonnie Miller-McLemore constructs a feminist maternal theology that seeks to make the flourishing of mothers and children within a feminist framework a possibility (Miller-McLemore 2002, 104). Since feminism primarily focuses on gender construction and not issues of race and class, I find womanist thinking a better location for this work at the present time. Therefore, I branch off and propose a womanist maternal theological method that particularly highlights the voices of mothers within this African Diasporan context, whether the mothers are biological or women who took responsibility for and helped to care for another's child. Womanist authors such as Teresa Fry Brown, Barbara Essex and Renita Weems address mother/motherhood, but none under the auspices of a womanist maternal theology.[1]

---

1. Brown 2000. Brown talks at length of the importance of African American grandmothers, mothers, and other mothers in handing on spiritual values or moral wisdom across generations of African American families, churches, and communities through their use of biblical mandates, precepts, and examples. Essex 1997 discusses the role of her grandmother and mother in her childhood and adult life. Weems 2002 highlights her relationship with her mother and its impact on her relationship with her own daughter.

This paper proceeds along three axes. First, I explore racial/ethnic concepts as a means of establishing the Canaanite mother, an ethnic outsider, as a typology for black mothers in the United States. Although Jesus comes to her non-Jewish territory, where technically she is the racial majority, the Gospel writer reverses the power dynamic. Thus the woman's gender relegates her to a person of minority status who needs resources from someone in power. Even in her own geographical location, she becomes decentered.

Second, this exercise seeks to construct a definition of "work" to ascertain how the "work" of the Canaanite mother correlates with current ideas of "work" among African American mothers. A definition of work as activity bringing children wholeness and health emerges as Matthew portrays the woman seeking her daughter's healing outside of the home. This paper questions whether such a definition aligns or contrasts with present-day mothers who may define work in more materialistic, concrete terms.

Lastly, I examine whether such "work" compromises family structure and family well-being. As the Canaanite woman, an ethnic outsider, addresses and implores someone of Jewish descent to provide her a service and publicly addresses Jesus amidst a male-dominated society, she dares to cross racial and gender boundaries. I wish to ascertain if these actions compromise not only her well-being and status but also that of her child. I also seek to determine if this Canaanite woman is a prototype for black mothers in the United States who, while working various and odd hours, simultaneously tear down walls of racism and sexism for the sake of their children. Yet, such work may endanger family construction. In other words, does a biblical mother or a black mother working become a biblical mother wrecking/black mother wrecking, one who wrecks or dismantles mother-to-child bonds and relationships in the name of work?

On Being a Racial/Ethnic Outsider

Matthew establishes Jesus as leaving the land of Gennesaret and traveling to parts of Phoenicia in the province of Syria. More specifically, Jesus enters the northern districts of Tyre and Sidon, which are under Roman rule. He encounters one labeled a "Canaanite" in this predominately Gentile territory. Unlike Mark, who identifies the mother as Syrophoenician, Matthew wants the audience to associate this Canaanite with the people who struggled with the Hebrews for the Promised Land. For Matthew's reader, this Canaanite is a reminder of the people God had to drive out for Abraham's seed to receive the promise. She is a reminder of an idolatrous people. This mother is a reminder and a remnant of a people who did not honor the God of Abraham and Sarah, Isaac and Rebecca, and Jacob, Leah, and Rachel. The author's mention of "Canaanite" also recalls the Matthean genealogy that lists other Canaanite women: Tamar (Matt 1:3) and Rahab

(1:5). Both Tamar and Rahab are also types of outsiders in that they are associated with prostitution. The Canaanite mother, Tamar, and Rahab all achieve their goals through skillful speech and deed while acknowledging Israel's precedence in salvation history. Whereas Levine maintains that Jesus is only on the outskirts of the area, I maintain that he physically goes into the city (Levine 1998, 346). Jesus, a Jew, dares not only enter into this Gentile district, but he dares to enter into conversation with a woman of this district.

Besides Herodias, who tells her daughter to request the head of John the Baptist (Matt 14:1–2), this Canaanite woman is the first woman to speak in the Gospel of Matthew. She is the first woman to speak to Jesus. Yes, the woman with the issue of blood encounters Jesus, but she talks to herself and never responds to him (9:18–26). Matthew mentions mothers (1:18–25), a mother-in-law (8:14–15), and motherhood (10:35–37; 12:46–50), yet up to this point no woman speaks to Jesus other than this ethnic outsider. The work she has to do on behalf of her daughter no longer warrants silence and does not leave place for marginalization or low self-esteem.

Whereas Jesus is in an area where he is now the racial minority, Matthew employs language that depicts him otherwise. Jesus has power; the Canaanite woman desires to access it. Using a rhetoric of marginalization, the Canaanite woman's language indicates powerlessness, even in her own hometown. She refers to Jesus as "Lord" three times (Matt 15:22, 25, 27). He is the "Son of David," an acknowledgment of the magnificence of Hebrew history (15:22). Jesus initially ignores the woman's presence and does not answer her at all (15:23). His disciples try to convince him to send her away because she is making too much noise (15:24). Jesus calls her a "dog" (15:26), a derogatory term the Canaanite woman uses in turn to refer to herself (15:27). Perhaps Matthew repeats the reference as a play on the Greek words for dog (*kynaria*) and Canaanite (*Chananaia*). This "dog" or Gentile only wishes for crumbs from the master's table (Matt 15:27). Finally, the Canaanite woman does not have a name. She is merely a woman who comes out and starts shouting at Jesus like a loose street dog that does not stop barking.

Assertive, strong-willed African American women also have to contend with being called a dog, the "b" word, or "bitch." Black women, who seem to have it all together and who really do it have it together, must fight and engage in verbal combat to get the healing they and their children deserve. Even in places or locales where African American women are the majority or are running the show as managers, supervisors, leaders, teachers, doctors, lawyers, or just being the heads of households, it is not unusual for someone to come into their home, their territory, their abode and try to reverse the power dynamic.

Black women get challenged by both men and women who question their authority. "Who does she think she is?" "She is not the boss of me!" Children who know that they know better will try to act grown from out of nowhere. "I didn't ask to be born anyway!" Students will say one thing to an African American female professor and yet remain silent and dumbfounded at the words of her white counterpart. Like this Canaanite woman, we black women know what it is like to have the tables turned and the roles reversed.

Outsider language or society's rhetoric of submission says that, "Yes, you are the doctor with a medical degree from Harvard, Vanderbilt, or Yale, but I want a second and third opinion." "Are you sure about this diagnosis?" Such language says, "Yes, you are the professor, but I am going to send the dean an email without sending you a copy." Outsider language is the government's welfare system penalizing our inner-city moms if the baby's daddy lives with them; yet, persons with privilege get welfare called tax breaks, and this behavior is acceptable. Outsider language says, "What does a black mother mean when she says she is a stay-at-home mother, home schooling her children? Don't you work?" Outsider language says to black mothers who work, "Why don't you stay at home? Daycares are not the place for children? Don't you miss out on their development when you work? Doesn't your husband make enough? Do you have a husband?" Even on our own grounds, in our native land, minding our own business, we African American women, like this Canaanite woman, can speak to reversals of power.

Trying to "Work" It Out

The Canaanite woman shouts at Jesus and pleads for mercy. She does not ask for anything nonessential. Her request involves life and death. She does not desire to kill a man, like Herodias, the mother before her (Matt 14:1–2), nor does she desire a place in the kingdom of God, like the mother of the sons of Zebedee after her (20:20–28). Her daughter is demon-possessed and needs deliverance. Her baby is not herself, and momma has done all she knows to do. So the Canaanite woman goes to work.

Matthew does not use the word "work" at all in this pericope. He does not describe the mother as working. I do. Yet interestingly enough, the writer employs the word *ergo*, meaning work, labor, or deed eleven times throughout this Gospel (5:16; 7:22; 11:2, 20, 21, 23; 13:54, 58; 14:2; 23:3, 5). Only once is work as "praxis," meaning function, deed, or office, utilized (16:27). I believe *ergo*, the source or root for "energy" and "energize," delineates much physical, social, mental, and emotional effort. It is exhausting while at the same time exhilarating.

So what do I mean by "work"? By "work," I mean the consistent, conscientious act of pursuing those in power and challenging authority for survival, healing, health and wholeness, and future security. To work, with or without financial remuneration, is not only to seek my welfare but to seek the well-being of persons in my family, my community, my race, and people of the world at large. Work is active, not passive. Work is what I/we do, not what is done to me/us. Such work requires the engagement and cooperation of mind, body, and spirit.[2]

The Canaanite woman works. She actively pursues Jesus because she believes that, as "Lord" and "Son of David," he has power. She works in that she does not stop shouting or pleading with Jesus to use his power to enhance her situation, although the disciples urge him to send her away. Recognizing the authority of Jesus, this nameless woman works because she challenges his hesitance to use this power to help a powerless one such as her. This mother works so that her demon-possessed daughter may be set free and thus survive, be healed, and be made whole. This mother works her faith and secures not only a present healing but a future promise initially reserved for the house of Israel.

The Canaanite mother sacrifices her body in that she dares to speak so boldly to a man in public in a patriarchal society. After all, Matthew does not say she is under anyone's authority, and thus she could be reprimanded by those in authority for her "out of place" actions. As the author does not mention a husband, perhaps the Canaanite is a single mom. Nonetheless, she puts her mental acumen and emotions on the table in that she engages in a verbal contest vis-à-vis Jesus and yields to his language of marginalization for the sake of her daughter. Her work is a sacrifice of her physical, emotional, and mental self. Yet, in the end, she also reaps spiritual benefits.

Patricia Hill Collins states that understandings of work, like understandings of family, vary greatly depending on who controls the definitions. Quoting May Madison, she maintains: "One very important difference between white people and black people is that white people think you are your work.... Now a black person thinks that my work is just what I have to do to get what I want" (Collins 2000, 48). Instead of conceptualizing work by typology, perhaps the motivation and the range of the work is a better grasp of value and worth. Too often those who earn better salaries with excessive fringe benefits and stock options easily attach self-worth with self-work. Thus, using Collins—and from a broader African American context—the work of mothers who clean the academic halls to survive, heal, and become whole is just as valuable as the work of mothers who teach in these same academic halls for survival, healing, and wholeness.

Work as alienated labor can be economically exploitative, physically demanding, and intellectually deadening, such as the type of work long associated with black women's status as "mule" (Hurston 2000, 17). Yet

---

2. The definition of work does not maintain that stay-at-home mothers do not engage in such pursuit, challenge, or advocacy. I believe another definition of "work" needs to be developed for the important work of such mothers, particularly since society tends to attach a negative connotation to the work of mothers who choose not to "go to work" outside of the home.

work can also be empowering and creative, even if it is physically challenging and appears to be demeaning. Exploitative wages that black women were allowed to keep and use for their own benefit or labor done out of love for members of their own family can represent such work (Collins 2000, 48). Although Collins particularly frames her definition of work in black feminist thinking, aspects of survival and wholeness as apparent in the pericope surrounding the Canaanite mother are present. Work is thus more than a reluctant, "I've got to go to work." It is an intense, focused, determined, "I've got work to do!" because life and soul are at stake. There is a spiritual element of the work mothers do on behalf of their children.

To Wreck or Not To Wreck

I included in my title the phrase "biblical mother wrecking/black mother wrecking." "Wrecking" is the pursuit of persons, the conscientious engagement in activity, the challenging of authority that endangers a child's life and stunts a child's mental, emotional, physical, social, or spiritual growth. It refers to a mother's "work" that is detrimental to her child or family in general. It means that the family suffers from this work. Does an African American mother who works wreak havoc and wreck a child's life? Before answering the question, there are some other issues that must be addressed.

First, we must bring to the surface the plethora of roles of mothers. Miller-McLemore maintains that the dilemma facing working mothers is the struggle between the procreative and the creative (2002, 91). The dilemma is the tension between wanting and needing to be mother and yet wanting and needing to be someone else—and being both/and all the time. It is the desire to be at home, at school events, at dance lessons or athletic events and the desire to write scholarly articles, teach classes, and attend professional meetings. The dilemma is a rope that pulls in at least two ways. It is "I am also a mother" language. In addition to who I am as professor, dean, lawyer, maid, clerk, wife, sister, I am also a mother.

Therefore, second, the history of black working mothers cannot be overlooked. "Also a mother" were the slave women who nursed master's children and picked and chopped in his fields and then went to make a home for their own families. These mothers took care of their own quarters after bearing their burden in the heat of the day. "Also a mother" included two million Reconstruction women who were the earliest housewives or stay-at-home moms. Yet, like the experience of the Canaanite woman, they represent a reversal of power. Reconstruction laws or black codes forced many of these postslavery mothers from their homes back into the fields. Black mothers who migrated to northern factories, those who took in laundry and took in children before there was an official cleaning business or KinderKare—yes, they were "also a mother." One cannot forget the triple consciousness of family, work, and community exemplified by clubwomen such as Ida B. Wells and Mary Church Terrell. As black women and black mothers, they did not relinquish their public duty. Wells "nursed her two sons, taking them on trains on the way to her lectures" (Parker 2005, 33). However, according to sociologists LaFrances Rogers Rose and Joyce Ladner, the story of African American motherhood did not begin here in the United States but has its roots in Africa. The close bond between black women and children did not lose its importance when African women were brought to America and enslaved (Williams 1993, 34).

Consequently, African American women and African American mothers have a history of work. Yet now, the so-called "mommie wars" challenge the relevance of such work and, perhaps in some ways, this history. This is a third element that impacts the possible work-as-wrecking line of thinking. There is a conflict between mothers who stay at home with their children and mothers who work outside the home. According to the article "Working vs. Stay at Home" in *Babytalk*, there are benefits to both sides; there are exceptions to both sides. Stay-at-home moms are the primary soothers and cuddlers and are there for those benchmark moments. Children do not necessarily have the separation anxiety sometimes experienced in daycare transition. Children of working moms benefit in that they have a broader social circle with daycare workers, other children, or babysitters. Working mothers also stay in their projected career paths (2006, 55).

The same article maintains that there are also drawbacks to each argument. Working mothers may experience guilt over missing a first walk or first word. For children, even the most sanitized daycares breed germs. Children are likely to attract colds and other illnesses from each other. Stay-at-home mothers deal with professional isolation, and the children obviously tend to be more attached to the mothers (2006, 56). Again, there are exceptions to both sides.

Does this mean that mothers who stay at home with their children are completely happy with their lives? Some are. Some are not. Does this mean that children of stay-at-home mothers are healthier or have a greater maternal-child bond? There are cases of both yes and no. Are children of working moms more socially developed? Are these working mothers climbing the corporate ladder with family in tow? I think the answers lie in each of our own lives and what "works" best in our own family situations. There are no absolutes, as perpetrators of these "mommie wars" would have us to believe. What is evident is that, in both cases, both sets of mothers do what they do in their children's best interest.

Most black women and black mothers have always worked and will continue to work. Some of the children who come from such homes are the most articulate, independent, socially adept, intellectually sound, and spiritually grounded persons. However, some children struggle. I cannot say what the defining line or determining factor is. I do not think that work in the sense that I have defined wrecks the lives of children. Yes, they may miss their mommie, and yes, mommie may miss an event or two. However, quantity of times present cannot be judged against quality time. I believe to each his or her own; to each mother, her own. She must use whatever "works" for her. Her situation will work, if she works it.

The Canaanite mother went to work. Apparently she left the child either at home alone or with relatives or neighbors, because the text does not record the daughter being present. Did the child suffer because of her mother's work? She was demon-possessed and already in harm's way. Her mother went to work to alleviate the torment. Did the daughter benefit from the mother's work? Matthew concludes that pericope with "and the daughter was healed instantly."

The Canaanite mother also benefited from this work in that she was persistent and unrelenting. She pursued the power source and became a beneficiary of that power. She gained in that she changed Jesus' mind. She was no longer an ethnic outsider screaming after Jesus, but she engaged him in an intense intellectual conversation. She gained in that her gender and her faith were affirmed. Jesus replied, "Woman, great is your faith. Let it be done as you wish" (Matt 15:28).

African American mothers who work benefit themselves in that they are allowed to pursue career goals that for some are divine callings. There is a spiritual connection to this work. They benefit because they are able to provide for themselves and their children. We benefit since we can engage in other forms of intellectual stimulus. We gain personal fulfillment. At the same time, such work is healing to our children. They get to see their mothers in another light, not as some demeaning object projected in music videos. Simple material accoutrements as food, clothing, health care, and shelter are also rewards of such work for both mothers and children. Love for their children drives most black working mothers to do what they do, just as it was the love of her daughter that drove the Canaanite woman to do what she had to do.

Conclusion

I began with a general portrait of media images of black working mothers and a history of black working mothers. Such a history includes black women as church mothers or the Mother Jones type. This portrait is broad enough to even cover mothers who specialize in tough love, perhaps lending themselves to the Mommie Dearest nomenclature. Yet readers are perhaps more comfortable with the nurturing, caring, Mother Goose type of mommie. Regardless, one can see that the continuum of black mothering is wide indeed.

Throughout this paper I integrated my own personal thoughts on working and black mothering, yet I did not reveal my own social location. Thus whereas I began in broad strokes, I end with a more refined brush. My own identity has informed my approach to this topic.

As an African American mother of two sons and one who has been called to be both an ordained minister and a professor, I have found myself grappling with the procreative and the creative in me. The day after I submitted the final draft of my dissertation, my first son was born. I commuted five hundred miles with my second son in utero to yield to the creative calling in me. Three months after delivering him, I sat inattentively in faculty orientation wondering, "What in the world am I doing here? I just gave birth." I have missed football games, a growth milestone here or there, and have experienced guilt for working. Yet at the same time, the loud voice that propels me beyond motherhood also confirms my work and affirms that everything is all right. The many hugs and smiles I get from my sons coming and going affirm this as well.

Where do we go from here? I think this analysis of the work of the Canaanite mother as a prototype of black working mothers leads to many places. First, in the academy we must talk more about family and family issues as an integral aspect of who we are as scholars. Many of us bring our families to professional meetings; yet, there is limited discussion on the intersection of family and career. We cannot overlook the "off the record" questions at job interviews about family or plans for children. Many pre-tenure females hear a "hint" or outright warning to wait to have children until after they have completed this matriculation process. Issues of maternity leave and timing and class coverage are the elephant in the academic room.

Second, I maintain that, whereas womanist methods take up the mantle of class and race not addressed in feminism, more must be done to highlight internal class issues between black women who teach in the academy and black women who cook and clean in the academies. We must look for ways in which our work gives voice to black mothers on welfare, black mothers who are the working poor, and black mothers who work for other black mothers.

Lastly, we must address the children. If one surmises that the Canaanite mother leaves her child home alone, then the daughter is a latchkey child. She is a child who in our modern time has a key to the house and enters an empty home to fend for herself until mother arrives. Our academic work must advocate for after-school networks, faith-based initiatives, and community programs to fill in the gap. We must send a clarion call to strengthen existing programs where surrogate mothers and neighborhood grandmothers step in until momma gets off work.

Works Cited

Brown, Teresa L. Fry. 2000. *God Don't Like Ugly: African American Women Handing on Spiritual Values*. Nashville: Abingdon.

Collins, Patricia Hill. 2000. *Black Feminist Thought*. 2nd ed. New York: Routledge.

Essex, Barbara J. 1997. Some Kind of Woman: The Making of a Strong Black Woman.

Pages 203–11 in *Embracing the Spirit: Womanist Perspectives on Hope, Salvation and Transformation*. Edited by Emilie Townes. Maryknoll, N.Y.: Orbis.

Hurston, Zora Neale. 2000. *Their Eyes Were Watching God*. New York: HarperCollins.

Levine, Amy-Jill. 1998. The Gospel of Matthew. Pages 339–49 in *Women's Bible Commentary*. Edited by Carol Newsom and Sharon Ringe. Louisville: Westminster John Knox.

Meyers, Carol, ed. 2002. *Women in Scripture: A Dictionary of Named and Unnamed Women in the Hebrew Bible, the Apocryphal/Deuterocanonical Books, and the New Testament*. Grand Rapids: Eerdmans.

Miller-McLemore, Bonnie. 2002. *Also a Mother: Work and Family as Theological Dilemma*. Nashville: Abingdon.

Mitchem, Stephanie Y. 2002. *Womanist Theology*. Maryknoll, N.Y.: Orbis.

Parker, Lonnae O'Neal. 2005. *I'm Every Woman: Remixed Stories of Marriage, Motherhood and Work*. New York: HarperCollins.

Weems, Renita J. 2002. My Mother, My Self. Pages 117–25 in idem, *Showing Mary: How Women Can Share Prayers, Wisdom, and the Blessings of God*. West Bloomfield, Mich.: Walk Worthy Press.

Williams, Delores S. 1993. *Sisters in the Wilderness: The Challenge of Womanist God-Talk*. Maryknoll, N.Y.: Orbis.

Working vs. Staying at Home. 2006. *Babytalk* February:54–56.

12

Motherhood Archetype
MOTHERS OF JUSTICE

Brenda Wallace

Introduction

Women are not foreign to the concept of being on the forefront of justice issues in the world. Women have served in every justice movement in history, and I ascribe them as archetypical "mothers of justice and activism." Women played necessary and vital roles from the beginning of human existence to the Christian movement, women's suffrage to the civil rights movement; they also carried on their husbands' legacies until this day. Jewish women followed Jesus to help propel the Christian movement by giving their time and resources, from preparing meals as Martha the sister of Lazarus, to the women in Luke 8:1–3 who followed, possibly serving meals to Lydia and the Samaritan woman who evangelized their communities. Biblical authors used women as metaphors for those worthy of the kingdom of God, and Jesus used parables to teach his followers important messages.

My essay engages a comparative analysis between a biblical example of a woman of justice, the widow in Luke 18, and a contemporary woman of justice, Mother Mary Harris Jones. In this essay, I propose examining the widow in Luke 18 from feminine instinctual qualities that form the basis for archetypal mothers of justice movements. After I begin with the work of male scholars and philosophers as a foundation, I then use feminist and womanist hermeneutics of suspension to interpret the text from a marginalized point of view. First, I provide my own translation of the passage under consideration and study. Second, using Hendrikus Boers's structural paradigm, I examine two characters in the parable: the widow and the judge. Third, I explore the meaning, as described by Jesus or the implied author of the text, in reference to need/lack; preparedness; performance; and sanction for the widow, judge, and Mother Jones. Fourth,

I analyze Paul Ricoeur's poststructural method of interpreting parables by identifying: (1) the role of story in the parable; (2) extravagance in the parable; and (3) time in the parable (Ricoeur 1981, 165–69). Fifth, I provide a possible interpretation of the parable engaging the prayers of African American slaves toward developing a "hermeneutic of the marginalized." Lastly, I explore how this passage about a widow might be read through the eyes of another widow, Mother Jones. Mother Jones was a justice seeker and activist. Do the actions of the widow in Luke 18 provide parallels for social justice activists and in the work of Mary Harris Jones?

The widow in Luke 18:1–8 is a prime example of a woman of justice. In the parable, this powerless widow faces a powerful judge and requests justice with the only resources she has: time and persistence. She shows up in his courtroom day after day seeking justice. Her persistence is a model for praying without ceasing. This widow encounters the judge and keeps coming to engage him until he finally exchanges his immoral actions for acts of justice on her behalf. Her nonviolent resistance so pesters the judge that in his self-talk he imagines the widow will do him harm by giving him a black eye (see Schottroff 1995, 101–20; Johnson 1981, 268–74). In my African American heritage, there were men such as the late Dr. Martin Luther King Jr., Jessie Jackson, and Al Sharpton who used nonviolent resistance to confront systems and change them. The threat of violence, of a black eye, is implied action that caused the judge to contemplate. The widow's nonviolent resistance is powerful. The tool of nonviolent resistance is not passive resistance. As seen by the judge, the resistance causes his active participation to grant justice. Resistance is a force and an energy that can make others react, as it does in the case of the widow.

The widow provides an archetype for how ancient women combated injustice. She also shows how nonviolence with a threat of violence is a powerful influence to bring about justice. Archetypical mothers, mothers, and widows, include, Joan of Arc (1412–1431), Sojourner Truth (1797–1883), Justine Wise Polier (1903–1987), Mary McLeod Bethune (1875–1955), Eleanor Roosevelt (1884–1963), Irene Morgan Kirkaldy[1] (1917–2007), Rosa Parks (1913–2005), Harriet Tubman (1820–1913), Ida B. Wells (1862–1931), Mary Church Terrell (1863–1954), Barbara Jordan (1936–1996), Corretta Scott King (1927–2006), Marian Wright Edelman (1939–), and others. Specifically comparing Mother Mary Harris Jones (1837–1930) to the widow in the text affords a mother-of-justice archetype. What is an archetypal mother of justice? What prayer might mothers of justice pray? How have women justice

---

1. Irene Morgan Kirkaldy was a forerunner to Rosa Parks as a woman of justice. She refused to give up her seat on a Greyhound bus in 1946. Thurgood Marshall and William Hastie argued her case before the Supreme Court. On June 3, 1946, the Supreme Court ruled in her favor, outlawing discriminatory seating practices in interstate travel (Goldstein 2007).

seekers caused powerful oppressive systems to change their actions? What are women persistently praying for today? Do modern-day oppressors still fear getting black eyes from mothers of justice? What oppressive systems of this day do archetypal mothers of justice change? What prevents twenty-first-century mothers of justice from speaking out against injustice? Where do women find the courage, compassion, and wisdom to become modern day mothers of justice? How do we use our faith as women of justice today to fight against wage and earnings inequities? How do we stand up for the thousands of women and children left fatherless because of a senseless war in Iraq? What does the "kingdom of God" look like today? Why are not more women crying out for child support to feed and care for their children? How are the voices of women of justice heard when their children are treated unjustly by the American criminal justice system? What is the responsibility of women of justice in the Jena Six situation in Jena, Louisiana, or in other similar cases across America?

The working definition for archetypal mothers of justice are women who may or may not be biological mothers, but their acts of wisdom, compassion, and activism—as persistent matriarchs of movements—encourage freed men, women, and children from oppressive systems of injustice. These were audacious women who stood beside men, helped men, cooked for men, were jailed at times with men, organized labor unions, fought against child labor laws, and stood up for the right to vote and other civil rights. They were activists and social reformers. These women engaged oppressive systems and by their persistence, wisdom, and courage they forced those who were powerful and powerful oppressive systems to grant justice. The widow in the text "is in a precarious situation regarding her 'shame' because she has no male to defend her and the honor of her children and household" (Neyrey 1991, 63; Camp 1991). These archetypal mothers stood in the gap for equality for all who experienced systemic injustices in one way or another.

Womanist scholars have the freedom to use all of their experiences and resources at their discretion: ways of seeing, of knowing, or of connecting. Our history of oppression gives us a unique perspective and the use of *every* available resource to determine the best points to make. Therefore, I choose the structural methodology of Boers and Ricoeur to develop a "hermeneutic of the marginalized."

Scholarly Exegetical Assistance toward a Hermeneutic of the Marginalized

I hold the structural methodology of Hendrikus Boers and the poststructural methodology of Paul Ricoeur in creative tension as I examine the plight of the widow in Luke 18:1–8 as a mother figure. Using these two methods, I develop a "hermeneutic of the marginalized." The constitutive elements are: (1) a crying out or calling out to God—an encounter; (2) meditating, inner contemplation, or an inner conversation with God—an engagement; and (3) a change in action or an incomprehensible decision—an exchange or a reversal.[2]

Initially I planned to compare the methodologies of traditional biblical exegetical methods (e.g., text, form, source, literary) of Luke 18 to Ricoeur's poststructural methodologies of philosophical hermeneutics. I soon moved to a comparison of structural methods because traditional biblical criticisms presuppose a historical analysis with some preunderstanding that the biblical text provides a gateway to understanding history. Conversely, structural exegesis assumes some form of a linguistic paradigm (such as Boers) that takes language into account as the category for analysis rather than as a gateway that accesses history (Patte 1976, 1). Shifting my focus affords a comparison of different methodologies towards a "hermeneutic of the marginalized."

Translation of Luke 18:1–8

(1) Then he told them a parable that it is necessary to pray always and not become weary.

(2) Jesus said, "In a certain city was a judge who was not fearing God and who had no respect for human beings.

(3) Now a widow was in that city, and she was coming to him [the judge] saying, 'Give me justice from my adversary.'

(4) And after a time he [the judge] did not want to; indeed, he said these things to himself, 'I am not afraid of God, and I do not respect a human being.

(5) Truly, I will give her justice because this widow gives me trouble [black eye] so that her coming might not wear me out.'

(6) Then the Lord commanded, 'Hear what the evil judge says,'

(7) And will not God do justice for God's elect who are crying out day and night, and will God delay for them?

(8) I say to you that [God] will grant justice without delay to them. However, will the Son of Man then find faith upon the earth when he comes?"

Structuralism toward Hermeneutics of Testimony to Suspicion

Biblical scholars began using structural methodologies and procedures to interpret the biblical text in the 1960s and 1970s because French and North American structuralist critics showed interest in the Bible.[3] Historically, structuralism began with the work of Ferdinand de Saussure, who argued

---

2. I have modified the elements of Paul Ricoeur in his presentation of the elements found in each parable.

3. For further discussion, see Barton 1988, 10–11.

that meaning is derived from the interlocking functions and interlocking relationships of linguists and language. The work of Saussure and Hermann Gunkel opened a gateway allowing New Testament biblical scholars to see the language of the text as a structure.[4] The works of other scholars in other fields, such as semiotics, added shape and form to structuralism. According to Daniel Patte, structural exegesis is "that which employs those exegetical methods which are deliberately derived from the methodologies of the linguist Ferdinand de Saussure, and of the anthropologist Claude Lévi-Strauss" (Patte 1976, 1). Building upon this foundation, Edgar V. McKnight and Hendrikus Boers expanded the methods of structuralism and structural exegesis for New Testament exegetes (see McKnight 1978; Patte 1976; Boers 1988). Therefore, structuralists assert that words have a relational meaning, not just an essential meaning. In the structural analysis of this essay, I rely heavily on Hendrikus Boers's work and his paradigm for interpretation developed from the analytical categories of A. J. Greimas. Later in this essay, I develop the relational, fixed, or objective meaning, which I shall label text-interpretations, to move me one step closer to a hermeneutic of the marginalized around the mother-widow, recognizing that there may be a plurality of vast possible meanings that are objective and that follow what is in the text.

During the same period that structuralism was surfacing in the 1960s and 1970s, there were reactions to this form of interpretation called poststructuralism or deconstructionism. Poststructuralism bases its methodologies on the works of Plato, Aristotle, Fredrick Schleiermacher, Wilhelm Dilthey, Jacques Derrida, Monroe Beardslee, Wolfgang Iser, and Paul Ricoeur, among others. Poststructuralism presupposes a careful or close reading of texts, "drawing attention not to the main lines of argument which they contain, but also to the metaphors in which the argument is expressed, and which, as it transpires, undermine the argument itself" (Davies 1992, 424–26). Unlike structuralists, poststructuralists chose to embrace the history surrounding a text, following the work of Jacques Derrida, who sought to take history sincerely and circularly without obtaining a final meaning. Paul Ricoeur might argue that the meaning of a piece of writing lies neither in the author's intentions nor within the words of the text itself but in the interplay between the text and the reader as the text comes alive (Ricoeur 1981).

I propose a creative new paradigm using the work of Paul Ricoeur and his paradigm for interpreting the parables of Jesus on the subject of the kingdom of God. Further, I propose a meaning, which I shall label self-interpretation, to move toward a hermeneutic of what I call marginalized.

Hendrikus Boers provides an introduction to a general methodology of interpreting biblical narratives. He applies the semiotic insights of A. J.

---

4. See McKnight 1988 for a review of linguistic history of reader-response and reader-oriented criticism.

Gremas to interpretation of scripture. Another level of interpretation can be found only when there is a question of meaning and what meaning is for C. Lévi-Strauss as quoted by H. Wayne Merritt, "What is the 'meaning of the meaning' of this literary, compositional technique that is presently, sufficiently established."[5] Boers uses a narrative schema to interpret the abstract structure of a text that includes Need/Lack, Preparedness, Performance, and Sanction as a means of analyzing that uses the work of A. J. Greimas (see the definition of the terms in the following chart).

Narrative Schema[6]

A. Need/Lack	B. Preparedness	C. Performance	D. Sanction
A subject of a circumstance, disjoined from a desirable object, or conjoined with an undesirable object	An active subject, willing or obliged, and able (having the power), to overcome the need, specified in A, by a performance	The active subject performing the action transforming the circumstances specified in A into its opposite	Recognition of the success or failure of the performance, or of the achievement of a desired value

These terms are a way to analyze the narrative trajectory, or the course of the discourse. Boers states that:

> This narrative schema is not merely the formalization of what is said in the text, but a structure which can clarify what happens syntactically. This is similar to our expectation of a sentence. . . . All four phases of the narrative schema do not have to be actually represented in the text; nevertheless they are presupposed by those that are represented. So for example, if one has only the *performance* of an action in a text, it presupposes a *need* that the performance has to satisfy, and a subject who is *prepared* to carry it out; it also anticipates a *sanction* indicating whether it is a success or a failure. (Boers 1988, 9).

Based on these definitions, I chart the format of the parable found in Luke 18:1–8 from the standpoints of both the characters in the text, the widow and the judge, and Mother Mary Jones.

---

5. See Merritt 1990, 97–108, quoting from Lévi-Strauss, "The Meeting of Myth and Science." According to Lévi-Strauss, "There is something very curious in semantics, that the word 'meaning' is probably, in the whole language, the word the meaning of which is the most difficult to find. What does 'to mean' mean?" (1979, 12).

6. Boers 1988, 9.

Point of View—Widow

Need/Lack	Preparedness	Performance	Sanction
Justice disjoined from justice and society	Powerless Willing yet unable	Repeatedly coming to the judge to request justice from the ruling class	Conjoined to society Disjoined from opponent
Conjoined to judge	Know-how to overcome is persistence		Justice granted

Point of View—Judge

Need/Lack	Preparedness	Performance	Sanction
Respect for God and humans	Powerful and has the know-how to grant justice	Has an internal struggle with self observed via self-talk and contemplation	Grants justice to the widow and is conjoined to the widow and society
Disjoined from God, the widow, and society	Able yet unwilling to grant justice		Justice granted
Conjoined to widow			

Point of View—Mary Harris Jones "Mother Jones"

Need/Lack	Preparedness	Performance	Sanction
Justice disjoined from justice and society	Powerless Willing yet unable	Repeated activist fighting for the rights of workers and their families	Conjoined to miners, Industrial Workers of America, Children's Crusade
Conjoined to political elite	Know-how to overcome is persistence and the ability to influence and organize workers and families	She confronted President Theodore Roosevelt, WV Governor William Glassock, and WV District Attny Reese Blizzard	Disjoined from opponent politicians Justice granted

The text-interpretation of the passage suggests that the widow has little power to overcome her circumstances, yet she uses what she has on her side: time. She has the time to keep coming to and bothering the judge until she receives a desired result, in this case justice. On the other hand, the judge is powerful and thinks he has no real need to be conjoined to the widow, but he engages in inner contemplation and self-talk; one could say the judge struggled with himself over his lack of fear of God and humans.

Therefore, he talks himself into granting justice, and perhaps in so doing he is conjoined not only to the widow but also to God and the society where he lives. God seems to use the judge's unwillingness to cause the judge to see and contemplate his frailness and callous behavior toward the widow.

In Paul Ricoeur's "The 'Kingdom' in the Parables of Jesus," first published in 1976 and translated into English in 1981, Ricoeur analyzes the parables by (1) the literary resources utilized; (2) the role of story in the parables; (3) extravagance in the parables; (4) time in the parables; and, (5) the worlds of the parables (Ricoeur 1981). I apply four of the five methods to develop a self-interpretation of the parable in Luke 18:1–8 to obtain additional elements for a hermeneutic of the marginalized.

In this parable the literary resources that Jesus uses are symbolism and hyperbole or exaggeration. According to Ricoeur, a parable "surprises, astonishes, shocks, provokes: exposing such and such a prejudgment. . . . it obliges one to reconsider things, to come to a new decision" (Ricoeur 1981, 166). In addition, Jesus teaches by means of metaphor; he begins by saying that there is always a necessity for prayer, yet there is no other reference to prayer or praying in the storyline or plot of the parable.

Ricoeur might argue that the role of the story in this parable is exaggeration. The parable of the widow and the judge is just an "ordinary story whose entire metaphorical power is concentrated in the moment of crisis and in a denouement that is either tragic or comic" (Ricoeur 1981, 167). In this particular case, the denouement is comic because it has a happy ending. The moment of crisis comes when the judge finally makes a decision after serious contemplation and internal struggle caused by the widow's persistent and bothersome request.

Ricoeur's third analytical trait is found in the extravagance in the parable. In this analysis there are several factors, or critical moments, that would surprise, astonish, or shock the reader. First, how could some judges grant justice to a person without receiving a bribe first, seeing that Jesus spoke out against tax collectors and others in powerful positions that accepted bribes (Reid 2002, 284–94; see also Weaver 2002, 317–19)? Or, what judge has no respect for humans? Second, what widow would risk bothering a high-ranking official, requesting justice without bribery or an influence over the judge? Or, what ancient widow would pester a man in public? Both of these characters operate from an exaggerated perspective, and readers and/or hearers are left with a paradoxical situation. In daily, ancient Palestinian life, if one wanted justice, one would expect justice only from a judge who had been bribed (Reid 2002, 284–94).

Widows in the Greco-Roman world were vulnerable, placed in harm's way, and often exploited and taken advantage of in the community (Price 1996, 1212). The widow in Luke 18 lost the protection of her husband; therefore, she faced socioeconomic oppression. This unnamed widow became the "target for exploitation" (Herzog 1994, 225). Specifically, financial oppression left her no choice but to seek justice and vindication from the courts. Jesus rewarded and commented upon this widow's great risk and her faithfulness. Perhaps if this widow had other means, such as bribe money or sons to plea-bargain for her, she would have received justice or vindication sooner. She did what I call P.U.S.H. Metaphorically, she Prayed Until Something Happened. Her strategy was not to give in to her unfair circumstances without at least confronting the judge and trying to persuade him to act favorably on her behalf. The persistent, constant prayer motif begets positive results; praying day and night delivers, and God answers and grants justice in this parable. The timing of God's actions can require centuries of prayer and faith before justice is granted, as is the case with American slavery.

Now, the extravagant thing in this parable is that the widow received justice without paying any bribe money; she used what little power she had: time and persistence. The elements that caused this surprising result came from a judge without pity or moral religious ethics; that is, he (or she) is without fear of anyone or anything, yet justice is granted. Disorientation or a distanciation, as Ricoeur would say (1981), takes place in dialectical opposition to reorientation or appropriation. That is to say, the widow is distanced from the justice, and the judge is distanced from society, and the vehicle of extravagance is the impetus for this disorientation.

The confusion that takes place in the extravagance of the parable is resolved when I examine the time elements that reorient the characters of the parable. Oddly enough, the storyline provides, in Ricoeur's words (1981), an encounter, an engagement, and a reversal. At this level, the parable speaks to us about prayer. I can decipher from the parable what prayer is like. There is a need for an encounter and engagement with God. As a result of this encounter and engagement, a reversal takes place. The surprise is not that the action of the widow astonishes us as much as the action of the judge surprises and astonishes us. The judge does not remove the widow from his courtroom, which is his privilege to do. The judge engages in a dialogue with himself, contemplates and perhaps meditates on the widow's request, such that a change takes place. Then the judge makes a decision, which is a reversal of a previous decision. He decides to see and do things differently. What he does definitely does not make sense. The judge is the one with the real encounter with God. Prayer after deep contemplation and inner self-talk changes us, though not necessarily the circumstances. In this parable, the judge is the one who changes.

Toward a Hermeneutic of the Marginalized

Tradition teaches us and some biblical scholars assert that the judge represents God when God responds to prayer and faith. What about another possible metaphor for God: the widow? Allegorically, this parable is about a widow, rather than a judge, who represents God. The widow, who is like God, comes to us over and over and over again until we meditate and contemplate within ourselves and make a decision to change our ways. We decide to do something that does not make sense. We forgive someone who has wronged us; we grant justice to someone whom we do not think deserves justice from us; we pray for someone who has used us. At that moment, we are engrossed in the power of prayer like the judge, and we contemplate. After we do some serious inner self-talk and meditation, we miraculously do the unexpected. I believe this is how African American slaves survived as chattel in a hostile world.

One can discern that the world in which African American slaves found themselves was a world that distanced them from mainstream society. The slaves operated in one world, yet through contemplation and meditation they appropriated themselves by transcending to another world and being present in the world of the here and now. Slaves received liberation as they distanced themselves from their circumstances, from a world of hostility, while working for justice in surreptitious ways in present time. They realized eschatology, in which they found themselves, and they appropriated a new world or a hermeneutic—a hermeneutic of the marginalized. Slaves sought a new worldview that one day would provide them, their children, and their children's children justice for all (Earl 1993). Luke 18:1–8 is about justice.

The Greek word ἐκδίκησις, which means justice, is found a total of six times in the New Testament, with the same case and number, twice in the current passage: Luke 18:7, 8; Acts 7:24; 2 Cor 7:11; 2 Thess 1:8; 1 Pet 2:14. The word is translated several ways in the New Testament: rendering of justice; avenge; punishment; retribution; vindicate; and revenge. I have chosen the meaning "rendering of justice" to emphasize that the widow seeks justice under the law from a judge. Since Luke's Gospel tends to spend a lot of time on the marginalized, it is possible that he was familiar with God's concern for justice for the poor, especially widows: "God's justice aims at creating an egalitarian community in which all classes of people maintain their basic human rights" (Mafico 1992, 1129). God's justice is the justice that African American slaves sought and is prevalent in the words of slaves.

The slaves' justice emerges in their words and prayers. According to Riggins Earl, the slaves "ingeniously reconstructed their masters' fragmented teachings of the Bible" (1993, 3). In so doing, they appropriated a new world, one that was forgiving and tolerable of their existence: through their prayers, the status of their being changed. They saw themselves not so much as the property of the slave masters but eschatologically as property of God. Earl says that "language [which included prayers] allowed slaves to make the transition from the status of being the master's property to that of being authentic members of the family of God" (3). Slaves appropriated a new world that distanced them from their present world. This new world allowed them to live a life so that they could tolerate and ultimately forgive those who persecuted them. The slaves' new world was "a metaphorical network" (Ricoeur 1981, 165–69) where they prayed, sang, reformulated the biblical stories, and worshiped their God together. I believe the slave transcendence was an ontological identity change. For me, ontological identity is developed through the integration of life experiences, the relationships one has made and continues to make, as well as one's personhood. During these times, they spoke of hope in an eschatological manner that propelled them to see justice as a part of the by-and-by, but also to see justice as a part of their own immediate righteous behavior. Following are examples of the prayers of two former slaves that demonstrate this point:

"A Slave Woman's Prayer" as Recorded in 1816

> O Lord, bless my master. When he calls upon thee to damn his soul, do not hear him, do not hear him, but hear me—save him—make him know he is wicked, and he will pray to thee. I am afraid, O Lord, I have wished him bad wishes in my heart—keep me from wishing him bad—though he whips me and beats me sore, tell me of my sins, and make me pray more to thee—make me more glad for what thou hast done for me. A poor [N]egro. (Washington 1994, 19)

"Always Pray" by Sojourner Truth 1878

> Oh, God, you know how much I am distressed, for I have told you again and again. Now, God, help me get my son. If you were in trouble, as I am, and I could help you, as you can me, think I wouldn't do it? Yes, God you *know* I would do it. Oh, God, you know I have no money, but you can make the people do for me, and you must make the people do for me. I will never give you peace till you do, God. Oh, God, make the people hear me—don't let them turn me off, without hearing and helping me. (Washington 1994, 57)

I believe the prayers of these slaves demonstrate that the slaves encountered God, and their prayers are the indication that they meditated and changed how they saw their world. In addition, there were slaves who protested their circumstances. Their stubborn agitation and possible uprising was a threat. There were slaves like Harriet Tubman who in nonviolent and violent resistance challenged the institution of slavery. Slaves like Denmark Vesey, Nat Turner, and others were responsible for hundreds of slave revolts that may have caused the escalation of President Lincoln's Emancipation.[7] The actions of slaves in nonviolent and in violent ways helped them to survive. The slaves recognized that there was no justice in the slavery institution and systems of oppression that their owners and

---

7. See "Slave Rebellions and Uprisings in the U.S." on the History Guy website http://www.historyguy.com/slave_rebellions_usa.htm.

masters employed. The slaves continued to pray, and they were persistent in their prayers for justice. They knew that there was justice and it was in the hands of God alone.

Mother Mary Harris Jones (1837–1930)

Oftentimes when tragedy befalls people, they become stuck wailing in their predicament. The widow in the text, African American slaves, and Mother Jones faced their predicaments head-on to obtain the justice they knew they deserved for themselves and others. Mother Jones survived the death of her husband and four children to yellow fever in Tennessee in 1867. She moved to Chicago only to survive the Great Chicago Fire in 1871. After enduring such heartache, she had a right to give up; it would have been understandable if Mother Jones had simply given up. Instead, Mother Jones is known for her famous words, "Pray for the dead, and fight like hell for the living" (Gorn 2001).

In Mother Jones's audacity, she confronted the oppressive systems of her day. She did not allow her status as a woman and widow to confine her to the status quo. She organized labor unions, wives of mine workers and "mop and broom brigades," and she embraced her role as a matriarch to overcome all of her obstacles to force change in America. This change occurred when women did not have the right to vote (Gorn 2001). Similar to the widow in Luke 18, she had no power, no voice, and no resources, yet she changed the world for the better by bringing to the consciousness of others the cruelty of working conditions for women, men, and children. She fought for, marched for, and got the results she sought: justice. Mother Jones's prayer was for the dead, and she used her marginalized status and the marginalized status of the working class to raise the consciousness of America. The current child labor laws in this country are essentially because of the work of Mother Jones. Mother Jones did not become weary in her old age after tragedy. She demonstrated her lack of fear of wealthy politicians. She used what she had: her ability to organize and influence the working-class majority to join in her protest. Elizabeth Gurley Flynn, a nationally known labor organizer, called Jones "the greatest woman agitator of our times." She was denounced in the United States Senate as the grandmother of all agitators. Mother Jones was proud of that title and said she hoped to live to be "the great-grandmother of agitators" (Hawse 2007). She was as stubborn an agitator as the widow in the parable, according to Luise Schottroff:

> The parable of the stubborn widow provides a cameo model and an example in which faith is pictured as the patient labor of resistance in everyday life, a crying for justice. The parable speaks of a widow because, within the context of biblical tradition, talk of widows conjures up the structural violence of patriarchy and God's partiality for its victims. What we see in the parable is not a victim to be pitied but a woman who fights

tenaciously and whom a sexist judge denounces as potentially violent. It is worth considering whether the stubborn widow does not hold up a better model for Christian women—and men—than the model of an innocent, nonviolent Jesus. . . . Resistance to sexism has to be seen as part of the resistance to violence in all its forms. (Schottroff 1995, 116–17)

Mother Jones fits the archetypal definition for a mother of justice. Her acts of wisdom, compassion, social activism, stubborn persistence, and courage helped move freed men, women, and children from systemic oppression, namely, classism and sexism. She encountered oppression, she engaged the oppressive systems, and she engaged those who were in powerful political positions and the powerful systems that kept oppression in place. Her encounter and her engagement were relentless until an exchange occurred. The former ways of systemic injustice were reversed finally to grant justice to all who experienced systemic oppression in the child labor laws of the United States. What would Mother Jones be doing today? I wonder if Mother Jones would be protesting against the war in Iraq? I wonder if Mother Jones would be protesting for the widows and children left fatherless because of the war in Iraq? I wonder if Mother Jones would protest the inequities of salaries of women who do the same jobs as men for less pay? Would Mother Jones be interested in the Genarlow Wilson case and other cases of injustice for young black men in America? What mother-of-justice archetypes in the vein of Mother Jones and Marian Wright Edelman will pick up the banner for justice of all children?

A Womanist Approach to a Hermeneutic of the Marginalized

By comparing the words of these prayers with the actions of the characters in the parable, I can develop a hermeneutic of the marginalized. There are similarities between the need for prayer and the need for justice in the parable and in the prayers of the marginalized. Oftentimes it is not easy to spell out exactly how such parables function. However, the metaphor and the narrative both appeal to something innate in the human psyche that involves the hearer more profoundly than either the statements or imperatives in the parable do. This appeal depends on an emotional, transcendent, and aesthetic stimulus, and it is possibly very necessary for us to confront ourselves. This parable serves to make prayer available to all—it also makes it necessary for all—rich and poor alike: it illuminates; it demands an encounter, an engagement, and a reversal with the rewards of a changed person or system.

The Lukan Jesus emphasizes action, a necessary quality for persons who are waiting for something that is not to be immediate. Many scholars note Luke's interest in oppressed people, especially women and the poor, and the several references to prayer (see Johnson 1986, 197–240). According to Goosen and Tomlinson, "Jesus insists that his disciples be people of prayer" (1994, 85). Luke's interest gives me the impetus I need to move toward a hermeneutic of the marginalized. Luke uses words in this parable that signal when the marginalized should pray. In verse 4, he uses "after a time"; in verse 7, he says, "crying out day and night"; and in verse 8 he explains, "without delay." These terms could be associated with prayer in this way: "after a time" could represent a past event; "crying out day and night could represent a continuous event; and "without delay" could represent a present event. I believe these terms represent a time to pray; that is, "after a time" means I must be patient and pray; "crying out day and night" means I must keep on praying; and "without delay" means I must pray immediately—now. This was the prayer hermeneutic of the slaves. They were patient and prayed, they kept on praying, and they prayed in their present situations. This is especially clear in the prayer of Sojourner Truth, an abolitionist born Isabella Baumfree (1797–1883). Now that I have a prayer hermeneutic of African American slaves and of the widow in the parable, I can formulate a hermeneutic of the marginalized. Mother Jones put a new twist on prayer. She suggested fighting for justice with whatever you have even if the only thing you have is your voice.

A hermeneutic of the marginalized can be found in the actions of the widow in the parable, in the actions and prayers of African American slaves, and in the actions of Mother Jones. The poor—the marginalized—in society have frequently resorted to the transcendent power of prayer to relieve their suffering. They have called out to God, meditated, and changed their outlook on their circumstances. The hermeneutic of the marginalized, therefore, requires first crying or calling out to God: an encounter. Second, it requires meditation and inner contemplation or an inner conversation with God: an engagement. Third, it demands a change in action or a decision that does not make sense or it is incomprehensible: an exchange or reversal. The result is a changed, transcended, whole person who is in right relationship with God. Luke pertains to holistic healing—a healing that takes place after an encounter, an engagement, and an exchange or reversal. Holistic healing means a person is wholly in right relationship with God.

I stand on the shoulders of women before me who stood up for justice. In the community where I serve mostly poor people (mainly women and children), I, too, have had to pray persistently, go to court, and face off with police to ensure justice. One incident in particular comes to mind. A DeKalb County policeman barged into an apartment where I was visiting to offer pastoral care. He asked where the mother's oldest son was. She said, "Upstairs." Without asking permission, the peace officer proceeded up the stairs and brought the boy down in handcuffs. I was livid; no rights were given, and the policeman sat the boy on the curb as the Friday night entertainment for the community. The mother did not say a word. My pastoral care chaplains' office is next door. I boldly approached the policeman, identified myself, and said to him that what I just witnessed was not justice. There was a crowd of people watching as the policeman scolded the boy for the entire neighborhood to see. I butted in and told the policeman this had to stop: either read the boy his rights and arrest him or bring him into my office to dispel the crowd. Luckily, the policeman decided to listen to reason and brought the boy into the office, where I questioned him and asked what happened. The boy told me that he was accused of breaking into a car. I asked him when this was supposed to have happened, all the while knowing, since I had been in conversation with the boy and his mother earlier in the day. The boy said he did not know. The person whose car was burglarized was identifying the boy for the police. There was no lineup, just this particular boy for her to identify. The justice system as I know it does not allow for single identification. The accused must be selected from several suspects. The next day, I relayed what happened the night before to my peer, a male chaplain, who said, "You are a powerful woman." I asked, "What does that mean?" He said that I was able to stand up for the boy without being carried off to jail with him. I merely used my power to help a helpless, powerless boy receive some justice. Justice seekers sometimes weigh the consequences, and sometimes they just act regardless of the consequences. My prayer for justice is similar to that of the many women whose acts of courage, wisdom, compassion, and stubborn persistence brought down cruel injustices so that the marginalized in their care might receive justice.

God in God's gracious wisdom gave us anger, and anger is how we mortal humans get in touch with the need for justice. I find that there are times when I am angry; God wants me to get in touch with the injustice around me. Anger is the fuel I need and use to combat injustice. I become angry enough to pray in the midst of and through my anger. I have to encounter my anger, stay close enough to my anger to see my way and what God wants me to do about the injustice I see. I have to pray long enough for my anger to advise me and engage my spirit to give me guidance. Prayer encourages my heart and mind. Prayer gives my spirit the strength to move from where I am to where I need to be. Prayer changes my anger and gives me the fortitude to act—clearly and precisely. Prayer gives me strength to put the information I receive from God in motion. And, the spirit of justice moves as I pray. My prayer is:

> Guide me, O Thou Great Jehovah, Pilgrim through this barren land.
> Guide me, O Thou Great Jehovah, Pilgrim through this barren land.
> I am weak but thou art mighty, Hold me with thou powerful hand.
> I am weak but thou art mighty, Hold me with thou powerful hand.
> Bread of heaven, Bread of heaven, Feed me 'til I want no more.
> Bread of heaven, Bread of heaven, Feed me 'til I want no more.
> (Williams 2001, 135).

God of Justice give me and other mothers wisdom, courage, and compassion.

Grant us the courage to stand in the face of injustice and petition for justice and equality for all. Almighty God, who sent your only begotten Son to bring good news to the poor and let the oppressed go free, help me and others to live up to this anointed call to ministry. God of justice grant me and other mothers the strength to face systemic oppression head-on so that oppressors will open their eyes to see their injustice before you exact punishment on behalf of the poor, the weak, and all those who live under systems of bondage. God of justice, hear my prayer as I come to you daily, morning, noon, and night. God of justice, grant us who seek justice on your behalf the resources to feed the hungry, to give living water and drinking water to those who are thirsty. God of justice, grant us who seek justice on your behalf the resources to welcome strangers, to cloth the naked, and to visit those in prison. God of justice, help me and other mothers who seek justice on your behalf the courage to encounter and engage oppressive systems, until those persons in control of oppressive systems exchange their ways for your ways and understand your distribution and retribution. This is my prayer. Hear me and grant justice, for I will give you no peace. Let the cries of women and men who fought for justice in times past, times present, and times to come worry you. Hear me in Jesus' name. Ashe, and Amen.

Works Cited

Barton, John. 1988. Reading and Interpreting the Bible. Pages 2–13 in *Harper's Bible Commentary*. Edited by James Luther Mays. New York: Harper & Row.

Boers, Hendrickus. 1988. *Neither on This Mountain Nor in Jerusalem: A Study of John 4*. SBLMS 35. Atlanta: Scholars Press.

Camp, Claudia V. 1991. Understanding a Patriarchy: Women in Second Century Jerusalem through the Eyes of Ben Sira. Pages 1–39 in *"Women Like This": New Perspectives on Jewish Women in the Greco-Roman World*. Edited by Amy-Jill Levine. SBLEJL 1. Atlanta: Scholars Press.

Davies, Margaret. 1992. Post-structural Analysis. *ABD* 5:424–26.

Earl, Riggins R. 1993. *Dark Symbols, Obscure Signs: God, Self, and Community in the Slave Mind* New York: Orbis.

Goldstein, Richard. 2007. Irene Morgan Kirkaldy, 90, Rights Pioneer, Dies. *The New York Times*. Online: http://nytimes.com/2007/08/13/us/13kirkaldy .html?partner=rssnyt&emc=rss.

Goosen, Gideon, and Margaret Tomlinson. 1994. *Studying the Gospels: An Introduction*. Ridgefield, Ct.: Morehouse.

Gorn, Elliot J. 2001. Mother Jones: The Woman. MotherJones. Online: http://www .motherjones.com/politics/2001/05/mother-jones-woman.

Hawse, Mara Lou. 2007. Mother Jones: The Miners Angel. *The Illinois Labor History Society*. Online: http://www.kentlaw.edu/ilhs/majones.htm.

Herzog, William R., III. 1994. *Parables as Subversive Speech: Jesus as Pedagogue of the Oppressed*. Louisville: Westminster John Knox.

Johnson, Luke Timothy. 1986. *The Writings of the New Testament: An Interpretation*. Philadelphia: Fortress.

———. 1991 *The Gospel of Luke*. SP 3. Collegeville, Minn.: Liturgical Press.

Lévi-Strauss, Claude. 1979. *Myth and Meaning*. New York: Schocken.

Mafico, Temba L. 1992. Just, Justice. *ABD* 3:1129.

McKnight, Edgar.1978. *Meaning in Texts.* Philadelphia: Fortress.

———. 1988. *Post-modern Use of the Bible: The Emergence of Reader-Oriented Criticism* Nashville: Abingdon.

Merritt, Wayne H. 1990. The Angel's Announcement: A Structuralist Study. Pages 97–108 in *Text and Logos: The Humanistic Interpretation of the New Testament.* Edited by Theodore W. Jennings Jr. Atlanta: Scholars Press.

Neyrey, Jerome H. 1991. *The Social World of Luke-Acts: Models for Interpretation.* Peabody, Mass.: Hendrickson.

Patte, Daniel. 1976. *What Is Structural Exegesis?* GBS. Philadelphia: Fortress.

Price, James L. 1996. Widow. Page 1212 in *The HarperCollins Bible Dictionary.* Edited by Paul J. Achtemeir. New York: HarperCollins.

Reid, Barbara E. 2002. Beyond Petty Pursuits and Wearisome Widows: Three Lukan Parables. *Int* 56:284–94.

Ricoeur, Paul. 1981. The "Kingdom" in the Parables of Jesus. *AThR* 63:165–69.

Schottroff, Luise. 1995. *Lydia's Impatient Sisters.* Translated by Barbara and Martin Rumscheidt. Louisville: Westminster John Knox.

Washington, James M. 1994. *Conversations with God: Two Centuries of Prayers by African Americans.* New York: HarperCollins.

Weaver, Dorothy Jean. 2002. Luke 18:1–8. *Int* 56:317–19.

Williams, William. 2001. "Guide Me, O Thou Great Jehovah." *African American Heritage Hymnal.* Chicago: GIA Publications.

13

"Mother Knows Best"

THE STORY OF MOTHER PAUL REVISITED

Margaret Aymer

In 1990, Beverly Gaventa drew academic attention to a curiosity within the writings of Paul of Tarsus: in at least three instances, (1 Cor 3:2; Gal 4:19; 1 Thess 2:7), Paul refers to himself in motherly language (Gaventa 1990; 2004). Gaventa notes, "The metaphor that underlies all three of these passages is 'I am your mother'" (Gaventa 2004, 86). Gaventa goes on to call these metaphors "squared" metaphors, for they involve not only a sig-nification on the object of the metaphor (the gospel as milk; the presence of either Christ or the community as a new-born infant; the community as infant children) but also a signification on Paul as mother (2004, 86–88). Gaventa's "metaphor squared"—perhaps more accurately, "metaphor queered"—raises the question of motive.[1] What possible benefit could attend the *über*-masculine Paul that he should choose to "metaphorize" himself, to use Gaventa's barbarism, as a mother (Clines 2003)?

Gaventa suggests a number of responses. She claims that, with mater-nal imagery, Paul is signifying upon the long-term relationship between himself and his congregations. His use of maternal imagery, she argues, differs from his use of paternal imagery in that the latter signifies "the initial phase of Christian preaching and conversion" (Gaventa 2004, 89). Further, she argues that Paul's use of maternal imagery signifies not so much on his "apostolic office" as his vocation (91). Particular to Paul's Galatian "labor pains" (*ōdinō*), Gaventa argues that this birth language "associates Paul's apostolic vocation with the anguish anticipated in an apocalyptic era and recalls to the Galatians their own crucifixion in Christ" (1990, 191).[2]

---

1. The "queerness" of Paul's self-identification as a mother begs addressing but cannot be tackled in this short essay.

2. Gaventa goes on to note that such a reading makes this "not an emotional outburst but an important theological link between this section of personal appeal

All of which still begs, for me, the central question: Why a mother? Surely other kinship metaphors, particularly those pertaining to "kinfolk" (*adelphoi*), would suffice to denote Paul's ongoing relationship with any of his "assemblies" (*ekklēsia*). Neither does Gaventa's argument that the use of maternal imagery denotes Paul's vocation answer the question of why, for it is not at all clear what would make motherhood more vocational than fatherhood, particularly to a first-century man of either Jewish, Roman, or, as in Paul's case, bi-/multi(ply)-cultured identities. And it seems odd that Paul would use his "labor pains" to denote apocalyptic anguish. Clearly, one can make such an argument with reference to the metaphoric description of the birth pains of the created order, of the whole community of God, or of the Deity. However, there does not appear to be any other canonical evidence for an actual human male self-signifying as a birthing or nursing mother.[3] What, then, is the "nursery rhyme" that Paul is spinning as the "Mother Goose" of the early church, and why is he spinning it?

Roman[4] Motherhood: A Short Excursus

Perhaps we might call this Pauline fiction "Mother Knows Best." Set in the first-century of the Roman-occupied world, it is a collection of three "stories" or "fictions" about the ideal child-nurse and/or Roman mother, in turns the "mammy" and "June Cleaver" of the ancient Roman world, and of her relationship with her recalcitrant children.[5] Paul, of course, is

---

and the remainder of the letter." I confess, working within the context of historically black theological education, I am puzzled by the distinction between emotion and theology.

3. Contrary to Gaventa, a brief survey of the Septuagint and Greek New Testament use of *ōdinein* shows that in no other text is a similar use found. The basic metaphor of the pains of the birthing mother is found in Ps 7:15, Sir 19:11; 34:5, Hab 3:10; and Isa 23: 4. The birth pains of Zion are recorded in Mic 4:10; Isa 66:7–8; and Jer 4:3; 12:2. The birth pains of the entire people of God are found in Sir 48:19; Isa 26:17–18; and Jer 49:22. But in no other instance does an actual male character refer to himself as being in birth pains; neither does any other narrator refer to an actual male character as being in birth pains, although Sirach makes a reference to a generic "fool" for whom the hearing of news causes him to have "birth pains" until it is delivered. Here further study is clearly warranted, to research the possible use of the metaphor outside of the canon.

4. This is not an argument about citizenship or geographic location, but rather one of culturally recognized type. Further research might demonstrate whether similar cultural tropes exist in other Roman-dominated groups; of particular interest to Pauline studies would be whether Jewish ideals of motherhood of the first century pattern themselves in any way after or over against Roman ideals.

5. As will be discussed below, most child-nurses (wet- and dry-nurses) were slave women (see especially Joshel 1986). Just as in ancient times, so also twentieth-century idealizations of the child-nurse and the mother center around male fantasies of the ideal mother-type, fantasies typified in some ways by "mammy," the African American slave woman and child-nurse typified by Hattie McDaniel's

the protagonist of each of these fictions. Very much like the contemporary fictions of mammy and June Cleaver, I propose that Paul's "fictions" about his "mammy/motherhood" are rooted in ancient images of ideal Roman maternity and that a study of these images may give us the beginnings of an answer to the question, Why a mother?

In her seminal text on Roman motherhood, Suzanne Dixon traces carefully the contours of Roman idealization of maternity. She notes that the preponderance of images of the Roman matron center around "a formidable stereotype, strongest within the aristocratic echelons, of the unbending moral mentor, guardian of traditional virtue and object of a lifelong respect comparable with, though not equal to, that accorded a *paterfamilias*" (Dixon 1998, 2, 6–7). According to the moralists, the Roman matron was expected to stand as a force with which even adult children had to reckon, and she was buttressed by a society in which "*pietas in parentes* is a virtue intended to apply until the death of the parents" (234).

By contrast, the child-nurse (*nutrix*) was frequently a slave and always a poor woman with few options except those afforded her by her bodily functions. Yet, in her helpful article on the role of the child-nurse, Sandra Joshel reminds us that not even the child-nurse was completely powerless; she held a position of power over the helpless master-infant, a power that was acknowledged by her charges even when they were adults (Joshel 1986, 10–11, 21). That nurses knew themselves to be powerful is reflected in the epitaphs that they wrote for children under their care who died in infancy. Joshel notes that in these epitaphs, they named themselves "nurse" rather than "freed slave" or "slave" of a powerful person, and in so doing nurses "announced that a socially prominent and powerful person once relied on" them (21). Indeed, child-nurses commanded such a level of respect that they were often freed in their old age and memorialized by their charges upon their death (19–20, 21).[6]

To be sure, free men, not women or slaves, had absolute legal and societal power in ancient world societies, and the power of *patria potestas* was reserved to the oldest free man in the Roman family unit. Nevertheless, Dixon's and Joshel's writings suggest that we should not necessarily conclude that when Paul "metaphorizes" himself as "mother" he is figuring himself as one in a position of weakness. Rather, a brief examination of Roman ideals suggests that, whether signifying on himself as child-nurse or as mother, Paul's "fictions" would likely have been understood by his

---

portrayal in the 1939 film *Gone with the Wind* and "June Cleaver," white U.S. matriarch typified by Barbara Billingsley in the 1957–1963 television serial *Leave It to Beaver*. To be sure, there are many others.

6. Joshel points out that, while epitaphs written by the elite for their nurses emphasize the nurse's station, either as slave or as freedwoman, epitaphs written by nurses themselves emphasize only their station: nurse of this particular elite person who "relied on them."

assemblies as a statement of his relative, although not absolute, authority and power.

Paul's "fictions," then, begin with a strong Roman mother or at least with a child-nurse, a woman authoritative relative to her charge; in either case she, Paul, is a formidable woman within the Roman cultural matrix. Mother Paul's specific social power rests in her role as the expected moral compass for her children, even her adult male children (Dixon 1988, 233). Suzanne Dixon's work is most helpful here. She shows that the Roman mother was expected to exhibit "strength and moral purpose" (188). In her adolescent children, she was

> expected to participate in decisions concerning an adolescent son's train-
> ing and career even if his father were alive.. . . She was generally expected
> to show a keen and detailed interest in her son's activities, to encourage
> and identify with his aspirations and to correct any wrong-headed youth-
> ful tendencies. (176–77)

Even in her adult sons, she was to "inspire and foster legitimate ambition" and to "curb mature excesses" (188). Moreover, and perhaps most aston-ishingly, "[they were] expected to defer to her wishes within recognised limits" (202–3).

Less power accrued to the Roman child-nurse; she was, after all, still a slave or a poor freedwoman (*liberta*). Yet the parodies of the satirists reveal that even the child-nurse could control the moral compass of her adult charge, whether for good or (more often among the satirists) for ill. Take, for instance, the supposed influence of the child-nurse on her adult female charge.

> [She] is portrayed as someone who encourages the tendencies of free
> women to resist traditional gender relations in which women are sub-
> ordinate and accessible. The poet or husband/author images that it is
> the nurse's intrusion, not the independent action of the woman, which
> thwarts his desire. (Joshel 1986, 10)

This is a remarkable amount of moral suasion to attribute to a mere slave, but, to the extent that one can make parallels between ancient slavery and slavery in the United States, one can argue that it is not out of charac-ter for the child-nurse commonly referred to in the south as the mammy. As Annie Laurie Broidrick of Mississippi confessed about her family slave nurse, "We had the greatest love for her, but it was tempered with fear, for she never overlooked a fault" (Joshel 1986, 12). If Broidrick's relationship to her child-nurse may be tentatively held up as an example of what one might expect, it is quite possible that child-nurses of the Roman-dominated region also held moral sway over their charges well into their adult lives.

None of this unequivocally negates the possibility that some mothers practiced maternal indulgence toward children in a manner more like our modern fictions of "motherhood." However, Dixon points out that, at least in the writings of ancient Romans, such *indulgentia* is associated with servants. The famous mothers [held up as *exempla* by the moralists] are admired for their *disciplina ac severitas*— their vigilance and high standards—rather than the "softer" qualities of patience or tenderness. (Dixon 1988, 3)

It is possible that the relationship between the child-nurse and her charge might have been one of *indulgentia*. Evidence suggests that the child-nurse was memorialized by her former nurslings as "freely loving and devoted" and "unambivalently committed and devoted to their charges" (Joshel 1986, 8). However, these memorials capture the concerns of the ruling classes rather than those of the women forced to feed and to nurture them.

Once again, we might turn with caution to African American slave women to discover parallel voices that might speak for those slave child-nurses silenced by ancient, elitist history. In listening to these voices, we find that, at least in the nineteenth century in the United States, slave child-nurses cared more about the fate of their own children, and the orphaned children of others within the slave community, than they did about their assigned charges. When it came to their duty, there was a limit to their affection (Joshel 1986, 12–14). While far more research is necessary here, one might surmise a similar limit to the affection of Roman child-nurses for their nurslings, that, with regard to the infants who would become their future masters, such affection (*indulgentia*) was, in part, an affectation unnecessary when the children in question were their own.

The evidence suggests, then, that the Roman mother and to some extent the child-nurse was a woman of authority, one whose accepted and expected social role was the moral formation of her children. To that end, she would use whatever techniques were necessary, including "entreaty and bullying," to ensure that her children grew in wisdom and virtue (Dixon 1988, 194). As will become evident below, it is she, rather than any of our modern idealizations, who is the pattern for "Mother" Paul.

Mother Paul

With this reimagined Roman mother-mammy in mind, let us consider, briefly, the ways in which Paul's self-figuration as "mother" plays itself out in the three key passages. To begin, let us look at the crisis in Corinth. In Corinth, Paul's "children" are divided over questions of patronage, or perhaps better, "paternity."[7] Some are claiming to be children of Apollos, others of Cephas, and still others of Paul (1 Cor 1:12; 3:4). In response, Paul presents an extended argument about the nature of the other-worldly, spiritual wisdom in which he ought to be speaking to the Corinthians. But, as chapter 3 opens, Mother—or at the very least mammy—Paul, steps

---

7. Later Paul reminds the Corinthian assembly that, origin notwithstanding, it was he who became "their father" (1 Cor 4:15), as will be discussed below.

forward, displaying all of the *disciplina ac severitas* expected of a Roman mother (Dixon 1988, 3, 182).

> I was not able to speak to you as spiritual people but as fleshly people, as infants in Christ. *Milk*, I fed you, not food, for you were unable. But you are still unable; you are still fleshly people. For since there is still jealousy and envy in you, are you not fleshly people and do you not walk just like other human beings? For whenever one says, "I am of Paul" and another "I am of Apollos," are you not mere humans? (1 Cor 3:1–3)[8]

Of note in this passage is Paul's claim to have been at the very least the child-nurse, if not indeed the breast-feeding mother, of the entire Corinthian assembly. *"Milk*, I fed you" suggests the dependency of the entire assembly on Mother-Mammy Paul for its existence and sustenance (1 Cor 3:2). As such, it underscores to them Paul's ongoing maternal authority among them, *regardless* of who their father was, with which maternal authority also follows Paul's right and responsibility to call them to virtue and morality. Standing on this maternal authority, Paul is then able to hold them accountable for their moral lapse—their "jealousy and envy," which he characterizes as "merely human" (1 Cor 3:3). Mother Paul, thus, stands firmly in her role as a moral agent to curb the immoral and childish behavior evidenced in the factionalism at Corinth. Further, "she" has a right to expect to be obeyed; filial piety (*pietas in parentes*) still applies even in adulthood.

A similar argument can be made when examining Paul's rhetoric in Gal 4:19.[9] In Galatia, the issue is famously that of circumcision, specifically of the external pressure being placed on some of the Galatian men to be circumcised. Joop Smit argues convincingly that Gal 4:19 falls in the *conquestio* or "appeal to pity" section of the epistle, Gal 4:12–20 (Smit 2002, 51). In a *conquestio*, one aspect of the appeal might be to "ask the audience to think of their parents" (51). This is what Paul is doing in Gal 4:19 as he "attributes to himself the role of their mother going through the pain of giving birth to them all over again" (52).

By assigning the text to the rhetorical category *conquestio*, Smit frees Gal 4:19 from readings in which Paul's birth pangs are seen as necessarily symbolic of "the apocalyptic events that transpire through God's intervention in human history" (Witherington 1998, 315).[10] Yet his reminder that the *conquestio* includes a reference to the parents of those in the au-

---

8. All translations are my own, unless otherwise noted.

9. Clearly there is no space in such a short exercise to summarize the entire discussion around the rhetorical structure of Galatians. Perhaps its most complete discussion to date can be found in the collection of essays edited by Mark D. Nanos aptly titled *The Galatians Debate* (2002).

10. Witherington gives a number of examples for his assertion. However, the examples from the Synoptics and 1 Thessalonians refer to birth pains of the entire created order, and the examples from Revelation and Isaiah to either general or

dience also forces a reading that takes the childbirth metaphor seriously, rather than glossing it over by rendering it "again in travail until Christ be formed in them," as do A. J. Goddard and S. A. Cummings (Goddard and Cummings 1993, 115).

Still, Smit seems unsurprised that Paul would choose to self-identify as the mother (rather than the father) of the community. It is one thing to remind an audience of its parents; it is quite another for a male speaker to argue his ongoing, birth-pain-filled maternity of his audience. A possible solution may be to read Gal 4:17–20 as the voice of Mother Paul, a voice more exasperated than "helpless" and calling on more authority than the opening "kinfolk" (adelphoi) would signify (Smit 2002, 52). It may well be Mother Paul who, taking over the letter, explains to her adult children the enemy's intentions (Gal 4:16). She then proceeds to remind her children what she has already taught them about being zealous, even in her absence (4:17–18). Finally, in exaggerated maternal entreaty, she cries out against the impiety of her children—who owe her their very lives—because they are "putting her through childbirth" all over again (4:19). At the crux of their impiety, to their shame, is that Christ has not already been formed in them (4:20). Surely such a reading could not be read as a gentle, pastoral rebuff but as another example of disciplina ac severitas (Dixon 1988, 3).

Quite different from the other two mother "fictions" that Paul spins is 1 Thess 2:7. Whereas the other two passages are examples of stern responses to unwelcome behavior, 1 Thess 2:1–12 is a rehearsal of the excellent imitation that the Thessalonian assembly has made of Paul (Gaventa 1998). Here there is no mother calling her children to piety, but there is a mother, and she should give one pause. Paul figures her in this way: "we became gentle in your midst, as if a child-nurse were cherishing her own children" (1 Thess 2:7).[11]

Already we have seen images of Paul as breast-feeding mother, literally feeding her Corinthian children out of her bodily substance, and Paul in Galatia, as we saw immediately above, is the birth mother to the Galatian community. However, in no other place does Paul so clearly identify

---

envisioned women. In none of these examples is a human male figure suddenly pregnant and going through birth pangs a second time.

11. Thalpē literally means "to warm" but can also be translated "to cherish." There is some discussion as to whether the word in 1 Thess 2:7 should be nepioi or epioi, but that is not immediately relevant to this short essay. My tendency is to agree with the assessment of D. Maguerat: "Mais il n'est nul besoin de s'émouvoir; car si le conflit divise les exégètes au niveau de la critique textuelle, l'établissement du sens n'en souffre pas: qu'on lise nèpioi ou (plutôt) èpioi, d'une façon ou d'une autre les apôtres opposent à l'arrogance des mauvais orateurs une attitude de petitesse, de tendresse, de fragilité" ("Whether we read it 'nèpioi' or (rather) 'èpioi,' one way or another, apostles contrast their meekness, tenderheartedness, and gentleness to the arrogance of bad orators/speakers") (Marguerat 2000, 386).

himself not with the matron but with the child-nurse, not with the free woman of means but with the slave woman or poor woman. To use an American-based metaphor, in 1 Thessalonians Paul and the apostles are not like the mother in the "big house" but like the mammy back in the slave quarters who *finally* gets to nurse her own children (Donfried and Marshall 1993, 17).[12]

To be sure, Paul here is playing on a well-known stereotype, the stereotype of the nurse who is "unambivalently committed and devoted to [her] charge," a common image of his day (Joshel 1986, 8). But to his credit, Paul does not idealize the devotion of the child-nurse to those she is forced to feed; instead, his inclusion of "her own" (*ta heautēs*) underscores that which Joshel has already shown: that regardless of the requirements of the "big house" and the master or mistress, the loyalties of the nurse-mammy rest with her own children and not with her nurslings (1986, 21).[13]

Paul's discourse in 1 Thessalonians, then, is striking not only for its similarity but even more for its dissimilarity with his other two extant uses of maternal imagery. If we may argue that the ostensibly free mother of Corinth and of the assemblies of Galatia is calling to recalcitrant children to remind them of their pious obligation, we have no such mother here. In fact, in an unusually insightful metaphor for a free man who flippantly employs metaphors both of slavery and of maternity, Paul here identifies himself with a woman who has no control over her body or its functions. If, as Paul reports with joy, the Thessalonian assembly has been imitating Paul and his colleagues, one wonders how they respond to being compared to slave children, pulled away from their mother by her master, so that she can give sustenance to other children, or to being called to abandon the children of their breasts for the sake of the gospel (1 Thess 1:6). Surely some of this is echoed in Paul's lament of how much he longed to be with the Thessalonians but has thus far been prevented (1 Thess 2:18);[14] it is as though Mother Paul, the slave-nurse, longs for her children but cannot return to them.

---

12. Karl P. Donfried and I. Howard Marshall (1993, 17) suggest a tie between the child-nurse (*trophos*) of 1 Thessalonians and those of the Dionysiac mysteries in Thessalonica. Although this may be true, it does not explain the presence of the *heautēs* that so pointedly changes the metaphor from child-nurses in general to a nurse caring for her own children.

13. As Marissa Myers, a colleague of mine, pointed out, this may say more than we might like to imagine about Paul's own infancy, for he, too, may have been nursed by a slave-woman who then had to return home to comfort her own children.

14. Of course, this raises all sorts of uncomfortable questions about the identity of Paul's slave-master, but then, any time Paul figures himself as a slave of the Deity, such theological questions ought to be raised.

Mother Goose: Fabulist Mother Paul

All of which brings us back to the question: Why a mother? Clearly no definitive answer can be given in such a short exercise; however, I would like to suggest a hypothesis, one that emerges from the position of the mother in Roman society. Here again, Dixon's work proves to be invaluable. She notes that, despite the recognized authority of the Roman mother, "in the last analysis, the mother did not have a legal sanction corresponding to *patria potestas* to enforce her authority if it were challenged" (1988, 6). Fathers, by contrast, through the life-or-death power of *patria potestes* had a great deal of power. Thus, as Dixon points out, "sons *chose* to defer to a mother. Paternal authority was different. Fathers who disapproved of their son's . . . actions did not write them emotional letters or stand anxiously at doorways—they could haul them off rostra or execute them" (Dixon 1988, 181). Dixon's work speaks not only to the power of the Roman mother but equally as pointedly to the limits of that power, limits that required of the mother the use of forms of persuasion, since she could use neither brute force nor command.

Paul intimates that he understands the power of a father in his Corinthian correspondence and that he might even be willing to exercise some of that power (1 Cor 4:15, 21). Yet that in his absence he succumbs to the need to "write them an emotional letter" suggests that there are limits even to Paul's power. This may be why, in addition to paternal threats, he also includes maternal admonition—admonition that, although it attributes to him less absolute power, nevertheless is no less stern and carries no less of an expectation of obedience. Yet he has enough cultural capital with the Corinthian community to intimate that if its members ignore their filial duty to Mother Paul, they might well face the "stick" of father Paul (1 Cor 4:21).

Paul also figures himself as a father in the Thessalonian correspondence, but, interestingly, in this "fiction" he invokes none of the *potestas* of the father. Rather, the father in 1 Thessalonians takes the role normally reserved to the pedagogue, the slave charged with the instruction and guardianship of the master's children (1 Thess 2:11). This, of course, parallels Paul as slave child-nurse tending her own children in the verses that immediately precede it (2:7). Strikingly, although Paul claims paternity here, he does not claim its power. That may not be as surprising in 1 Thessalonians as it would be in other texts, for Paul does not claim his maternal authority in this text either. It seems with the Thessalonians, at least in this letter, he has no complaint, and thus he has no need.

Whereas Paul claims his paternity both in Corinth and in Thessalonica, he makes no such claim to the assemblies of Galatia. This is particularly surprising. One would expect that, given the tenor of the Galatian correspondence, Paul would waste no time in establishing his paternal authority over the Galatian assemblies and reminding them of their moral obligation to immediate and unconditional obedience. But in this letter, Paul is decidedly not the father of the Galatian assemblies; he makes no pretense that he has the power of *patria potestas* over them. Perhaps he knows that his distance and the power of the opposition make him unable to exercise paternal authority, the power to "haul them off rostra," the power to "execute them" (Dixon 1988, 181). What power he does have is that of entreaty and especially of threat: threat not about what *he* will do if they do not obey but about what "their father" (read the Deity) will do if they do not obey.[15] As a result, he writes an "emotional letter" to the assemblies of Galatia, one that plays on social expectations of *pietas* and that underscores his relative authority—authority not as all-powerful father but as Mother Paul, she who, out of filial piety if for no other reason, ought to be obeyed.

In these three texts, Paul is spinning a series of "fictions," perhaps even "nurse(ry) stories"—stories about a birthing, nursing mother who, just like a good Roman mother or a devoted child-nurse, calls her children to a life of virtue, using whatever means she has at her disposal. She is not all-powerful, as is the father, but she comes with authority that demands filial piety. Paul's "fictions" are striking precisely because they uphold the authority not only of the ancient father but also of the ancient mother. In fact, not only does Paul elevate this authority as just; he claims it as his own.

Nevertheless, it would be foolish to figure Paul as an unqualified ally for mothers (or women), ancient or modern. As I have pointed out in an earlier paper, neither of the two other mothers in Galatians get the kind of respect from Paul that he commands to himself. Hagar, the flesh-and-blood slave mother, is treated to what I have called "a rhetorical hysterectomy":

> She . . . is doubly signified upon as womb and a slave; [and as such] she is doubly cast out. Paul participates in this exclusion . . . which comes about precisely because of her societal location as a slave, which is, in turn, denoted by her essential woman-ness [or her motherhood], her fleshly, child-bearing womb. (Aymer 2004)

The other mother in Galatians does not fare much better.

> She gives birth, but not according to the flesh; indeed she is signified upon as the "barren one," the one who does not have birth pains (*odino*). Her children, although many (4:27), are elusive, consisting of breath (*pneuma*) (4:29) and promise (*epaggelia*) (4:23, 28). These are children of the mouth, not the womb; her essential woman-ness, her womb, is excised from the discourse. (Aymer 2004)

Thus we should not be under any illusions that Paul here is championing actual motherhood. His motherhood is in fact a "fiction," a "nurse(ry)

---

15. The ultimate of these threats is, according to Paul, permanent subjugation under the law, and, as the law has been figured as the *pedagogue*, this suggests a state of permanent immaturity, of never attaining the age of majority and thus becoming heirs.

story" told to children to teach them morality and virtue in ways that they can understand. Paul is playing on recognized themes: the virtuous mother and the gentle but persuasive mammy/nurse. But he retains the right to be mother and to define motherhood; not every mother counts in Paul's family.

Retelling the Story

This short essay makes an attempt to take Beverly Gaventa seriously in her call to reexamine these texts. In particular, it seeks to propose a preliminary response to her question: "What cultural codes are enforced or violated when Paul images himself as a woman in labor or a nurse caring for her own children (2004, 92)?" This is an important question, but I suggest that its answer may lie less in Pauline theology and more in the social history of ancient, particularly Roman, motherhood. Many more such questions need to be posed. What influence, if any, might Jewish understandings of motherhood, particularly Hellenistic Jewish understandings of the first century, bring to Paul's discourse? How should Paul's *über*-masculinity be refigured in light of these maternal images, or is it possible that Paul is signifying on the masculinity inherent in maternity, just as he signifies on the victory in crucifixion and on the strength in undergoing persecution?

Other questions also attend, questions not so much of ancient context as of contemporary contextualization: chief among them, in this era in which contemporary fictions of motherhood impact even Supreme Court decisions about women's reproductive health, is: To what extent have we turned the biblical mother, even the biblical mother Paul, into "June Cleaver," and whom does that serve? And what communities—and here I am intentionally thinking about mother- and grandmother-led African American households—might benefit from the image of a mother as deserving filial piety, mother as "she who ought to be obeyed"?

Beverly Gaventa's challenge has been before us for nearly two decades. This essay is a brief attempt to take her challenge seriously. I hope it reopens the discussion that she first proposed, a discussion of what these strange texts might signify, for Gaventa points us to a remarkable set of "fiction," yes of "nurse(ry) stories," stories that bear the unlikely beginning: "Once upon a time, there was a mother named Paul."

Works Cited

Aymer, Margaret. 2004. Don't Bring that Seminary Stuff Back Here. Paper presented at the Annual Meeting of the Society of Biblical Literature, Atlanta, Georgia.

Braxton, Brad R. 2002. *No Longer Slaves: Galatians and the African American Experience*. Collegeville, Minn.: Liturgical Press.

Clines, David J. A. 2003. Paul, the Invisible Man. Pages 181–92 in *New Testament Masculinities*. Edited by Stephen D. Moore and Janice Capel Anderson. SemeiaSt 45. Atlanta: Society of Biblical Literature.

Dixon, Suzanne. 1988. *The Roman Mother.* Norman: University of Oklahoma Press.

Donfried, Karl P., and I. Howard Marshall. 1993. *The Theology of the Shorter Pauline Letters.* New Testament Theology. Cambridge: Cambridge University Press.

Gaventa, Beverly Roberts. 1990. The Maternity of Paul: An Exegetical Study of Galatians 4:9. Pages 189–201 in *The Conversation Continues: Studies in Paul and John in Honor of J. Louis Martyn.* Edited by Robert T. Fortna and Beverly Roberts Gaventa. Nashville: Abingdon.

———. 1998. *First and Second Thessalonians.* IBC. Louisville: John Knox.

———. 2004. Our Mother St. Paul: Toward the Recovery of a Neglected Theme. Pages 85–97 in *A Feminist Companion to Paul.* Edited by Amy-Jill Levine. London: T&T Clark.

Goddard, A. J., and S. A. Cummings. 1993. Ill or Ill-Treated? Conflict and Persecution as the Context of Paul's Original Ministry in Galatia (Galatians 4.12–20). *JSNT* 52:93–126.

Joshel, Sandra R. 1986. Nurturing the Master's Child: Slavery and the Roman Child-Nurse. *Signs* 12:3–22.

Marguerat, Daniel. 2000. L'Apôtre, Mère et Père de la Communauté (1 Thessaloniciens 2/1–12). *Études Théologiques et Religieuses* 75:373–89.

Nanos, Mark D. ed. 2002. *The Galatians Debate.* Peabody, Mass.: Hendrickson.

Smit, Joop. 2002. The Letter of Paul to the Galatians: A Deliberative Speech. Pages 39–59 in Nanos 2002.

Witherington, Ben. 1998. *Grace in Galatia: A Commentary on Paul's Letter to the Galatians.* Grand Rapids: Eerdmans.

Responses

14

Learning to Know about Mothers Who "Know Best"

Tat-siong Benny Liew

Persons of many different cultures have written about the importance of mothers. The French psychoanalyst, André Green, for example, writes of a "dead mother complex" in which a child, because of his mother's depression, develops a form of "blank" or perpetual mourning that manifests itself through both a loss of meaning and a "cold-core" subjectivity (1986, 142–73). Claudia Tate, a literary scholar of African American descent, credits W. E. B. Du Bois's mother for defining for Du Bois "a resolute belief in education as the means of self-perfection" (1998, 187). In addition, Tate proposes that Du Bois's equation of racial uplift or assault with female approval and rejection has much to do with his mother's idealizing gaze at and aspirations for her son despite their material impoverishment (184–88).[1] Pippin's reference to the work of Slavoj Žižek also underscores in a way the significance of motherhood, though in a way that is not only sexist but also the opposite side of Green's "dead mother." For this Slovenian critic, as Pippin points out, "pathological narcissism" and dysfunctional familial relations are all results of an overbearing mother who takes things over in the absence of the father.

Gafney is therefore right on target when she wonders aloud about

---

Following the request of the volume editors, this essay is written in response only to the essays by Britt, Crowder, Gafney, Pippin, and Wallace.

1. For Tate, this is evidenced by Du Bois's choice to (1) identify *Dark Princess*, where heteroerotic satisfaction functions as a parallel to or metaphor for racial advancement, as the favorite of his own writings; and (2) represent his first memorable encounter with racism when he experienced a casual rejection by a female classmate in high school.

the paradox of how motherhood is both ubiquitous and obscure, although this paradox is not limitable to the patriarchal tendency of biblical gene-alogies that Gafney identifies. Toni Morrison says as much when one of her characters, Hannah, has difficulties bringing up the subject of mother love even as a grown woman. All Hannah can do is to stammer and dance around the subject, saying to her mother, "I know you fed us and all. I was talking 'bout something else. Like. Like. Playin' with us. Did you ever, you know, play with us?" (Morrison 1973, 68). Of course, Hannah herself is overheard by her daughter talking with two other women about the agonies of childrearing, though none of them could admit that mothering might be a smothering duty rather than an expression of love. Trying to reassure one of the women as well as herself, Hannah says, "Sure you do [love your child]. You love her, like I love Sula. I just don't like her. That's the difference" (57). If, as Gafney states, "[n]ot all are or will become moth-ers, but all have had mothers" (23) then we may add that, as a follow up, most if not all—mothers or not—find it difficult to talk about mothering.

Britt, Crowder, Gafney, Pippin, and Wallace should be commended, therefore, for their attempts to talk about not only this difficult subject but also how it relates to a much-talked-about but no-less-difficult book known as the Bible. The ubiquitous obscurity surrounding mother-talk may have much to do with the widespread and deep-rooted beliefs that "all women need to be mothers, that all mothers need their children and that all chil-dren need their mothers" (Oakley 1974, 186). These "all"-inclusive beliefs about "needs" ignore the multiple roles or "complex personhood" of moth-ers (Gordon 1997) and hence cover over the many conflicts of interests that may exist between them and their children. Both Gafney and Pippin point to the complexity of motherhood and mothering in their respective essays. For Gafney, Naomi is both a Mommie Dearest and a Mother Jones. For Pippin, who fantastically turns Ernest Käseman's famous statement about "apoca-lyptic is the mother of all Christian theology" (Käseman 1969, 102) into a reading of the mother in Christian apocalyptic, Mother Goose and Mom-mie Dearest turn into one another almost seamlessly. Gafney and Pippin thus effectively deconstruct the binary oppositions that not only ground the dominant ideologies of mothering but also group or categorize mothers into separable "good" and "bad" types. The very construction of Mommie Dear-est as abusive, self-centered, and manipulative—and thus undesirable and even despicable—functions, for example, to reinforce that "good" mothers should be or must be selfless in caring for the needs of their children.

"Complex personhood" means not only that the same person may be a "good" and a "bad" mother at the same time but also that mothers actu-ally have complicated and conflicting needs and desires. While Wallace's parallel reading of both the widow in Luke 18:1–8 and Mary Harris Jones as "mothers of justice" reminds me of Ruth Wilson Gilmore's well-known essay about mothers and prisoners in contemporary California (Gilmore 1999)—particularly how injustice would so incur the righteous indignation

of mothers that it will turn them into "mothers of revolution," and those
who act unjustly would end up dislodging a boulder that might fall on their
own heads—I am bothered by the fact that mothers are still viewed here as
activists and spokespersons for only their children's well-being instead of
their own needs and desires. I will have more to say about mother's needs
and desires; let me point out here that this question is related also to Gafney's important discussion of "maternity by force" in Ruth, as well as the
theme of sacrifice or self-sacrifice that Britt helpfully points to in the same
book. At issue here is not only whether motherhood is chosen or imposed
(a question that Gafney also wonders about in relation to Mary becoming the mother of Jesus), but also how motherhood in general—because
of the neat and tidy "all-need" beliefs identified above—makes ambivalent or unaffectionate feelings of mothers like Hannah unspeakable and
contradictory practices "invisible." As Crowder points out, many African
American women "need to work in order to survive"; as a result, mothering
is often a communal rather than a private undertaking. Furthermore, black
working mothers have, since the time of slavery, often been employed as
domestic workers, including the job as caregivers to other people's babies
and children. In other words, what Britt calls a "displacement" of mothers
may actually involve some mothers "outsourcing" parts of the mothering
role or function to others. Patriarchy is thus not only the result of displaced
or absent mothers (as Britt argues) but also operates *through* mothers (as
Gafney suggests with her reading of Naomi).

In recent years, more and more Latina and Asian American women (especially those of Southeast Asian origin) have joined their black sisters in
becoming professional caregivers of and for other people's children. Doing
so means not only that they have to provide alternative care for children of
their own, but also that they can be insidiously stereotyped as inadequate
and irresponsible mothers. This is all part and parcel of what Crowder
identifies as the "mother working/wrecking" dynamics. What Crowder's
essay exposes, then, is that mothering is—in contrast to Wallace's questionable appeals to "instincts," "archetypes," and structuralism—not only
a social construction but also one that genderizes and racializes. As social constructions, motherhood and mothering involve social, economic,
and political conditions as well as institutions beyond not only the narrow
confines of the family but also the power differential in terms of gender.
Gafney's translation of Ruth 3:12, particularly her use of the words "warrior-woman" to describe Ruth, immediately reminds me of Maxine Hong
Kingston's *Woman Warrior* (1989), which is not only about mother-daughter
struggles but also the interlocking structures of gender, race, class, sexuality, and imperialism.[2] All the essays that I have read from this volume deal

---

2. Since *Woman Warrior*'s emphasis on gender, race, and imperialism should
be more or less self-evident, let me just point to two episodes to indicate its relation

with some of these interlocking structures. For example, Wallace focuses on the intersection between gender and class or status, and Britt highlights the ethnic and colonial dynamics in his intertextual reading of Ruth with not only Coetzee's *Disgrace* but also Ezra-Nehemiah.

As helpful as Britt's essay is in reading the mothering story of Ruth, it has—like the other essays that I have read from this volume—failed to make a connection between motherhood and (anticolonial?) nationalism. This is all the more surprising given not only Britt's references to "motherland" but also Pippin's mention of "Mother Jerusalem." This issue is especially significant given how Britt tends to follow previous scholarship in reading Ruth as a book of protest against the narratives of another group of returnees, namely, the "restoration" project of Ezra-Nehemiah, under which "foreign" mothers and their children were banished to "purify" an ethnic or a national community. This removal has something to do with the ideology that women, as mothers, reproduce not only children but also citizens through their faithful cultivation or reproduction of indigenous or national culture in their children. As such, mothers are also "mothers of the race" (Edwards 2003, 165), or "mother[s], moulder[s] of the nation" (Young 2001, 368). It is because of this ideology that we will find in the apocryphal vision of 4 Ezra the appearance of Zion as a mother, whose loss of a son represents the loss of a nation (4 Ezra 9:26–10:59). For the same reasons, Du Bois would also talk not only about Africa as his "motherland" rather than "fatherland" (1968, 116) but also repeatedly told a story about his "grandfather's grandmother" singing a Bantu song that—despite not being translatable into English—has been passed through the generations (DuBois 2004, 136; 1968, 114–15). Mothers are the guardians of not only children but also culture; as the last bastion against foreign corruption or invasion, they must be protected and put under surveillance. Focusing only on the tropes of Mother Goose, Mommie Dearest, and Mother Jones, these essays end up forgetting to deal with the constructions of Mother-City (see also Pearce 2004) or Mother-Land and what they may imply about various kinds of power relations.

I am also disappointed that neither Gafney nor Britt—in putting mothering in the intersection of gender and ethnicity—deals with sexuality in Ruth, even though (1) others have explicitly read Naomi and Ruth as having something akin to a lesbian relation (e.g., Duncan 2000; West

---

to class and sexuality. In terms of class, there is the episode about Moon Orchid coming from China to the United States to reclaim her husband, who is now not only a successful medical doctor with an office in a "fine" building with a "chrome and glass" lobby where "ashtray stands and plastic couches [are] arranged in semicircles" but also the husband of another woman (Kingston 1989, 113–54). In terms of sexuality, there is not only the story of the "no-name woman" who killed herself and her child because of an illicit affair (1–16) but also the story of the gender-crossing and cross-dressing Fa Mu Lan (19–45).

2006); (2) Gafney herself talks about the queer but frequent use of Ruth's vow to Naomi in heterosexual weddings; and (3) Britt himself mentions a lesbian relationship between Lucy and Helen in Coetzee's *Disgrace*. I refer to this not only because—as the contemporary debate over lesbian mothers shows—motherhood is often assumed to be a heterosexual privilege, but also because lesbian motherhood helps in a way to raise the question of how motherhood or mothering may be separated and separable from both biological reproduction and paternity. Given how the book of Ruth ends with the neighborhood women declaring not only that Ruth is more than seven sons to Naomi but also that "a son has been born to Naomi" (Ruth 4:15, 17), Naomi's feeding, caring, and nurturing of Obed (Ruth 4:16) may signal the displacement of both Naomi's sons as well as Obed's father, Boaz.[3] Instead of—or in addition to—reading Ruth as a surrogate mother, as Gafney does, I would propose reading Boaz as a sperm donor. In other words, Boaz and Naomi's sons, Mahlon and Chilion, are to a degree interchangeable, as are Boaz and the "other kinsman" (Ruth 3:10–13; 4:1–13). Naomi and Ruth basically use Boaz's sperm to have a child. In contrast to a patriarchy that insists on paternity so children are born to a man by one woman or a number of women (as Gafney's citing of Jesus' genealogy in Matt 1:1–16 demonstrates), Naomi and Ruth work together so that a child is born to *Naomi* with the sperm of a displaceable or substitutable male candidate.

I am not trying to dismiss here Gafney's excellent point about how the plot of Ruth "turns on the axes of [male] progeny and provision." Ruth's story undeniably assumes the importance of having husbands and sons. That "need" is—again, as Gafney points out—precisely what Naomi emphasizes as she urges Orpah and Ruth to return to Moab rather than accompanying her back to Judah (Ruth 1:8–13). The clincher of the story— the very naming of David not once but twice at the end, with the second time in the form of a traditional genealogy that centers solely on fathers and sons (Ruth 4:17–22)—also confirms Simone de Beauvoir's exposition of the myth in *The Second Sex* that "every mother entertains the idea that her child will be a hero ... [a] son [who] will be a leader of men, a soldier ... and his mother [Ruth and/or Naomi?] will share his immortal fame" (de Beauvoir 1968, 497, 516). Ruth as a birth mother is in some way not unlike Ruth as a worker who gleans grains in the field (Ruth 2:17–23); she provides marginal and disposable labor that is necessary to produce what Naomi needs. What I am trying to suggest, however, is that even as the

---

3. As an intertext of Ezra-Nehemiah, Ruth's displacement of fathers—particularly the death of Elimelech, Mahlon, and Chilion—may also be related to a critique of both Babylonian and Persian imperialism. I am thinking of something along the lines of Hortense J. Spillers's (2003, 203–29) reading of (single) motherhood in African American communities with the popular phrase "Mama's Baby, Papa's Maybe."

book of Ruth assumes—and thus affirms—the system of patriarchy, it also picks or chips away at the emphasis on paternity, which is one of patriarchy's major pillars of support. Just as one should not or cannot categorize mothers into neatly separable opposites, one must not lose sight of Ruth's oppressive *and* liberating dimensions or potentials. Britt, in addition to referring to Ruth's protest against ethnic proscriptions found elsewhere in the Hebrew Bible, is certainly correct to suggest that the narrative presents its protagonist as both victim and agent. Even a woman's emphasis on having a son may involve something more than meets the eye.

Commenting on another South African novel, Lauretta Ngcobo's *And They Didn't Die*, Anne McClintock talks about a "political motherhood" in which a woman may use her child or children as an insurance to secure the return of her husband (1995, 386–87). If we examine Ruth and Naomi as having a kind of "holy union" relations, what we may get from McClintock's reading is that Ruth's maternity may not simply be—as Gafney suggests—forced or imposed, especially given Naomi's initial suggestion to Ruth that they should part ways. This shift of perspective will further turn the object of maternal desire from the child to the mother's adult partner, although in Ruth's case the "reproduction of mothering"—*pace* Nancy Chodorow (1978)—ends up reproducing and complicating an eroticism that is not necessarily or merely heterosexual.

In a recent book, Emily Apter discusses how lesbian relations have been presented with or as "a figure of the sui generis Mother" (2006, 216). Regardless of how one reads the relations between Ruth and Naomi, Naomi's use of both Boaz and Ruth as surrogates does turn her into a "*sui generis* Mother." Note how the narrative links Naomi's nurturing of the child (Ruth 4:16) with the child being born to Naomi (4:17). Crowder talks about how African American women often take responsibility "for any and every child in the community long before daycare became a business" to become "'other' mothers or 'neighborhood' mothers," while Wallace talks about Mother Jones as a mother of many working-class men, women, and children. What they show is that mother-child relations are not inevitably biological, a thought that is further confirmed by Britt's emphasis on displacement of mothers as a transfer of affect. I do not have the space to develop my thoughts here fully, but what I am trying to get at is whether one may shift the emphasis on and the use of mother from being a noun to that of a verb. Put differently, I am questioning if mothering can be viewed more as a function characterized by the provision of care and nurture.

This shift of emphasis will bring about not only a change in the object but also the subject of mothering (see also Wong 1994). In terms of object, one will no longer limit mothering to a person nurturing and caring for someone younger than herself. Instead, one may question, for instance, in what ways Ruth may actually be mothering Naomi through not only her journey with Naomi to Judah but also her birthing of Obed to Naomi. Reading Ruth as mothering Naomi complicates in turn several sets of relations. First, Naomi's position as Ruth's mother-in-law or mother—a blurring within Ruth that Britt astutely observes—is inverted. Second, Ruth's mothering of an older person intensifies the conflicts of interests or even power struggles that I alluded to earlier about mothering. What does one do when one has to mother someone not only older but also more powerful? Does mothering then involve also a caretaking or nurturing of that person's ego or honor, as clients are supposed to do for their patrons in exchange for material benefits? The widow whom Wallace studies (Luke 18:1–8) does not do that with the judge, but is that what Ruth does for Boaz in their exchange in Ruth 2:8–13 and 3:8–9? If so, then, finally, Ruth's identities as "mother" and "lover"—vis-à-vis Boaz *and/or* Naomi—are also seriously confused.

In terms of subject, we have already seen from the paragraph above the "complex personhood" of someone who is mother, client, and lover all at the same time, but we may also ask if the mothering function of giving care and nurturing should be limited to women. Since I started this re-sponse with references to a couple of Lacanians (Green and Žižek), let me point out here that psychoanalysts after Freud have routinely compared the psychoanalytic relation with and as "mothering" (Luepnitz 2003, 232). The *male* psychoanalyst's job is to play the role of a "good enough mother" who would recognize *her* child and make up for whatever bad mirroring *his* client may have suffered in childhood. In his reading of John Singleton's 1991 film *Boyz N the Hood*, the African American scholar David Marriott suggests a very similar blurring of roles and blending or bending of gender. According to Marriott, Singleton's idealized black fatherhood in the film is a form of "fraternal mothering" in which a father becomes to his son(s) "a brother who does what a mother does," namely, to raise a child or children with love and in fraternity (Marriott 2000, 113–14). Wallace and Pippin have, each in her own ways, wondered about the motherhood of God or God as mother. Within the Buddhist traditions, Buddha is likened to a mother so much that Susanne Mrozik can actually write about the formation of a Buddha-mother figure (2006, 30–33).

What I am getting at is that mothering needs not be constricted to or conflated with women.[4] Following up on Pippin's suggestive reading of Jesus' lament over Jerusalem in the Gospel accounts, I would propose that Jesus in drag as a "mother hen" means that mothering is performative rather than biologically determined. I mentioned earlier that patriarchy is built upon binary oppositions; one of those binary oppositions is the rigid division between male and female. I have also mentioned that the ideolo-gies surrounding motherhood and mothering involve more than gender,

---

4. This does not deny the fact that, given the conventional conflation of women and mother, the dominant society is—as Wong (1994) suggests—more ready to acknowledge and assign mothering roles for racial/ethnic minority men who are already feminized.

but that does not mean that gender does not matter. A significant question, then, is whether our work on motherhood and mothering helps us to rethink not only the assumed practice of mothering (like the typecasting of mothers into Mother Jones or Mommie Dearest), but also the assumed identity or gender of mothers. This is again where studies of sexuality, and their destabilizing of gender binarisms, may be both interesting and important. Going back to the book of Ruth, one may ask, for example, how one may read Naomi's gender in light of the juxtaposing statements about her nursing or nurturing Obed and "a child being born *to Naomi*" (rather than "to Boaz") in Ruth 4:16–17. If one wants to read 4:16–17 as mainly a "displacement" of Ruth—as Gafney and Britt do—one may similarly ask what this would imply about Ruth's gender, given (1) the comparison being made between Ruth and "seven *sons*" in 4:15; and (2) Naomi's lament in 1:11–13 that she is too old to have a husband to bear sons for her daughters-in-law. Ruth's vow of loyalty in response to Naomi's lament (1:15–17) and her actions afterwards may be read as Ruth replacing Naomi's dead sons and/or playing the role of Naomi's "husband" to give her the son she thought she would never have.

I realize that this suggestion to change the subject of mothering practices may be viewed as yet another "displacement" of mothers and hence of women.[5] This, I believe, goes back to the debate of whether an emphasis on mothering is good for feminism and even to the paradox of feminism itself. Joan Wallach Scott has, for instance, indicated that, while (French) feminism tends to make claims from a seemingly universal ground of "woman," it also critiques and criticizes the categorical and naturalized split between "man" and "woman" (Scott 1996, xi, 3). It is at least partly this paradox or dilemma that helped lead to the development of the "New Gender Politics," or the nonlinear movement from feminist to queer and then to transgendering concerns (Butler 2004, 4–11). In this new politics or set of theoretical practices, gender and sexual differences are simultaneously analyzed and questioned as "the foundations of cultural and human communicability" (Butler 2004, 208–9). Perhaps the kind of ambiguity or messiness that sexuality studies offer will help us think differently about mothering in terms of both its practice and its practitioners. Pippin should know, however, that I am not pinning any apocalyptic hope on this *nonlinear* movement. Motherhood is not an ideal state, and mothering will continue to be done imperfectly (whether by women and/or by men). Mothering relations will also be revealed as—and become—profoundly unstable when queer, transgendering, and other important concerns are considered. I do not know—and I certainly have my share of doubts—if

---

5. Note, however, that Sara Ruddick (1983) would push my direction even further. Identifying the paternal function as authoritative power without attentive love, she dreams of a world—in contrast to Žižek—in which there will be no fathers but only mothers of both sexes.

mothers really "know best." I do know that I have learned a lot from these essays, but I also know that there is still much about mothers and mothering of which I know little and I must learn more.

Works Cited

Apter, Emily. 2006. *The Translation Zone: A New Comparative Literature*. Princeton: Princeton University Press.

Butler, Judith. 2004. *Undoing Gender*. New York: Routledge.

Chodorow, Nancy. 1978. *The Reproduction of Mothering: Psychoanalysis and the Sociology of Gender*. Berkeley and Los Angeles: University of California Press.

De Beauvoir, Simone. 1968. *The Second Sex*. Translated and edited by H. M. Parshley. New York: Knopf. [Orig. 1952]

Du Bois, William Edward Burghardt. 1968. *Dusk of Dawn: An Essay toward an Autobiography of a Race Concept*. New York: Schocken. [Orig. 1940].

———. 2004. *The Souls of Black Folk*. Boulder, Colo.: Paradigm. [Orig. 1903]

Duncan, Celena M. 2000. The Book of Ruth: On Boundaries, Love, and Truth. Pages 92–102 in *Take Back the Word: A Queer Reading of the Bible*. Edited by Robert E. Goss and Mona West. Cleveland: Pilgrim.

Edwards, Brent Hayes. 2003. *The Practice of Diaspora: Literature, Translation, and the Rise of Black Internationalism*. Cambridge: Harvard University Press.

Gilmore, Ruth Wilson. 1999. You Have Dislodged a Boulder: Mothers and Prisoners in the Post Keynesian California Landscape. *Transforming Anthropology* 8:12–38.

Gordon, Avery. 1997. *Ghostly Matters: Haunting and the Sociological Imagination*. Minneapolis: University of Minnesota Press.

Green, André. 1986. *On Private Madness*. Madison, Wisc.: International Universities Press.

Käseman, Ernst. 1969. *New Testament Questions of Today*. Translated by W. J. Montague. Philadelphia: Fortress.

Kingston, Maxine Hong. 1989. *The Woman Warrior: Memories of a Girlhood among Ghosts*. New York: Vintage. [Orig. 1976]

Luepnitz, Deborah. 2003. Beyond the Phallus: Lacan and Feminism. Pages 221–37 in *The Cambridge Companion to Lacan*. Edited by Jean-Michel Rabaté. New York: Cambridge University Press.

McClintock, Anne. 1995. *Imperial Leather: Race, Gender and Sexuality in the Colonial Contest*. New York: Routledge.

Marriott, David. 2000. *On Black Men*. New York: Columbia University Press.

Morrison, Toni. 1973. *Sula*. New York: New American Library.

Mrozik, Susanne. 2006. Materializations of Virtue: Buddhist Discourses on Bodies. Pages 15–47 in *Bodily Citations: Religion and Judith Butler*. Edited by Ellen T. Armour and Susan M. St. Ville. New York: Columbia University Press.

Oakley, A. 1974. *Woman's Work: The Housewife, Past and Present*. New York: Pantheon.

Pearce, Sarah. 2004. Jerusalem as "Mother-City" in the Writings of Philo of Alexandria. Pages 19–36 in *Negotiating Diaspora: Jewish Strategies in the Roman Empire*. Edited by John M. G. Barclay. New York: T&T Clark.

Ruddick, Sara. 1983. Maternal Thinking. Pages 213–30 in *Mothering: Essays in Feminist Theory*. Edited by Joyce Trebilcot. Totowa: Rowman & Allenheld.

Scott, Joan Wallach. 1996. *Only Paradoxes to Offer: French Feminists and the Rights of Man*. Cambridge: Harvard University Press.

Spillers, Hortense J. 2003. *Black, White, and in Color: Essays on American Literature and Culture*. Chicago: University of Chicago Press.

Tate, Claudia. 1998. *Psychoanalysis and Black Novels: Desire and the Protocols of Race*. New York: Oxford University Press.

West, Mona. 2006. Ruth. Pages 190–94 in *The Queer Bible Commentary*. Edited by Deryn Guest, Robert E. Goss, Mona West, and Thomas Bohache. London: SCM.

Wong, Sau-ling C. 1994. Diverted Mothering: Representations of Caregivers of Color in the Age of "Multiculturalism." Pages 67–91 in *Mothering: Ideology, Experience, and Agency*. Edited by Evelyn Nakano Glenn, Grace Chang, and Linda Rennie Forcey. New York: Routledge.

Young, Robert J. C. 2001. *Postcolonialism: An Historical Introduction*. Malden, Mass.: Blackwell.

15

Reading Mothers and Motherhood by the Godly Standards of Scripture

Alison Jasper

What first strikes the reader about this collection of essays linking mothers and motherhood with the Bible is the variety of concerns addressed and approaches taken. Some essays are pastoral in tone, some seem like cultural criticism, and some are more strictly exegetical. It seems that the editors care to read about biblical mothers and motherhood using a wide range of critical approaches and methodologies. But the selection of essays—and of the theme itself—shows that they are also interested in the much more difficult question of whether it could be said that the Bible, as a whole, takes a position on the issue of motherhood. The various authors recognize that these ancient texts are products of particular times and particular communities and clearly want to allow them to speak for themselves, but in bringing this project to birth, both authors and editors are also addressing a community of men and women readers whose concerns are perhaps slightly different from those of the scholar. The academic theologian or biblical scholar has her or his own ideological perspective or faith standpoint, of course, but such scholars do not necessarily seek actively to apply the knowledge gained through their scholarly work on the Bible in their lives as, for example, preachers, counselors, or parents. On the other hand, projected readers clearly belong to a community of people—no doubt including theologians and biblical critics—that asks the question: What have biblical representations of mothers and motherhood to do with the expectations we place upon mothers today? In the face of a lethal, sexually transmitted condition such as AIDS, for example (see Mbuvi), or as we begin to talk more openly about the damage caused by domestic violence against women and the parental abuse of children (see McClenney-Sadler), how should we place ourselves in relation to those scriptural traditions? What can we reasonably expect to gain from them? How do we understand their authority in our lives, if indeed—say as feminists—we could or should?

Feminist writing in particular has challenged the assumption that scriptural authority always underpins public morality or familial pieties benignly. The Bible as a collection of images, narratives, and metaphors, just as much as a collection of explicit rules or instructions, does not consistently and explicitly "oppose" sexual and physical violence against women or children, for example, though it may at times speak prophetically about a responsibility toward widows and orphans or legislate against incest or rape. The abhorrence of domestic abuse and violence against women is something we should be surprised—possibly horrified—to see challenged in print today. Yet it seems that reading the Bible for unambiguous guidance on these important issues is more than we can hope for. It might be more reasonable to view the work of reading scripture, in J'annine Jobling's helpful words, as a venture into "heterology" (2008, 91). Heterology, as she uses the term, is the attempt to return the known to the unknown: "heterologous interpretation exploits the shiftiness of the reading process, its destabilising moments," looking for the ambivalences, for the repressed, for the abjected elements of the text and acts as a means of challenging casual or entrenched forms of sexism, racism, or any other oppressive political ideology that gestures toward scriptural authority. In this sense, heterologous interpretation refuses any interpretative monopolies, but equally cannot authorize any more or less liberal or feminist approaches either.

In "Rethinking the 'Virtuous' Woman (Proverbs 31): A Mother in Need of Holiday," Cheryl A. Kirk-Duggan voices a key note of caution somewhat along these lines: paying attention to the cultural, historical, or literary context of biblical texts makes problematic any simplistic view of them as sources for "good" or "bad" mothering. Readers will find Kirk-Duggan's essay clarifying the suggestion that biblical references are highly nuanced and culturally situated, and she is acutely aware that the biblical texts need to be handled carefully. Even biblical models of women that appear positive should not be referenced indiscriminately. Used without recognition of how movement from cultural context to cultural context through time unavoidably entails new readings, readers of the Bible are in danger of compounding the struggle faced by today's overburdened mothers—our increased expectations of them are not necessarily balanced by correspondingly supportive structures of pay, health care, or education—by forcing them to strive for ideals that are at best context specific and, at worst, completely misread and misunderstood.

Linda S. Schearing's essay puts the spotlight on a historical case in point. This study—which will also be very useful for cultural scholars of Christianity—illustrates the ways in which some key biblical texts have influenced historical attitudes toward the treatment of a mother's pain in childbirth. Focusing on the distinction between physical pain and maternal anguish to which discussion of the Hebrew text of Genesis appears to bear witness, Schearing notes that nineteenth- and twentieth-century Western exegetical scholarship provided a critical response to the prevalent view, shared by many medical practitioners of the time, that a mother's pain in labor was just punishment for the sin of her biblical foremother, Eve, in which she shared. Schearing's implication is, of course, that biblical texts cannot be taken at face value and that carelessly decontextualized readings may end up being invoked to support cruel or damaging practices quite improperly. Readers with a traditionalist perspective on biblical authority may find it harder to acknowledge that our understanding of biblical language and cultural values are inevitably transformed to some degree, in the face of technological, political, and environmental changes, but it is vital to recognize this, lest we fall into the trap, for example, of equating biblical authority with a culturally contextualized patriarchal authoritarianism.

The discussion of biblical hermeneutics in recent years has generally reflected the view that biblical texts, so freighted with past and present longing for unproblematic truths and moral guidance are, more often than not, opaque and ambiguous. This opacity is due not simply to the varying and unfamiliar historical and cultural contexts within which biblical texts have been composed but also to the mosaic of moods, associations, desires, and assumptions—including those to do with Christian faith—made by every different biblical reader. This does not make the attempt to read biblical texts a fruitless one, however, since the mosaic brought into being by biblical reading understood in this way is undeniably richly colored, emotionally and sensually rewarding, and, as this collection also reveals, intellectually and theologically challenging. But forms of more recent literary and cultural criticism and theory chime in with a series of older and more traditional hermeneutic approaches—not excluding biblical texts themselves that tell listeners how everything comes in parables—in warning us not to expect biblical reading to clear away every confusion or to reveal a pristine meaning for all times. A collection such as Pippin and Kirk-Duggan have compiled powerfully invokes this reflection and cautions us strongly against trawling the biblical texts for normative conclusions on the maternal theme.

This is not to say, as Frank Yamada argues, that there are no patterns prevailing across the millennia or that we cannot, for example, identify the patriarchal structures invariably reflected in the biblical texts. In his essay, he draws the reader's attention to the relationship between mother and son in the hugely popular animated "sit-com" *The Simpsons* in order to make an interesting parallel with a biblical narrative. In *The Simpsons*, the fantastically blue-haired mother Marge is represented as resourceful, intelligent, somewhat compassionate, but above all else, loyal to a set of conventional moral and domestic codes. Bart, the "bad boy" son, plays the rebel and the nonconformist, but in the end his rebellion is more apparent than real. He is not excluded from his home or from his mother's love. He is never permanently excluded from school, and, essentially, his behavior does more to confirm than to challenge the ideological—and patriarchal—framework that his mother Marge is marshaled to defend in this series. Typically demanding the restoration of order while her menfolk play the fool (however disarmingly!), she features as the acceptable face of contemporary patriarchy. Yamada makes a connection between this pattern of rebellion and restoration of order in *The Simpsons* and a similar pattern he detects in Judg 13. In Judg 13, the unnamed wife of Manoah, like Marge, is clearly more intuitive and intelligent than her husband and, moreover, more in touch with the divine power of—patriarchal—order to which Samson's boorish and unpredictable behavior is ultimately forced to conform in the final "comedic collapse" at the end of the chapter. The comparison makes the point that biblical texts reflect patriarchal ideology and in ways that are still being echoed in popular culture. What it clearly does not do is translate into helpful hints for hard-pressed moms or, in this instance, fuel for social revolution.

Mignon R. Jacobs's contribution follows a similar line of thought, drawing attention to the biblical character of Bathsheba in a close reading of 1 Kings. Her piece gives readers a fascinating portrait of Bathsheba as a considerable character: the mother of undivided loyalty, playing the skilful politician surrounded by potential enemies. She manages the wavering, volatile, but still powerful King David to maintain her advantage in circumstances where the stakes are enormous: great power behind the throne, on the one hand, as the mother of the future king, and, on the other, annihilation of both son and mother. Once again, there is no explicit suggestion that the system in which she has no independent status as a woman could or should be changed. However, we are left to reflect on the uneasiness of the head that wears the patriarchal crown when surrounded by women of this calibre.

These scholarly readings of biblical mothers show us women who would probably not have been able to make much sense out of a Christian rhetoric that claims that "godly standards of scripture"[1] are an unmixed blessing for women. What the biblical narratives do reflect, however, is the stressful reality for women made vulnerable or powerful through motherhood in situations where men were actually accorded legally unrestricted

---

1. This term is in fact taken from the website Ladies against Feminism: (http://www.ladiesagainstfeminism.com/starthere.htm), which seeks, from the perspective of a group of conservative evangelical and predominantly American women, to encourage and support women and men in adopting what it views as a more biblical approach to life.

power over or granted very considerable cultural license in respect of women. In contemporary circumstances within which people—including actual or potential mothers—continue to turn to the Bible for exemplars, role models, or even minimally for some point of reference or comparison, it is, therefore, only prudent to suggest careful, critical reading as a precaution against the worst excesses of ideologically driven interpretation. The biblical passage read closely with benefit of critical interpretation is not thereby diminished, as this collection shows. It still constitutes a site for serious theological reflection on the nature of divine providence or our vulnerability and responsibility as providers of biological or emotional mothering. What the Bible does not do is provide any incontestable rule to follow in the complexities of twenty-first-century living.

I have suggested that this collection of essays as a series of exercises in pastoral theology, cultural criticism, or biblical exegetics explores texts about biblical mothers with a recognition that they have their own contexts, that we cannot take anything for granted, and certainly that we cannot imagine that they constitute an unproblematic pattern for proper mothering. On the other hand, there are good literary and theological reasons for continuing to read the biblical texts whether we view them as the starting point for reflection or regard the reading process as, in any case, a heterologous process that invariably confuses or trips up attempts to corral biblical texts into ideological contests in the interests of driving us to think and take responsibility for our own readings. Let me add another example of my own to those addressed by authors in the collection to illustrate this point.

I have suggested that the question that might lie behind the project of this book as a whole is: What have biblical representations of mothers and motherhood to do with the expectations we place upon mothers today? For me, this immediately raises a question about relationships between mothers and daughters and presses the point that the biblical texts, however nourishing and fruitful for critical readers and however important and significant for communities of readers, cannot be more than a limited resource within our contemporary Western world. I understand our contemporary Western world to be characterized by ongoing attempts by academics, politicians, and community and religious leaders to mediate between—sometimes, still to compete against—very different political, cultural, and theological agendas. In the example I have taken, which prioritizes mother-daughter relationships, the relentlessly patriarchal context of scripture seems to have bleached out the vitality and significance of this type of maternal bond. Bathsheba, the Virgin Mary, Samson's unnamed mother, and all the mothers of Israel were potential or actual mothers of daughters as well as sons. Yet—outside the book of Ruth or perhaps the story of the Syrophoenician woman's daughter—the Christian Bible gives few illustrations of mother-daughter relationships and even fewer hints about what might be the function of this relationship, for example, within the sacred community. In contrast, other relational bonds such as fathers and sons or fathers and daughters are amply illustrated in biblical narratives or metaphors concerning the nature of Jesus' filial relationship to God, for example, or God's paternal relationship to the people of Israel as child or erring wife. In sum, it could indeed be said, in one sense, that the Bible takes a view that mother and daughter relationships do not greatly matter.

Feminist theory has made us very aware that within a masculinist economy women have a role to play but that typically this role presents them as a sexualized commodity in exchanges between men. In relation to men, women's sexuality, their insignificant female genealogy, and their general—whether essential or constructed—difference from men becomes meaningful preeminently as the means to produce more of the same: sons who will become fathers of sons. Mothers of daughters or daughters of mothers have no function in this process, and neither can they signify within its productive economy except extrinsically as mothers of sons. Of course, if the feminist theorists have it right, it really is not surprising to find mother-daughter relationships so thin on the ground in biblical texts and thus also within this collection of essays! In fact, it is, perhaps, quite surprising to find any at all. In a contemporary context, if we simply read biblical texts with the view that they can determine a proper view of which relationships matter and which matter less, this will inevitably put us somewhat at odds with any more liberal thrust toward political or social equality. It will also put us at odds with a series of very different cultural contexts in which the relationship of mothers to daughters plays a much more significant role within the sacred community.

But if feminist theorists are right, it is important that we not lose sight of these mother-daughter relationships, even—or perhaps especially—in the context of Christian and biblical traditions. Feminist philosophers such as Luce Irigaray, for example, have proposed that there is strength and significance in the relationship between mothers and daughters precisely because in their terms women escape the economy that figures them as mere objects to be used by and exchanged between men (Whitford 1991, 45). Rather than suffering the torment of giving birth as a punishment for her part in her foremother Eve's sinfulness, for example, Irigaray envisions a eucharistic celebration of the relationship of daughter and mother:

> A woman celebrating the Eucharist with her mother, sharing with her the fruits of the earth she/they have blessed, could be delivered of all hatred and ingratitude towards her maternal genealogy, could be consecrated in her identity and her female genealogy. (Whitford 1991, 46)

Of course, we cannot escape from the fact that writing about mothers and daughters in relation to Christian scripture is inherently more difficult because there are so few actual references to mother-daughter relationships—either good or bad. Historically, of course, in the Western world there have been other imaginative resources to make up in some ways for this lack. Within Greek mythology, for example, there are stories about Demeter, the goddess of the harvest, and her daughter Persephone. Demeter's anger and grief at the rape and kidnap of her daughter in these stories plunges the world into dry desolation and is thus associated with the devastating power of the nonhuman world, which is also the *magna materia* from which we are all ultimately drawn as embodied beings. This is indeed an important image, and it indicates some cultural recognition of the sustaining and destructive forces this all-female relationship disposes. It gives some warrant to those who continue to configure the mother-daughter bond as a significant one. The power and significance of the mother-daughter relationship within Western cultures can also perhaps be traced in the tradition of fairy or folk tales transmitted orally across the European continent and carried abroad in the context of Western colonial expansions alongside Christianity. Stories about beautiful young girls and their wicked stepmothers, written down more recently by collectors such as Perrault—author of the original stories that have become commonly known as the tales of Mother Goose—or the Grimm brothers, may contain the veiled presence of this mother-daughter relationship otherwise so poorly represented. The ugly and wicked (step)mothers who seek to separate the beautiful girl from her prince or her wedding day are generally viewed, in a patriarchal light, for example, as evil witches, but they are perhaps merely the traces of women who have resisted the force of dominant patriarchal ideology that seeks to devalue any relationships except those with men. (Estes 1992, 70–110).[2] Of course, neither classical mythology nor folk stories have acquired the privilege of Christian scripture, so the voices and images of mothers and daughters have been resolutely bracketed off in elite contexts.

Challenging the characteristic privilege afforded to mother-son relationships in biblical texts, however, Madeline McClenney-Sadler's piece ("'For God's Sake Mommie Help!' The Mother-Daughter Dyad in Leviticus 18 and the Biblical Directive for Equity in the Family") focuses boldly on the book of Leviticus and demands that we look fairly and squarely at the uncomfortable issue of child abuse, specifically the sexual abuse of girls by their fathers. Drawing poignantly on her own pastoral experience, McClenney-Sadler considers the position of women who fail to defend their daughters against abusing fathers. Taking an example from within the church community, she indicates, if proof was needed, that the sexual abuse of little girls by their fathers is a problem within communities identifying themselves as Christian just as it is outside those boundaries and that figures of authority cannot be trusted always to respect female vulnerability simply because they are Christians. She recognizes that, in spite of

---

2. Estes develops the theme of the witch figure who protects and initiates the younger woman, particularly in her reading of the Russian folk tale of Vasalisa.

unmistakeable prohibitions on all forms of incestuous sexual contact in the biblical text, mothers may be so disempowered as women by patriarchal structures sustained by Christian churches that they are incapable of taking advantage of the protection the biblical injunctions might afford them in order to bear witness to and to contest the suffering of their daughters. A continuing privileging of male voices within both domestic and church contexts effectively silences them and all too often delivers the killing blow by subsequently judging these disempowered women as "bad mothers."

To sum up so far, collectively these papers reveal the unmistakeable marks of the Bible's varied cultural but invariably patriarchal origins—illustrated for me most symptomatically in their overall indifference to the mother-daughter relationship. The project is timely because, in continuing to focus on "the authority of scripture," some contemporary Christians are clearly still failing to recognize that the erasures of Western patriarchy—given expression in the scriptural "aporia" in relation to mother-daughter relationships, for instance—represent an increasingly real and visible divergence from wider social and cultural values. If we agree, for example, with McClenney-Sadler that mothers need to defend their daughters (or sons, for that matter) against the violence, neglect, or sexual abuse of men who are generally accounted powerful in Christian communities, we have also to acknowledge that scriptural resources of direct relevance to this issue are a little thin on the ground. The situation is powerfully compounded when women are denied access by patriarchal structures to leadership roles within those communities and cannot make their particular experience useful.

A final reflection on the theme of this collection brings me to the underlying convention of motherhood. Allowing ourselves, as women, to be defined by our biology—or by our ability or inability to have children—is something of which feminist theorists have been immensely wary since at least 1949, when Simone de Beauvoir wrote so ambivalently about motherhood in her groundbreaking work, *The Second Sex*. The barren woman is a typical biblical trope associated with the miraculous power of God to bless with new (male) life but also, of course, derives from and reinforces all the pejorative social and cultural implications of childlessness that exacerbate the sometimes acute personal suffering it causes. Mary's willingness, as a key figure in the church's tradition, to play the part of receptacle or human chalice in a divinely patriarchal story is preserved within scripture and still elevated within some Christian communities as an exhortation to all women. If I am concerned about the lack of biblical reference points for the important relationship of mothers to daughters, I should perhaps be equally concerned with the comparable and, contextually speaking, understandable failure of these ancient texts to offer representations of women who wish to put aside motherhood and mothering in favor of work unrelated to motherhood or even mothering. The Bible's limited representation of mother-daughter relationships and women who have chosen not to be mothers seems to me clear reason why the biblical reader needs to be extremely cautious about drawing up rules or conventions based upon biblical texts. This is not to suggest that the biblical emphasis on mother-son relationships places these texts somehow beyond the pale as resource for genuine spiritual reflection or theological discussion. It does not put them beyond the pale even as points of comparison or reference within any discussion of mothers and motherhood. However, I make the point in order to emphasize once again how important it is that we recognize the reality of cultural divergences between different contemporary as well as different scriptural contexts and to bring that divergence into sharp relief so that we can see what is really at stake when someone in authority talks sweepingly about "a scriptural view."

I began this piece by noting how the authors within this collection of essays respect and defend the integrity of the ancient texts within their own cultural and historical contexts, but also sensing a further question about whether the Bible, as a whole, could be said to take a view. Could it be said that these collected texts actually take a position on the issue of mothers or motherhood such that it could be applied to the lives of men and women in the contemporary Western world, for example? What have biblical representations of mothers and motherhood to do with the expectations we place upon mothers today? How should we place ourselves in relation to those scriptural traditions? What can we reasonably expect to gain from them? How do we understand their authority in our lives, if indeed we should? I have argued that, while it is certainly wrong to say that these biblical texts provide us with nothing to nourish or challenge us intellectually, theologically, or ethically as readers, it is very problematic indeed to try to derive normative principles of motherhood from them in a contemporary context. The texts themselves, as our authors ably demonstrate, are varied and disparate in character. Readers, too, bring their own complex assumptions and agendas to the task, and it appears as if both biblical writers and readers have recognized at various points that the most profitable way to read is to acknowledge the ambiguities that result from this intertextual encounter. If some in the past have believed that the Bible contained hidden or esoteric knowledge understood only by the initiated, recent biblical readers who reflect the far greater philosophical and cultural complexities of our global community have opted to understand reading practice as, in Jobling's words, heterologous, exploiting the shiftiness or destabilizing moments of the reading process to allow new meanings to emerge and to guard against the distortions produced when privileged—for example, patriarchal—reading communities remain unchallenged. In sum, the editors and authors in this collection have done a good job in presenting us with a wide variety of different and relevant texts and in encouraging readers to recognize their complexity and subtlety as products of a wide variety of different cultural contexts. Although I have argued that in some ways all these texts have been written under the erasures of patriarchal convention, implicitly what the collection of essays does is demonstrate the extreme difficulty of deriving any authoritative view—even a patriarchal one—from scripture and the importance of not abrogating responsibility for our own reading of scripture to others, when they invoke church or biblical reading traditions in order to wrest it from us.

Works Cited

Estes, Clarissa Pinkola. 1992. *Women Who Run with the Wolves: Contacting the Power of the Wild Women*. London: Rider.

Jobling, J'annine. 2008. *Post-Christian Feminisms: A Critical Approach*. Edited by Lisa Isherwood and Kathleen McPhillips. London: Ashgate.

Whitford, Margaret, ed. 1991. *The Irigaray Reader*. Oxford: Blackwell.

Contributors

Margaret Aymer is Associate Professor of New Testament at the Interdenominational Theological Center in Atlanta, Georgia, and is the author of *First Pure, Then Peaceable: Frederick Douglass, Darkness, and the Epistle of James* (Continuum, 2008).

Brian Britt is Professor of Religious Studies at Virginia Polytechnic Institute and State University. His research combines the analysis of biblical texts with problems of contemporary culture. In addition to articles in religious studies journals, his work includes two single-authored books—*Walter Benjamin and the Bible* (Continuum, 1996; Mellen, 2003); and *Rewriting Moses: The Narrative Eclipse of the Text* (T&T Clark, 2004)—and the co-edited volume (with Alexandra Cuffel) *Religion, Gender, and Culture in the Pre-modern World* (Palgrave, 2007).

Stephanie Buckhanon Crowder is Assistant Professor of Religion/New Testament at Belmont University, Nashville, Tennessee. She is an ordained Baptist and Disciples of Christ minister and a married mother of two sons.

Wil Gafney is an Episcopal Priest and Associate Professor of Hebrew and Old Testament at the Lutheran Theological Seminary at Philadelphia. Her book, *Daughters of Miriam: Women Prophets in Ancient Israel,* was published in April 2008 by Fortress, and she is a co-editor of *The People's Bible* (Fortress, 2008).

Mignon R. Jacobs is Associate Professor of Hebrew Bible/Old Testament at Fuller Theological Seminary and author of *Gender Power and Persuasion* (Baker, 2007), and *Conceptual Coherence of the Book of Micah* (Sheffield, 2001).

Alison Jasper is a lecturer in the School of Languages, Cultures and Religions at the University of Stirling. Her main area of research is in feminist theology. She is the author of *The Shining Garment of the Text: Gendered*

Readings of John's Prologue (Sheffield Academic Press, 1998) and numerous articles.

Cheryl A. Kirk-Duggan is Professor of Theology and Women's Studies, Shaw University Divinity School, Raleigh, North Carolina, and an Ordained Elder in the Christian Methodist Episcopal Church. She has written and edited over twenty books, has memberships in several professional guilds, is featured in Malka Drucker's *White Fire: A Portrait of Women Spiritual Leaders in America,* (SkyLight Paths, 2003), and is the 2009 recipient of the Excellence in Academic Research Award, Shaw University. With degrees in music and religious studies, Kirk-Duggan's research is interdisciplinary, spanning religious and women's studies. An avid athlete and musician, she resides in Raleigh with her beloved husband, Mike.

Tat-siong Benny Liew is Professor of New Testament at the Pacific School of Religion in Berkeley, California. He is the author of *Politics of Parousia: Reading Mark Inter(con)textually* (Brill, 1999); and *What Is Asian American Biblical Hermeneutics? Reading the New Testament* (University of Hawaii Press, 2008). He also edited "The Bible in Asian America" for the journal *Semeia* with Gale A. Yee (Society of Biblical Literature, 2002), as well as the volume *They Were All Together in One Place? Toward Minority Biblical Criticism* (Society of Biblical Literature, 2009) with Randall C. Bailey and Fernando F. Segovia.

Madeline McClenney-Sadler holds the doctor of philosophy in Hebrew Bible from Duke University, with minor concentrations in Islamic Law and Women's Studies. She is the author of *Re-covering the Daughter's Nakedness: A Formal Analysis of Ancient Israelite Kinship Terminology and the Internal Logic of Leviticus 18* (T&T Clark, 2007). She is also the founder and president of Exodus Foundation.org (http://www.exodusfoundation.org). Its national vision and mission is to stop the flow of African Americans to prison.

Andrew M. Mbuvi is Associate Professor of Biblical Studies and Hermeneutics at Shaw University Divinity School (High Point Campus). A native of Kenya, Mbuvi has published *Temple, Exile, and Identity in 1 Peter* (T&T Clark, 2007), essays in *Encyclopedia of African Religions* (Sage, 2009), and is currently working on two book projects: a commentary on Jude and 2 Peter for Cascade Publishers and a book on African novels and the Bible.

Tina Pippin is Professor and Chair of Religious Studies at Agnes Scott College in Decatur, Georgia. Her research interests are in apocalyptic culture (*Apocalyptic Bodies: The Biblical End of the World in Text and Image* [Routledge, 1999]) and in activist educational theory and practice.

Mark Roncace is Associate Professor of Religion at Wingate University, Wingate, North Carolina. He is the co-editor of two books: *Teaching the Bible: Practical Strategies for Classroom Instruction* (Society of Biblical Literature, 2005); and *Teaching the Bible through Popular Culture and the Arts* (Society of Biblical Literature, 2008).

Linda S. Schering is Professor of Hebrew Scriptures at Gonzaga University, where she has taught since 1993. She has co-authored two books: *Eve ande Adam: Jewish, Christian, and Muslim Readings on Genesis and Gender* (Indiana University Press, 1999); and *Those Elusive Deuteronomists: The Phenomenon of Pan-Deuteronomism* (JSOT Press, 1999).

Brenda Perry Wallace is currently a certified Associate Supervisor with the Association of Clinical Pastoral Education. She is currently serving as a CPE Supervisor and chaplain for the James A. Haley Veterans' Hospital in Tampa, Florida.

Deborah Whitehead is Assistant Professor of Religious Studies at the University of Colorado, Boulder, where she teaches courses in United States religious history, Christianity, North American religious thought, and gender studies in religion. Her research interests include American pragmatism and Christianity and culture in the United States.

Frank M. Yamada is Assistant Professor of Old Testament at Seabury-Western Theological Seminary in Evanston, Illinois. He has written and presented several essays in the areas of postmodernism, postcolonialism, ethics of interpretation, violence in the Hebrew Bible, culturally-contextual hermeneutics, and Asian American biblical interpretation. His forthcoming book is entitled, *Configurations of Rape in the Hebrew Bible: A Literary Analysis of Three Rape Narratives* (Peter Lang).

Index of Subjects

Index of Ancient Sources

Breinigsville, PA USA
16 November 2009
227638BV00002B/2/P